Beyond Graduation

The College Experience

JOHN HARLAND
and
IAN GIBBS

The Society for Research into
Higher Education & NFER-NELSON

Published by SRHE & NFER-NELSON
At the University, Guildford, Surrey GU2 5XH

First published 1986
© John Harland and Ian Gibbs

ISBN 1 85059 013 3
Code 8951 021

Library of Congress Cataloguing-in-Publication Data
Beyond Graduation.
1. Teachers college graduates – Employment –
Great Britain. 2. Teachers colleges – Great Britain
– Curricula. 3. Occupational mobility – Great
Britain.
I. Harland, John. II. Gibbs, Ian. III. Society
for Research into Higher Education.
LB1780.B49 1986   370.7'1'0941   86–8565
ISBN 1–85059–013–3

Typeset and Artwork by FD Graphics, Fleet, Hampshire.
Printed and Bound by Antony Rowe Ltd., Chippenham

Contents

Preface and Acknowledgements

In late October 1979, a conference held at the Royal Festival Hall proclaimed the emergence of an 'alternative way' through higher education. In addition to courses in universities and polytechnics, prospective students were to be offered a third route towards a degree, namely, non-teaching degree programmes in colleges of higher education. Seven years later, this book surveys the experiences of some of the first graduates who pursued the 'alternative way'.

The book is based on research involving a number of colleges of higher education, whose co-operation and encouragement we acknowledge with thanks. Likewise, the many students and graduates who responded to our questionnaires and requests for interviews deserve our special thanks. The research was about them, and we would like to think that publication of this volume is a reflection of the importance of the things they had to say. Although we as authors must accept final responsibility for the book's defects, its undoubted merits, of which we are confident that there are many, reflect the help and encouragement of numerous colleagues and staff in the institutions who in one way or another took part in the project.

We would first like to acknowledge the valuable contribution made by Sally Cree as Research Assistant to the project before leaving us to join the BBC. We would then like to thank the following people for reading the manuscript in its various stages of development, and for offering many useful suggestions for its improvement : John Barnett, John Bennett, Ned Binks, Gordon Brand, Norman Evans, Colin Greaves, Len Iggulden, Ian Lewis, Geoff Pacey, Allan Pattie, Michael Shattock, Roy Smith, John Stocks, Jason Tarsh, Graham Vulliamy and Ralph Wilkinson.

Ultimately, of course, responsibility for the views expressed here must remain with us; they do not necessarily reflect those held in the participating institutions.

Introduction

In 1970, institutions known as colleges of education were almost wholly concerned with the task of teacher training and education. By 1980, after a decade of closures and amalgamations, most of the surviving institutions had adopted the new, status-enhancing title of college or institute of higher education. In addition to courses leading to teaching degrees, they were also offering first degrees (usually in the humanities and social sciences) that were ostensibly unrelated to the teaching profession.

This broadening of the college curricula beyond that of a single or monotechnic concern with teaching was widely alluded to as 'diversification'. Although diversification in some colleges included vocationally-oriented courses for occupations other than teaching (eg social work, occupational therapy), the introduction of non-BEd and occupationally-unspecific degree courses was the most prevalent form of diversification. In college curricula parlance, the new courses quickly became known as the 'diversified degree programmes'.

In 1979 the first substantial group of graduates to complete the new programmes left the colleges and embarked on careers. What happened to them in the wider world of work and employment? Did they, as the term commonly used to refer to their degrees suggests, enter a diversity of occupations and professions? What was the nature and level of employment they found? How did their experiences compare with those of graduates from other sectors of higher education? Were they satisfied with the progress of their careers and the demands of their work? It was such questions as these that the research reported in this book set out to answer.

Adopting a methodological approach which permitted the juxtasition-ing of qualitative with quantitative data, the research is based on two main phases of data collection: the first destination statistics and other biographical details concerning the 1979 diversified degree graduates from eighteen colleges of higher education; and a postal questionnaire of 1979 diversified degree graduates from sixteen colleges of higher education, which we called the 'Beyond Graduation' survey. The bulk of the empirical material upon which the analysis is based consists of the findings of the latter, survey part of the research.

With regard to graduates from former colleges of education, the findings were that the teaching profession constituted the main employment outlet of the diversified degree programmes, that a notable share of the sample was 'filtering down' the labour market to jobs unaccustomed to graduate entry (eg secretarial and clerical work), and that graduates in such lower status occupations were frequently dissatisfied with their work, for which they often appeared to be overqualified and in which they were underemployed. In comparison to graduates from other sectors of higher education, including the proto-polytechnic type of college of higher education, graduates from the former colleges of education had greater difficulties in obtaining professional employment commensurate with, but outside of, the teaching profession.

Reinforcing many of Bone's (1980) observations on the effects on women's career opportunities of teacher training cuts, finding satisfying and suitable alternatives to teaching proved particularly difficult for female graduates, who together comprised a significant majority in the colleges' student constituency. The study highlights the harshness of an economic structure and socialization process that continues to limit the chances of women graduates finding work that makes real demands on the general skills and abilities acquired through an extended education.

The findings also confirm that the majority of diversified degree students in the former colleges of education came from middle-class families, had lower A level grades than their university counterparts, and registered for degrees which combined subjects in the arts and social sciences. With a few exceptions, the career and employment trends displayed by these respondents were common to graduates of all subject specialisms and combinations. Similarly, the findings fail to establish any immediately recognizable employment advantages to be gained from careers education or work experience components in the new courses. The graduates of the main institution initiating any such scheme were among the least successful in terms of salaries, level of employment, and satisfaction with jobs obtained and degree currency.

The belief that the skills acquired in degree courses had a direct relevance to occupational performance was largely restricted to graduates in the teaching profession or in jobs of a corresponding status. The vast majority of respondents, mainly irrespective of occupational circumstances, considered that employers used degrees as indicators of a high level of general intelligence and mental capacity. Graduates' retrospective accounts suggested that they typically sought both intrinsic and extrinsic rewards from higher education and a very similar combination of expectations was associated with their attitudes towards employment. Most indicated a preference for stimulating work, especially of a caring, altruistic kind, which would offer more than just instrumental rewards.

It is hoped that the portrayal of college graduates' early careers presented here will be of value to those responsible for providing, and devising policy for, higher education courses, expecially within the college sector. In proposing and planning the implementation of the diversified degree programmes, the official documents (Department of Education and Science 1972b, 1973, 1974) gave scant attention to the question of whether or not such courses possessed any economic or employment relevance. In gaining approval for them, colleges were not required to provide evidence that they offered any prospects of suitable employment. Nor were the colleges obliged to demonstrate that the programmes were responsive to unfilled gaps in employers' demands for highly qualified personnel. As a result, hardly any empirical evidence of the prospective or retrospective employment orientations of the diversified degree programmes has been marshalled, and very little discussion of the associated policy issues has been presented. It is believed, therefore, that the information drawn from the present research will make a useful contribution to the existing literature on the early careers and attitudes of diversified degree graduates from colleges of higher education.

The only alternative source of information on the employment orientation of diversified degree programmes is to be found in the colleges' own annual compilations of first destination statistics (eg Association of Careers Advisers in Colleges of Higher Education 1979). Valuable as these are, like corresponding publications from other sectors of higher education they provide only a very basic classification of occupational circumstances up to a period of only six months after graduation. The present study extends these sources by offering a wider range of more detailed data over a much longer period of time.

While previous analyses have usefully focused on other aspects of diversification in the colleges (Adelman and Gibbs 1979; Locke 1979; Locke and Russell 1979; Lynch 1979; Pratt et al. 1979; Stodd 1980), none has yet included any examination of the career dimensions of the new programmes. Here we do investigate this important but neglected element of the colleges' curricula. Furthermore, although the study's sample is a restricted and specialized one, its analysis has a wider relevance in so far as it engages a number of general themes arising from two major surveys of graduates from the main sectors of higher education (Kelsall et al. 1970; Williamson 1981). Likewise, by providing a detailed portrayal of graduates' actual career achievements and experiences, it is hoped that the study will produce some interesting points of contact and comparison with the research recently completed by Brunel University's cross-sector project on the 'Expectations of Higher Education' (Brunel 1984).

Not only has there been a lack until now of empirical data relating to the subject, but discussion of the policy and curricula issues surrounding the employment relevance of diversification has to date received only sketchy and cursory treatment in the literature. Successive government reports and white papers have only included one or two paragraphs touching on the subject (Committee on Higher Education 1963; DES 1972a, 1972b); DES circulars setting out the procedures for inaugurating diversification hardly mention any employment considerations (DES 1973, 1974); and the mere handful of papers and articles which include references to the topic allude in most cases only to the lack of economic demand for non-technical degree graduates (Hampson 1977; Murray 1978; Catto et al. 1981). Consequently, it is hoped that by extracting some policy-oriented proposals from the research findings, this study will go some way towards meeting an apparently pressing need for more open and informed debate about the diversified role of colleges in the overall provision of higher education.

Before considering specific policy implications for the colleges, our discussion centres on the wider significance of two particular problems pervading the research findings. They represent crucial issues confronting future policy formation in the area of higher education and its responsiveness to economic demands: they are the continuing oversupply of graduates in non-applied subjects and the mounting hierarchy among the different sectors of higher education. Following a brief assessment of various alternative corrective measures, two are pinpointed: a broadening of the number and distribution of occupational tasks demanding discretionary work, and integration of the various sectors offering advanced further education into a single, comprehensive system of higher education. It is suggested that following such measures the colleges might more clearly conceive their immediate policy and curricula development. The study closes with an estimate of its implications for the policy decisions now facing the colleges.

In addition to any lessons that might be offered to the institutions which are the 'providers' of higher education, the accounts and experiences presented here should prove useful to the students who are their 'clients' and 'consumers', and to the students' teachers and advisers. The findings will assist in improving the quality of decision-making among large numbers of applicants to higher education. The repercussions and implication of the data for this particular audience are seldom clearly articulated, but the graduate experiences revealed by this present research provoke a whole range of questions that obviously need to be carefully considered before taking up higher education. For example, prospective students should carefully consider the career implications of particular courses at particular institutions, the possible 'trade-offs' that may need to be made between 'intrinsic expressive' and 'extrinsic instrumental' rewards, the 'utilities' and probabilities of entering certain occupations, and the requirements and criteria used by employers in their selection processes. The complexity of these issues, the more immediate pressures of A level examinations, and the temptation to view the offer of a place on a degree course as a gratifying end in itself should not be allowed to deflect applicants from considering them. In many cases, and particularly in view of the current state of the labour market, more careful deliberation before starting courses will have important consequences for determining whether, upon graduation, students will find satisfying and rewarding employment. The accounts volunteered by graduates in this study are littered with examples of 'learning too late that . . . ' or 'if only I knew then what I know now . . . ' These graduates' hindsight perceptions can usefully inform the foresight of prospective students.

In addition to the potential educational value of our research to the 'providers' and 'clients' of higher education, it is also hoped that the analysis has something useful to say on a wider political level. It is argued that many of the career problems encountered by graduates, especially women, ultimately reside in the established practices governing the social organization and allocation of work. The scope for developing this interpretation has been severely limited, but it is hoped that the results may at least constitute one more pointer to the urgent need for political agencies to give more than lip-service to ideas for restructuring the ways in which work is traditionally designed and distributed.

Having outlined the nature of the empirical and policy-related contribution the study makes, a brief overview of its structure may be helpful. Chapter 1 presents an historical background to the institutions in question, then outlines the issues to be addressed by the research and reviews the literature on the associated policy implications and trends in the wider graduate labour market. Chapter 2 identifies the broader methodological approach, summarizes the context in which the research was carried out, and describes the particular methods and techniques used in the data collection and analysis.

The research findings are presented and interpreted in Chapters 3 to 7: Chapter 3 examining the first destination details of 1979 graduates, and laying the foundation for a more extensive look at their subsequent careers in the following chapters; Chapters 4 and 5 setting out the early career patterns and attitudes of respondents to the 'Beyond Graduation' survey. Having subjected the data to closer cross-tabulation analysis, Chapters 6 and 7 examine a number of biographical and institutional factors which may have influenced the early career experiences of the college graduates. The main findings of the research are summarized in Chapter 8, and the final chapter discusses their implications for the policy issues raised in Chapter 1.

1

New Graduates from Colleges of Higher Education

Aims of the Study

Although a major reason for the present study was the need for a more informed and open discussion of the inherent policy issues, additional reasons originated in a wider concern for the economic relevance of higher education. The following pages concentrate on the specific details and background of the case in question, but first a brief impression of the study's wider concerns may illustrate, in a very general way, some of the arguments and assertions of the rhetoric of the public debate.

A pivotal and widespread assumption which has traditionally under-scored the provision of advanced further education is the belief that, whatever else it should do, higher education should make a positive contribution to the economic well-being of society. It is often proposed that economic benefits should be derived, not only from higher education's research function, but from its teaching function as well. Consequently, the 'products' of higher education should, as a result of their extended learning, bring to their occupational performance such qualities as creativity, specialist knowledge and advanced intellectual capabilities.

A question often put is, 'In what ways, and to what extent is higher education accomplishing this task?' The anxieties lying behind such questions are expressed in a number of ways.

For example, from a perspective of economic accountability, it is generally held that society can expect a contribution to economic prosperity in return for its considerable investment in higher education. For many, the expected economic benefits represent the most convincing justification for maintaining the allocation of large amounts of public subsidy. Accordingly, if the economic returns argument is abandoned for one that views higher education solely as an opportunity for personal growth or as an alternative to unemployment, then the rational grounds for such subsidy are no more nor less valid than the arguments for subsidizing a whole range of cultural activities currently purchased privately, such as evening classes, adventure camps, holidays and social clubs.

A similar concern is voiced over the alleged need for advanced further education to be more responsive to the requirements of scientific and technological progress. Thus, it is frequently contested that, in order to sustain a rate of technological development comparable with that of foreign competitors, employers require workers who have acquired, and can apply, areas of knowledge which are presently housed, developed and transmitted in institutions of higher education. During recent years, the view has constantly been expressed that graduates are often ill-attuned to economic needs and technological requirements. Likewise, it is often stated that higher education itself is insensitive to the requirements of our economic and occupational structures. At a popular level, much resentment can be heard over the large quantities of taxpayers' money spent on providing an élite and privileged middle class with the luxury of not having to work for three years, after which they collect the cream jobs, even though many possess little practical knowledge or experience of the realities of work. In the political arena, over the past ten years, the major parties have emphasized – as least in speeches, if not in deeds – the importance of increasing the occupational relevance and benefits to be derived from all levels of the education service, including higher education.

Thirdly, in spite of the diminution in graduate opportunities in recent years, the vast majority of entrants to higher education still seem to anticipate, whether consciously or tacitly, that the results of their advanced studies will enable them to offer employers an enhanced occupational performance for which they can reasonably expect additional material and psychological rewards. Certainly, the prospectuses of individual institutions and the literature published by graduate careers agencies continue to promote the view that the private returns for investment in higher education remain very attractive. By way of illustration, the 1983 report on the predicted demand for graduates published jointly by the Standing Conference of Employers of Graduates (SCOEG), the Association of Graduate Careers Advisers (AGCAS), and the Central Services Unit (CSU) concluded:

> . . . The increasing complexity of many activities means that those with a high level of education have a great advantage in the search for employment, and this advantage over non-graduates is likely to continue. (Syrett 1983)

Despite these claims, scepticism over the purported employment benefits of higher education is more prevalent than hitherto and the recognition that a degree no longer guarantees entry to a high status profession is more apparent in popular conceptions. Consequently, prospective applicants may have to give greater care to assessing the extent to which higher education will deliver the enhanced career prospects it alleges it can.

In addition to improving the efficiency of productive enterprises, some commentators maintain that only in the context of a direct and constructive interrelation between higher education and the economy does it appear plausible that institutions of higher education might have a major contribution to make towards constructing a fairer economic and social structure.

Consequently, it is assumed that, in view of the doubts and questions surrounding its social and private returns, its efficiency and equity, the relation of higher education to economic processes constitutes a major social problem, and continues to require research and analysis.

As a reflection of the above, the focus of the research done for this study is predominantly, though not exclusively, concerned with the economic relevance of higher education rather than its intrinsic benefits or the cultural enrichment of its recipients. In economists' terms, the principal concern is with 'education as investment' rather than 'education as consumption', although aspects of the latter arise at various points. It is certainly not being suggested that intrinsic outcomes are of little importance in higher education, only that, in the opinion of the authors, issues of economic and employment relevance, with their associated policy complications, are currently more urgent and problematic than issues of consumption.

In considering how to render this very general topic more precise and manageable, at least three different types of approach to the problem can be identified. The most methodologically developed is that of the 'human capital' school of educational economists. Applying a 'cost-benefit' framework, this attempts to quantify the private and social returns on different types of investment in higher education. In the case of social returns, it typically calculates the costs of providing courses and uses gross earnings as a measure of social benefits, on the assumption that earnings signify the value of a worker's marginal productivity. The Department of Education and Science (DES) have carried out rate of return analyses (see Morris and Ziderman 1971) and other examples of the method can be found in Morris, (1973), Woodhall (1973) and Ziderman (1973).

Citing the ubiquitous imperfections in the wage-labour market which invalidate the 'income as value of productivity' principle and the intractable difficulties of quantifying economic benefits, Berg (1970) provides an alternative and more direct method of analysing graduates' contribution to economic productivity. Recognizing the difficulties involved in measuring standards of occupational performance, Berg, by examining such data as productivity rates, absenteeism and job satisfaction, contrasts the actual job performances of graduates and non-graduates in identical or similar jobs.

By a third approach, general indications of the nature and extent of the economic benefits graduates bring and of the contribution they make can be gained from surveys of their early career and employment patterns. For instance, valuable inferences concerning the economic relevance of different academic disciplines are provided in Tarsh's (1982) analysis of graduate unemployment rates six months after graduation. Offering similar indications from labour market trends, Williamson (1981) covers a much longer time scale and includes a greater range of relevant data.

The present study has adopted the latter approach. Accordingly, data on the early careers of graduates have been used to extract and interpret a variety of signals about the quality of the degree courses' relevance to occupational and economic needs. An important advantage of this approach is the scope it allows for the study to combine a range of 'objective' behavioural indices (eg unemployment rates, occupational areas entered, status and levels of employment, sector of employment, salaries, and so on) with a variety of 'subjective' attitudinal items (eg job satisfaction, evaluations of degree currency, career aspirations, etc.). As a result of incorporating behavioural and attitudinal elements, the method has qualitative and sociological dimensions which are usually lacking in the quantitative and largely income-based rates of return method. Furthermore, in contrast to the methods developed by Berg, it has the advantage not only of including the experience of those in full-time employment, but of providing a full cross-section of graduates' career experiences (eg as housewives, temporary workers, or unemployed).

Admittedly, of the three approaches, the early careers approach adopted here is arguably less direct and more inferential than the other two, but it should be stressed that the alternatives also depend on fundamental assumptions and inferences. Another limitation of the early careers approach, is that it does not allow for any reasonably direct analysis of actual job performance, such as those carried out by Berg. Initially, it was hoped to overcome this weakness by supplementing the early careers survey with follow-up interviews of respondents and their employers, during which job performance would have been a major topic. Unfortunately, neither time nor resources permitted such an extension to the research, although, as a compromise, a sufficient number of respondents volunteered written comments to permit an indirect analysis of the skills level demanded by various occupations.

Finally, it must be conceded that, compared with the lifelong age-earnings profiles common to many rates of return analyses, the time span feasible in early careers approaches is short. It is nevertheless believed that the length of time covered by this study (the thirty months following graduation) is sufficient to allow a comparative assessment of graduates' employment and occupational standing. On balance, although the early careers approach is not without shortcomings, its strengths, particularly its scope for embracing quantitative and qualitative data across the full spectrum of career patterns, are considerable.

Diversified Degree Graduates

The research for this study centres upon the BA/BSc graduates – sometimes referred to as the diversified degree or non-BEd graduates – from colleges and institutes of higher education. As will be outlined below, there are several reasons why this group constitutes an interesting case *sui generis*. In addition, while appreciating that the characteristics of the group are sufficiently atypical as to preclude simple generalizations to a broader population, it is considered that interpretations arising from their particular case contain important lessons for the wider field of graduates.

Precise classifications of colleges and institutes of higher education are unavailable, but according to the 1982 *Handbook of Degree and Advanced Courses* (Central Register and Clearing House 1982), sixty-three such institutions then qualified for the title. All but three of these were also included in the 1982 *Guide to the Colleges and Institutes of Higher Education* (Standing Conference of Principals and Directors of Colleges and Institutes in Higher Education 1982).

Largely under the auspices of this latter organization, the colleges and institutes of higher education have taken some steps towards presenting a collective identity. It would, however, be mistaken to think of them as a homogeneous group and, for the purposes of this study, it has proved useful to distinguish between three different types.

As indicated in Table 1.1, the largest group (A) are the voluntary and maintained colleges which have diversified, either as free-standing institutions, or through amalgamations with other colleges of education, from a teacher training base. The thirty-nine colleges and institutes of higher education of this type are referred to here as 'former colleges of education'.

A FORMER COLLEGES OF EDUCATION
Institutions which diversified from a teacher training base[a] – sometimes through amalgamation with another college of education

(i) Voluntary	V[c]	N[d]	(ii) LEA Maintained	V[c]	N[d]
Bishop Grosseteste[ab]	U	500	Avery Hill[a]	C	700
Chester	U	1,000	Bangor Normal[b]	U	400
Christ Church	U	850	Bath	C/U	990
De La Salle	U	900	Bretton Hall	U	750
Homerton	U	700	Bulmershe	C	1,000
King Alfred's	C	1,100	Charlotte Mason[a]	U	300
La Sainte Union	U	650	City of Liverpool	U	1,100
Liverpool Institute	U	1,500	City of Manchester	U	1,000
Newman[a]	U	640	Crewe & Alsager	C	1,600
Roehampton	U	2,500	Edge Hill	U	1,300
Ripon & York St. John	U	1,550	Hertfordshire	C	700
St. Mark & St. John	C	650	Ilkley	C/U	800
S. Martin's	U	730	Matlock	U	450
St. Mary's Fenham	C	320	Nonington	U	300
St. Mary's Twickenham	U	1,200	North Riding[a]	U	350
St. Paul & St. Mary	C	1,250	Rolle	U	500
Trinity & All Saints	U	900	West Midlands	C	800
Trinity Carmarthen	U	450	Worcester	C	1,000
Westhill[a]	U	530	TOTAL STUDENTS		14,040
Westminster	C	400			
West Sussex	C	1,000			
TOTAL STUDENTS		19,320			

B COMBINATION COLLEGES
Institutions including a college of education and a college of further education or art

	V[c]	N[d]		V[c]	N[d]
Bedford	C	1,600	Hull	C	3,000
Bradford	C	2,600	Luton	C	1,500
Bucks	C	1,800	Nene	U	1,400
Chelmer	C	1,300	New College, Durham	C	1,500
Colchester[b]	C	2,000	North Cheshire	U	450
Derby Lonsdale	C/U	1,500	N.E. Wales	U	960
Doncaster	C	2,000	South Glamorgan	U	3,600
Dorset	C/U	1,500	West Glamorgan	U	900
Gwent	U	1,200	West London	U	2,500
			TOTAL STUDENTS		31,310

C PROTO-POLYTECHNICS
Institutions not including initial teacher education courses

	V[c]	N[d]		V[c]	N[d]
Bolton	C	1,000	Harrow	C	1,200
Cambridgeshire CAT	C	2,000	Slough	C	900
Ealing	C	2,000	Southampton	C	1,500
			TOTAL STUDENTS		8,600

OVERALL NUMBER OF STUDENTS 73,270

Notes

a Colleges so marked have not diversified to the point of providing non-teaching first degree programmes, though they may offer diplomas in non-teaching subjects.

b Apart from these, all the other institutions shown in the Table were included in the 1982 Guide to the Colleges and Institutes of Higher Education.

c Validating body: U = University; C = CNAA.

d Approximate number of full-time students on AFE courses. The numbers are approximate because it is not clear from the source whether 'full-time' or 'full-time equivalent' figures are presented.

Source Central Register and Clearing House (1982)

Table 1.1
The colleges and institutes of higher education.

In addition to providing BEd programmes, the majority of the former colleges of education have diversified to the extent of offering BA/BSc[1] first degree programmes; the few (6) which have not are identified in the table.

A second group (B), here termed 'combination colleges' constitute those colleges of education which joined forces with colleges of further education, or, in some cases, colleges of art. Eighteen institutions are of this type. A third group (C), possessing a technical or arts college tradition, offer no initial teacher education courses and have no links with colleges of education. The six institutions fitting this description are here called 'proto-polytechnics'.

It should be stressed that such terms as 'combination colleges' and 'proto-polytechnics' were adopted for no other purpose than ease of identification in this study. Institutions were assigned to the categories according to the nature of any recent amalgamations and whether they incorporated teacher training courses. The meaning of the terms is entirely limited to these criteria and no prescriptive connotations regarding the status of the institutions are intended.

In order to extend the scope for comparative analysis, a small number of combination colleges and proto-polytechnics have been included in the research, but the major concern has been with the former colleges of education, especially those which have diversified into BA/BSc first degree programmes. Without replicating the valuable existing historical accounts of this type of institution (eg Dent 1977; Hencke 1978; Lynch 1979), a brief summary of the background to its recent emergence may prove helpful to readers unfamiliar with this sector of higher education.

Historical Background to the Colleges

Although the earliest teacher training establishments in England and Wales date from the very beginning of the nineteenth century, it was not until the middle of that century that systematic teacher training reached any significant scale. Then, by 1850, there were over thirty teacher training colleges, most of which were residential, Anglican foundations. Several commentators have noted that many of the problems vexing training colleges over the years can be traced to the original qualities and values of these founding institutions (Hencke 1978; Lynch 1979): the absence, for example, of a claim to a university tradition or connection, which evoked and perpetuated an image of the colleges as the poor relation of post-secondary education, despite their imitation of university architecture and trappings; education's lack of academic respectability as a discipline of knowledge; a shortage of students with high levels of intellectual calibre; and curricula which attempted to combine personal education with a craft apprenticeship approach to professional training.

Usually adopting the Anglican model, other voluntary organizations established more colleges throughout the latter half of the nineteenth century, and when, following the 1902 Education Act, local education authorities opened more colleges, they too, by and large, followed a similar pattern. The expansion of teacher training colleges which followed the entry of local authorities into the field, though slow at first, was eventually so extensive that by 1960 there were approximately one hundred and fifty colleges. Only a third were run by voluntary bodies, the remainder were local authority maintained.

During this period of development, entry to the teaching profession was typically through one of three routes: college certificates based on two years' concurrent training; one year consecutive training in a University Education Department following graduation; or untrained, graduate entry from universities. In terms of obtaining employment, academic achievements were superior to craft-based skills, and the cream of teaching appointments generally went to university graduates, who were often untrained, in preference to college trained applicants. With the greater involvement of government in all aspects of educational provision, the criticisms of the low academic standards of many colleges received stronger political support, and a succession of reports were commissioned to inquire into the state of teacher training.

In an effort to improve the academic credibility of colleges, the Burnham Committee recommended in 1925 that colleges should develop closer ties with universities, which would assume responsibility for validating their two-year training certificates. In 1942, the Government set up the McNair Committee, but this failed to reach agreement on vital issues concerning the colleges' future development. Half the committee wished to see all teacher training establishments integrated into a single administrative system under the universities. The other half recommended that, by placing them both under the auspices of area training services, the individual identities of colleges and of university education departments should be preserved. Integration was rejected and subsequent development reflected a compromise between the two proposals.

After the Second World War, the colleges experienced two waves of rapid expansion. In response to the postwar increase in the birthrate, the raising of the school leaving age to fifteen in 1947, and the growth of secondary modern schools, the first expansion involved the establishment of emergency training colleges by local education authorities. Then, following a brief oversupply of teachers in the mid-1950s, when, as a way both of avoiding closures and improving standards, the two-year course was extended to three, a second phase of expansion began in 1960. This was precipitated by a further increase in the birthrate from 1957, and a realization that there would be insufficient higher education places available to accommodate the immediate postwar generation that was then approaching university entry age. It was against this background that in 1961 a committee under the chairmanship of Lord Robbins was charged with the task of examining the capacity of the entire higher education system to meet future national needs.

In an effort to improve the academic standing of the colleges, the Robbins Report (Committee on Higher Education 1963) recommended a change of name from 'training colleges' to 'colleges of education', the introduction of a four-year BEd degree which would be comparable in standard with the BA degree, and the establishment of Schools of Education, under which the colleges would enjoy closer links with universities but without sacrificing their independence or their links with local education authorities. The latter recommendation was not implemented. Robbins also advocated a large increase in the colleges' student intake, as well as a general commitment to opening up advanced education access to what had been identified as a predominantly working class 'reserve of untapped ability'. With regard to these latter proposals, from the early sixties through to the mid-seventies the colleges substantially increased their student numbers and research suggests that, relative to the universities, the college constituency contained a higher proportion of students from working class backgrounds (Halsey et al. 1980). During this period, for many such students, the colleges of education provided an avenue to occupational and social mobility that was difficult to find elsewhere.

In spite of Robbins' encouraging recommendations and the second wave of expansion, the latter half of the 1960s held a mounting store of problems for the colleges. The post-Robbins compromises failed to dispel continuing tensions between the universities and the colleges over academic status; the precarious position of the colleges was shaken still further by the designation of thirty polytechnics and the consequent creation of a binary system of higher education; the birthrate began to fall – thus starting a trend which would have a profound impact on the colleges in the mid-seventies; and searching questions were being widely asked about the quality of the colleges' curricula. Amidst growing criticisms of the lack of coherence in the BEd degree and of unity between subject specialists and professional training, a Parliamentary Select Committee on Education and Science (see Willey and Maddison 1971) recommended another, major inquiry into the organization of teacher training.

In December 1970, the Secretary of State for Education, Margaret Thatcher, appointed a committee under the chairmanship of Lord James of Rusholme to look into the future of teacher training. In addition to examining the organization of courses and the roles of all higher education institutions vis-à-vis teacher training, the committee was specifically requested to consider:

> . . . whether a large proportion of intending teachers should be educated with students who have not chosen their careers or have chosen other careers; . . . (DES 1972a, p.iii)

The James Report (DES 1972a), published in February 1972, proposed a novel, but inevitably contentious, teacher education scheme consisting of three cycles. In an effort to reduce the tensions between subject specialisms and professional training, Cycle 1 would consist of a two-year Diploma in Higher Education (DipHE) at a college of education (first proposed as a two-year degree) or a three-year university or polytechnic first degree; Cycle 2 would provide a two-year period of pre-service professional training and induction, after which a BA (Education) would be awarded; Cycle 3 entailed a planned programme of in-service training and professional development. As far as the colleges were concerned, the crucial feature of Cycle 1 was that students who intended to become teachers would study for the DipHE alongside other students who could proceed to take a first degree or enter alternative careers.

Reactions to the Report were mixed, but in general, perhaps predictably, the 3-cycle teacher education scheme did not gain widespread approval. The Government's response was delivered in a White Paper, *Education: A Framework for Expansion* (DES 1972b). While accepting the objectives of an expansion in in-service provision (Cycle 3) and the progressive achievement of an all-graduate profession, the White Paper rejected Cycle 2 on the grounds that it allowed insufficient time for teaching practice. It gave guarded support to the introduction of the DipHE, but neither potential students nor employers appear to have been substantially attracted by this qualification.

Following Hencke (1978), it is arguable that if the James Committee had explicitly addressed the really crucial, but at the time not widely appreciated, difficulties facing the colleges – namely, the fall in the birthrate and the consequential drop in demand for teachers – response to the Report would have been very different. Although it implicitly assumed the probability of a fall in the demand for teachers, the James Report contained no detailed or explicit analysis of manpower forecasts for them. This was an astonishing omission, especially since officials from the DES, the main public body to support the setting up of this inquiry, had already intimated, albeit reluctantly, that in terms of the future demand for teachers, the colleges looked to be seriously over-committed. Hencke (1978) has maintained that, not only were the James Committee aware of the impending over-supply, but their draft report did contain a chapter presenting details. Such information would have strengthened the arguments for using any spare capacity that might exist in the colleges to improve and extend the overall period of teacher training or to diversify into the field of non-teaching degrees and diplomas. That chapter, however, did not appear in the final version – perhaps because of a disagreement between the DES and the committee over its policy implications – and the public remained largely unaware of the seriousness of the potential mis-match between teacher supply and demand. Hencke (1978) writes:

> One can only speculate on the response the James Report might have had from the same organizations which criticized the proposals if the figures had been known publicly at the time. What happened was that hostile public opinion, which had not been given a true picture, turned against the majority of the James proposals. This reaction resulted in a delay until the Department had worked out its policies to be published in the White Paper. (Hencke 1978, p.46)

The Government's policy responses to the decline in the birthrate were stated in the 1972 White Paper and the circulars (DES 1973, 1974) which followed it. As a result of negotiations between the DES, local authorities and voluntary bodies, some colleges would close completely, some would be absorbed by, or amalgamated with, other institutions of higher education, some would remain monotechnics (ie offering only teaching degrees), others would be allowed to diversify and develop into free-standing 'major institutions of higher education', offering first degree programmes ostensibly unrelated to teacher training. Notwithstanding a few brief references to educational objectives, such as the capacity for students to defer their commitment to teaching (DES 1974), the Government provided little overall guidance and coherence for the emergence of these 'major institutions' (Locke and Russell 1979; Locke 1979) and few doubt that the proposals were more financially and politically motivated than educationally inspired.

For the Government, this approach achieved the closure of several institutions at a time of growing financial stringency, pre-empted full-scale opposition by offering the larger colleges the incentive of diversification, and avoided the political embarrassment which would have followed such a draconian number of closures if some diversification had not been allowed. Diversification into first degrees in general arts[2] subjects would also increase the capacity of the higher education sector to provide sufficient places to meet the demand from the growing number of eighteen-year-olds, which would peak and then decline in the early 1980s. For the colleges, although severely reduced in number, survival was the achievement, and the capacity to diversify into the arena of non-teaching degrees was a significant step forward in their long search to be recognized as a legitimate member of the family of higher education institutions.

The impact of these policies threw the colleges into a period of turmoil and trauma. Following two rounds of closures and many institutional re-groups, all of which are well documented in Hencke (1978), Lynch (1979) and Locke and Russell (1979), the college of education sector gradually disappeared during the second half of the seventies. In its place there emerged an important new sector and force within higher education in England and Wales. Aspiring to the status implied by the 1972 White Paper's phrase 'major institutions of higher education', the new institutions which were forged out of the reorganization of the colleges, in the absence of any directive from the DES, led the way in adopting for themselves and similar establishments the title 'college of higher education' or ' institute of higher education'. With only a few of them remaining monotechnic, the majority participated in the process of diversification and, by the beginning of the academic year 1976, were registering undergraduates on BA/BSc non-teaching degree programmes. The shift from an exclusive concentration on teacher education to the provision of diversified degree programmes was so widespread that by the close of the decade, many colleges of higher education had as many BA/BSc as BEd students, if not more. Again in the absence of any government initiatives, and in order to provide a corporate identity and platform for the sector, in February 1978 the Standing Conference of Principals and Directors of Colleges and Institutes in Higher Education was formed. Membership consisted of higher education establishments, other than universities and polytechnics, in which a significant proportion of courses had been validated at degree level. The 1981 membership amounted to sixty institutions, including thirty-seven former colleges of education, seventeen combination colleges and six proto-polytechnics.

Table 1.1 shows that approximately 73,000 students were enrolled on full-time courses in the college of higher education sector. While 55,000 were on advanced further education (degree and degree level) courses, the remaining 18,000 were on non-advanced further education courses, the vast majority of which were provided by the combination colleges (B in the table) and proto-polytechnics (C in the table). The 55,000 undergraduates on degree or degree level courses in the college of higher education sector represented 12 per cent of all full-time students in higher education in England and Wales. The corresponding percentages for polytechnics and universities were 32 and 56 per cent respectively. These figures give an indication of the comparative size of the college of higher education sector, but it should be noted that the numbers include undergraduates on teaching and non-teaching degree programmes. The present study centres upon the early career patterns of graduates of the latter, non-teaching courses, predominantly, but not exclusively, from the former colleges of education.

Empirical Questions for the Research

Throughout the founding stages of the colleges of higher education, certain leading principals were convinced that a critical factor in securing the success of the diversified degree programmes was the extent to which they reflected and responded to the employment needs of the country. For example, in his opening address to the 'Higher Education: An Alternative Way' conference (30 September 1979), Mr. J.V. Barnett, Chairman of the Standing Conference, emphasized the need for the new courses to be relevant to economic requirements and said:

> One of the challenges facing the colleges and institutes is whether they possess the imagination and resourcefulness to develop in particular new insights into the vocational preparation of the non-technical graduate whether employed in the public or private sector.

As another indication of the colleges' concern for the occupational outlets of their new graduates, they formed, under the aegis of the Standing Conference, the Association of Careers Advisers in Colleges of Higher Education (ACACHE) in order to promote college careers advisory services and to monitor graduates' first destinations. In 1979, approximately two thousand non-teaching degree graduates (eg BA/BSc) were believed to have left the colleges. Using coding and recording procedures identical to those used by universities and polytechnics, ACACHE (1979) mounted a pilot first destinations survey which covered about half of the 1979 graduates. In 1980, on the basis of more comprehensive surveys, ACACHE recorded 2,747 graduates with non-teaching degrees from the colleges of higher education, and by 1981 the corresponding total had risen to 3,409.

In order to prepare the way for an evaluation of the employment currency of the new programmes, it was first necessary to provide an empirical account of the early careers of non-teaching degree graduates from colleges which had diversified from a tradition of teacher training. But no comparable study was available.

The absence in the literature of a retrospective study of college graduates' careers is largely explained by the simple fact that the colleges did not produce a substantial output of non-teaching degree graduates until 1979. Consequently, without severely reducing the time allowed for graduate career patterns to emerge, an earlier version of the kind of study attempted here would scarcely have been possible. The sources of information closest to the present undertaking are the annual first destination statistics provided by ACACHE, which, like their counterparts from other sectors of higher education, perform the valuable but necessarily limited task of producing data on graduates' circumstances immediately after graduation. Although these sources, especially those relating to 1979 graduates, have been immensely valuable, it was intended that the present research should extend the depth and scope of analysis beyond that made possible by first destination statistics alone.

In addition to the understandable absence of retrospective studies of college graduates' careers, the remaining literature also contains very few general references to the prospective employment orientations of diversified courses. Dent (1977), Hencke (1978), Lynch (1979), Russell and Pratt (1979), Campbell-Stewart (1980) and Gedge (1981) provide useful accounts of the development up to, and through, the process of diversification, but seldom and only tangentially do they comment on aspects relating to careers and employment.

Adelman and Gibbs (1979, 1980a, 1980b) provide an important case study of three former colleges of education which were among the first to offer a greater diversity of courses and programmes of study. The focus of their research was largely on the experience of undergraduates as they entered and progressed through their colleges, and on the changes to the colleges' organization and curricula. Although they present some interesting findings on students' early career aspirations, they had little to say about graduates' initial employment trends and were unable to follow their main cohort, based on the 1976 entre, after they had left college.

Studies by Locke and Russell (1979), Locke (1979), Pratt et al. (1979) and Russell and Pratt (1979), although providing a useful overview of all colleges in this sector, remain essentially re-analyses of already published official statistics. Concentrating on the state of general policy formation during the period of diversification and amalgamations, they say little about the students' experience of the colleges, and even less about the career expectations and employment patterns of college graduates. A more recent study, McNamara and Ross (1982), included nine colleges in its sample of seventeen institutions. However, their survey was predominantly concerned with BEd students and only incidentally with diversified degree programmes. The cross-sector project, 'Expectations of Higher Education', recently completed at Brunel University, will produce some information relevant to this area.

It is intended that the present study will go some way towards remedying the lack in the existing literature of any descriptive and empirically-based account of the early careers of non-teaching degree graduates from colleges by providing a basis for addressing issues of economic relevance. Consequently, once having documented the main trends and patterns of graduates' early careers, the plan is to interrogate the empirical findings from the perspectives and priorities offered in the opening sections of this chapter. At an empirical level, the question is, 'What indications of the economic contribution of diversified degrees emerge from the portrayal of college graduates' early careers?' More specifically, this raises the following kinds of questions:

1 As indications of economic contribution, what were the main early career and employment patterns displayed by the 1979 non-teaching degree graduates from colleges of higher education which diversified from a teacher training base?

2 As a further indication of economic contribution, at what levels of occupational status were graduates with non-teaching degrees finding employment?

3 Are there any sub-groups among these graduates whose early careers were markedly different from the rest of the group?

4 How did the early careers of college graduates compare with graduates from other sectors of higher education?

5 To what extent were college graduates satisfied with their degree currency and occupational circumstances?

6 Does the diversified degree appear to enhance the career prospects, employability and salaries of it holders?

Important as they are intrinsically, the answers to such questions have a wider significance. At one level, they engender important policy implications for the colleges' institutional and curricula development; at another, they provide a useful basis for exploring general problems in the wider graduate labour market. Taking each of these levels in turn, the remainder of this chapter delineates areas of particular interest to the present study.

Employment-related Issues for College Policy

The empirical material gathered for this study offers an opportunity for a review of policy in three main areas:

A In view of the early career experiences of diversified degree graduates, would (i) the extending of the occupational relevance of teaching degree programmes or (ii) the continued provision of non-teaching courses, represent the most efficient and resourceful method of giving the colleges the required stability to respond flexibly to a fluctuating demand for teachers?

B Assuming the desirability of some provision of diversified courses, do the early career experiences of non-teaching graduates from the former colleges of education lend support to the strengthening of (i) liberal arts degree programmes or (ii) more vocationally-specific courses?

C Assuming the continued provision of diversified liberal arts degree programmes, do the results offer encouragement for any distinctive curricula innovations, such as careers education courses, which might enhance the economic relevance and marketability of college graduates?

A brief examination of the recent development of these policy issues soon reveals the enormous influence the DES have wielded in shaping their direction. Although it would be mistaken to conceive of the colleges' internal policy bodies as entirely passive, throughout the last decade the DES constraints imposed on them have often been so restrictive that internal academic policy-making has had very little room to manoeuvre. Several commentators have already noted that government policy towards the colleges has frequently been characterized by fragmented and negative adminstrative constraints rather than constructive and integral planning (Hencke 1979; Locke 1979). In such a climate, policies regularly seemed to progress by default rather than by avowed intention and design. For readers unfamiliar with this sector, it may be useful at this point to offer a brief outline of their recent background.

First, the decision to increase the flexibility of the colleges' output by introducing diversified programmes, as opposed to making the BEd less of a single occupation qualification, rested heavily on the DES's fundamental assumption that a BEd non-teacher was a wasted resource, and by implication, that a BA/BSc non-teacher was a less wasteful resource. Effectively, it was assumed that, in periods of reduced demand for teachers, adding to the stock of arts and social science graduates represents a more efficient use of resources than increasing the number of BEd graduates. Despite the importance of this point, there was in the official publications which precipitated the introduction of BA/BSc degrees in colleges, not only no analysis of this assumption, but an almost total absence of any kind of reference to the potential employment outlets for the non-teaching degree graduates.

The most influential antecedent to the introduction of diversified degree courses was the Government's 1972 White Paper (DES 1972b). In proposing that some colleges should diversify, it is interesting to note that the only indication of the possible employment relevance for the proposed new courses was the vague reference to 'other professions':

> Some colleges either singly or jointly should develop . . . into major institutions of higher education concentrating on the arts and human sciences, with particular reference to their application in teaching and other professions. (DES 1972b, p.44)

Likewise, in the two DES circulars 7/73 and 6/74 that were intended to implement the developments proposed in the White Paper (DES 1973, 1974), no further guidelines on employment orientations were offered and, moreover, in setting out their criteria for assessing local authority plans for developing the colleges, no mention was made of the need to evaluate whether or not an employment demand existed for graduates of diversified courses. This is a curious omission, particularly since the major political parties have increasingly proclaimed their commitment to the criteria of economic relevance in the planning of higher education. Why then should such an important policy document so conspicuously ignore the employment implications of the courses they proposed?

A closer reading of the relevant documents suggests that the DES and the government were clearly aware of the possible employment problems likely to face diversified degree graduates, but chose not to highlight them and, in effect, left the colleges concerned to cope as best they could.

Two extracts from the 1972 White Paper's general sections on higher education are worth juxtaposing:

> The motives that impel sixth formers to seek higher education are many, various and seldom clear-cut . . . . But not far from the surface of most candidates' minds is the tacit belief that higher education will go far to guarantee them a better job. (DES 1972b, pp.30–1)

> The expansion of higher education provision has already reached the point where employers' requirements for such highly qualified people in the forms of employment they traditionally enter are, in the aggregate, largely being met . . . there seems little doubt that the continuing expansion of higher education will more than match the likely expansion of graduate employment opportunities as they are understood today. (DES 1972b, p.34)

It is difficult to imagine that the tensions between these two statements were not lost on DES officials and government ministers. Given, on the one hand, continued graduate expectations of career benefits, and on the other hand, a likely oversupply of graduates, with all its associated problems of underemployment and 'filtering down' in the labour market, the prospect of a considerable mis-match between expectations and outcome cannot have been totally unpredicted. Furthermore, information was available to indicate that general arts graduates were particularly vulnerable to the problems of oversupply and lack of demand (eg Hebron 1971). Yet, contrary to offering the colleges the resources and encouragement to broaden the occupational scope of their teaching degrees or to develop new and more economically-relevant courses, the government emphatically restricted them to diversified versions of their existing BEd curricula:

> Institutions applying for this more general authority [to diversify their courses][3] will need to show that such courses are wholly or mainly constituted of elements common to existing or proposed courses of teacher education or to other advanced courses already approved and that no additional staff will be required. (DES 1974, p.46)

In view of the lack of positive and detailed directives, and of the enforcement on the colleges of such limits to their curricula development, the Conservative Government of 1972 must bear a heavy responsibility for the employment experiences of diversified degree graduates from colleges of higher education. It was left to a study conducted in 1981 by the Department of Employment, at the request of the DES, to give the first signs of recognition of the lack of policy with respect to the employment outlets of college degree graduates:

> ... more information is needed about the growing number of graduates from institutions of higher education in England and Wales other than universities and polytechnics so that the degree courses provided by these institutions can be more closely related to the demand for graduates. (Catto et al. 1981, p.13)

By way of responding to this recommendation, it is hoped that, in this first of the selected policy areas, the present research findings can be used to assess the assumption that, in terms of a variety of employment outlets, the diversified degree programmes represent a better investment of resources than teaching degree courses.

Secondly, given the colleges' dual tradition and expertise in professional training and subject specialisms, principally in the liberal arts, the potential for diversification could be advanced along two main paths: one, building on professional training, would provide specific vocational preparation for other occupations apart from teaching; the other would offer a combination of the established subject areas as first degrees in their own right. Examples of the former are training courses for social workers and occupational therapists; an example of the latter, a BA in history and English. From the perspective of 'ideal' institutional models, the accent on a diversity of vocationally-related courses would make the colleges resemble small polytechnics, whereas emphasis on general arts degrees would cast them in the mould of small universities.

The Robbins Report (Committee on Higher Education 1963), the first official document in modern times to hint at diversification in the colleges, sought to encourage experimentation with both types:

> ... Some colleges will wish to broaden their scope by providing courses, with a measure of common studies, for entrants to various professions in the social services. We think they should be allowed to do so as soon as practicable, although we believe it would be wrong to suppose that the needs of these professions are likely to be such as to require large-scale provision in the generality of colleges. Other colleges may wish to provide general courses in arts or science subjects. (Committee on Higher Education 1963, p.108)

A decade later, during which time thirty polytechnics had been created, the James Report (DES 1972a) commented on the prospects for diversification in the colleges. In contrast to Robbins, however, the James Committee rejected the idea of a plurality of specific professional training courses and opted for the provision of general courses in the shape of the proposed DipHE:

> The colleges would contain a large range of students who, on completing the diploma course, would proceed on a number of different paths. The colleges would therefore be no longer training teachers in isolation. This solution to the problem of isolation would be better than the 'diversification' often urged, which seems to imply an unrealistic proliferation of specialist training courses for different professions, within the same institutions. (DES 1972a, p.69)

Apparently accepting this argument, the Government also favoured the generalist type of diversification policy and pursued it, not only through the DipHE, but also by allowing some colleges to offer first degrees, predominantly in the arts and social sciences. These policies were implemented through the 1972 White Paper and subsequent circulars (DES 1973 and 1974). In theory, colleges were free to explore the possibility of mounting alternative professional training courses, and some in fact succeeded in doing so. However, the DES restrictions controlling the setting up of vocational courses (eg through the approval of Regional Advisory Councils, limitations on recruiting new staff, etc.) were generally instrumental in reducing the chances of this form of diversification becoming the dominant mode. In the absence of any publicly available analysis of the respective employment relevance of the two modes of diversification, it is hoped that the present research results will provide some broad indications of the consequences and advisability of sustaining the current weight of emphasis between them.

This third policy issue involves an examination of the extent to which the results offer any pointers to the kind of distinctive curricula developments (eg work experience or increased student choice of course components) that may enhance the employability and economic relevance of diversified degree graduates. Although an empirically-based analysis of such a question is notably absent from the available literature, a number of commentators have emphasized or predicted the need for it. Catto et al. (1981) have already been quoted to this effect and Murray (1978) has indicated the degree of controversy which may surround the issue of the economic relevance of the colleges' diversified curricula:

> Serious problems of graduate unemployment seem unavoidable. The kind of courses many former colleges of education are best equipped to provide will certainly come under increasing criticism in relation to the manpower requirements of a sick economy. (Murray 1978, p.59)

In addition to the absence of particularly employment-related commentaries on diversified courses, there is also a shortage of literature on general aspects of the diversified curricula. However, according to the few available sources, it is widely accepted that, as a consequence of the Government's restrictions on the development of diversified courses and the recruitment of new staff, the non-teaching degree programmes were largely confined to the liberal arts emphasis characteristic of the BEd and Certificate of Education (CertEd) tradition. Having very little room for manoeuvre or real innovation, the former colleges of education devised non-teaching degree courses which closely paralleled their BEd origins (Locke 1979;

Locke and Russell 1979; Adelman and Gibbs 1980a,1980b; Murray 1978). Indeed, in many colleges, especially those validated by universities, subjects could be studied in groups which contained some students reading for BEd degrees and some for non-teaching degrees such as a BA or BSc (McNamara and Ross 1982). Because of the limitations on staffing and the necessity of avoiding direct competition with the universities for student enrolments, the vast majority of diversified programmes were not single subject degrees, but combined degrees, usually in two subject areas. Similarly, to secure safe and speedy passage through the necessary validation procedures, most courses were designed according to established and reputable academic procedures and did not risk less conventional proposals. As a result, the colleges have been criticized for 'aping the universities' and extending still further the process of 'academic drift'. Raggett and Clarkson (1976) were among the first commentators who regretted the lack of imagination in most of the new course offerings and observed that:

> . . . colleges have played safe and reproduced their existing teacher education main subject courses as new degrees and avoided the harder, more perilous development of new and untried areas. (Raggett and Clarkson 1976, p.163)

More stringent criticism was levelled against the subject orientation of the diversified courses by the Conservative MP, Keith Hampson, who argued:

> The people that the country lacks most are technicians, not degree people, and especially not people with degrees in humanities . . . . All too often . . . diversification and amalgamation have meant that liberal arts courses are being substituted [for teacher training]. Perhaps this was inevitable, given the sort of staff and facilities which most of the colleges of education had . . . . The result has been a proliferation of degree courses of a kind and quality which the country and our students simply do not need. (Hampson 1977)

A further reasonably widespread feature of the newly introduced diversified curricula was the adoption of modular or flexible programme structures, whereby students could select course units in line with their developing interests and career aspirations (Murray 1978; Lynch 1979; McNamara and Ross 1982). Following up recommendations expressed in the James Report, the 1972 White Paper and subsequent DES Circulars (DES 1972a, 1972b, 1973, 1974), a key claim made for unit-based schemes was that they provided opportunities for undergraduates to defer their commitment to teaching or alternative occupations. The extent to which transfer between teaching and non-teaching degree programmes was possible, the relative degrees of student choice in modular structures and its consequences for the institutional deployment of resources, are aspects of unit-based curricula which are well observed by Adelman and Gibbs (1979, 1980a, 1980b).

Thorburn and Parker (1978, 1980) have produced two rare sociological critiques of the curricula effects of diversification in the colleges. In the first, they maintain that during the period of diversification some key institutional changes have taken place: an increasing bureaucratization; a growth in courses with all-embracing inter-disciplinary labels; and a spread of a vocational orientation which involves much more instrumental appraisal of means and ends in higher education courses. In the later paper

(1980), Thorburn and Parker develop their notion of a vocationalist orientation by distinguishing between colleges' 'traditional (true) vocationalism' — clearly-defined ends and means related to teacher training — and a 'new vocationalism', which is characterized by a 'lack of clear occupational ends combined with a variety of uncertain educational means' (p.63). It is suggested that colleges are experiencing the trauma of attempting to adopt 'new vocationalism', while simultaneously preserving the atmosphere of a monotechnic and its commitment to 'traditional vocationalism'. Asserting that claims for the 'new vocationalism' are merely rhetorical, the authors remain extremely sceptical of its relevance to the problems currently facing the colleges:

> Dimly perceived notions of the constitutive elements of this new form of vocationalism have been presented as part of the rationale of many of the recent courses . . . . This new vocationalism, with its dependence upon eclectic academic enquiry, and only vaguely formulated occupational ends may well have flourished in the more experimental and expansionist educational climate of a decade ago, but had become increasingly out of phase with the changed economic situation of the 1970s. (Thorburn and Parker 1980, pp.63-4)

In its place, these sociologists advocate:

> Ours has been an academic's message. We have argued for the retention and strengthening of traditional main subject areas where possible. Indeed the natural grouping of small numbers of lecturers around their disciplines represents, for us at least, a last chance to provide centres of excellence in particular areas while simultaneously retaining many of the face-to-face relationships associated with the older collegiate structures. (Thorburn and Parker 1980, p.69)

Adopting a position which is diametrically opposed to the ones just considered, Stodd (1980, 1981) has argued that the process of academic drift in the colleges has resulted in a lack of distinctiveness in many diversified course offerings, when compared with similar ones provided in the universities and polytechnics. Consequently, in view of forecasted smaller age cohorts, static age participation rates and financial restraints, Stodd maintains that the continued development of a traditional academic and liberal arts curricula, as a pale reflection of that which is already available in universities and polytechnics, will severely jeopardize the colleges' changes of survival. As a counter measure, he counsels the taking of positive steps to create a new and qualitatively different curricula for the colleges. It is suggested that a group of colleges should combine to operate a flexible credit transfer scheme, which would allow for different preferences in modes and phasing of study. Of particular relevance to our present interests, Stodd also advocates the inclusion of life skills and work experience schemes within the diversified curricular. A small number of colleges have in fact already introduced such components (Binks 1979) and it is upon the graduates' evaluation of these that much of the attention in this policy area is directed.

The Wider Graduate Labour Market

It would be misleading to consider the early careers of college graduates in isolation from recent trends in the graduate labour market as a whole. As a group, college graduates certainly possess a number of distinguishing features, but as graduates pure and simple they have much in common with their counterparts from other sectors of higher education and all confront the same present conditions of graduate employment. The employment patterns of college graduates are thus only fully understood when seen against the backcloth of the overall market for the highly qualified, and, indeed, in our final chapter here, policy issues of specific relevance to the colleges are prefaced by a discussion on the research's policy implications for the wider market. Meanwhile, a brief summary of recent trends in the early careers of all graduates is an essential preliminary to inspecting the experiences of college graduates in particular. The following points summarize the main trends in recent years.

For some time now, there have been substantial increases in the total number of first degree graduates from universities and polytechnics. Output from UK universities has risen from 57,000 in 1975 to 65,000 in 1979, and 67,000 in 1980[4]. The number obtaining full-time and sandwich degrees from polytechnics in England and Wales has increased from 14,000 in 1977 to 19,000 in 1979, and 19,500 in 1980[5]. Throughout the 1970s, there was a tendency in both sectors for the number of women graduates to increase at a greater rate than men, and the proportion of degrees in the arts and social sciences rose, while those in science and engineering fell (Catto et al. 1981).

According to the annual first destination statistics (UGC and PCA), the 1970s witnessed an upsurge in unemployment among new graduates, despite a very slight but temporary improvement in 1978 and 1979. These sources indicate that the rate of unemployment among new polytechnic graduates has tended to be higher than that of their counterparts from universities.

In the Unit for Manpower Studies (UMS) survey of 1970 new graduates from universities and polytechnics, Williamson (1981) found that those with a good class of first degree spent less time in unemployment, especially those who were subsequently engaged in public adminstration and industry. On the basis of first destination statistics for 1980 university graduates, Tarsh (1982) provides more recent evidence that a better class of degree is associated with a higher success rate in finding permanent employment.

Information derived from Catto et al. (1981, pp.78-9) indicates that during the late 1979s, the proportion of unemployed university graduates from engineering, science and social studies actually fell; in contrast, the corresponding proportion from the arts increased. By 1979, arts-based graduates from universities and polytechnics were respectively about five and seven times more likely to be unemployed than their colleagues in engineering. 1979 was a particularly difficult year for arts graduates, especially from the polytechnics, where one in four were unemployed. In all subjects, apart from engineering, the polytechnic rates were significantly higher than the universities. This may suggest that the perceived status of the sector in which a graduate studies is an important determinant of graduate employment patterns and prospects (see Bacon et al. 1979), although alternative explanations – more detailed subject differences, variations in A level grades – could also be important.

Covering the period 1976–1980, first destination statistics (UGC and PCA) show that for both universities and polytechnics, a slightly greater proportion of new female graduates accepted temporary work than did their male colleagues. Likewise, a slightly larger share of women was not available for employment. The universities generally had similar percentages of each gender in the 'believed unemployed' category, but the proportion of women polytechnic graduates in this category was usually a little higher than that of men. A large part of these tendencies seems to be operating independently of other factors such as subject area or institutional status.

Between 1975 and 1979, the number of university graduates undertaking further academic study or training declined, while the number entering permanent employment rose (University Grants Committee 1980, p.5). A smaller proportion of polytechnic graduates undertook further education or training, but they too displayed a similar decline: 25 per cent of all known first degree graduates in 1975, falling to 20 per cent in 1979. A slightly larger proportion of polytechnic graduates than of university graduates found permanent employment, and a similar, if less marked, increase was also evident for the polytechnic graduates: 53 per cent of all home graduates entered permanent employment in 1976, compared with 57 per cent in 1979.

The DES Statistical Bulletin 2/80 (DES 1980) reveals that the proportion of first degree graduates from universities entering industry and commerce increased over the 1970s. This was mainly due to a rise in the numbers entering commerce, a major outlet for the growing number of women graduates. In contrast, the proportion absorbed by the public service fell, especially in the civil and diplomatic services. The percentage of full-time polytechnic graduates who entered industry and commerce was similar to that of universities, but for those on sandwich courses[6] the polytechnic proportion was much higher.

The same source indicates that for 1977 and 1978, whereas 40 per cent of arts-based graduates undertook further study or training, only 30 per cent entered permanent home employment. By way of comparison, almost half of the social studies and science graduates, and two-thirds of engineering graduates, found permanent home employment. In addition, arts graduates frequently formed the highest share of those who were not available for employment. Of those arts graduates who entered permanent home employment, the highest proportion, approximately one-third, accepted jobs in commerce. Traditionally, the largest proportion of graduates absorbed by the public service and education are arts graduates (Catto et al. 1981). Alternatively, almost three-quarters of science and maths graduates who found permanent employment, did so in industry and commerce, as did 60 per cent of social studies graduates.

As a general rule, a greater proportion of male first degree graduates entered permanent home employment than female. In 1978 for example, of all male university graduates whose first destinations were known, 53 per cent entered permanent home employment, compared with 44 per cent of female graduates. In polytechnics, the corresponding figures were 57 and 52 per cent. Despite a recent increase in the proportion of women graduates going into industry, in 1978 nearly a quarter of men, but less than one tenth of women university graduates did so. For polytechnics, the percentages were slightly lower for women. There was seldom any difference between the sexes of those entering commerce.

Comparing the results of the research done by Kelsall et al. (1970) with the UMS survey, Williamson (1979b) concludes:

There is some slight evidence that the large increase in the overall numbers of graduates between 1960 and 1970 may have led to some filtering downwards into work traditionally regarded as non-graduate in nature. The percentage of graduates entering social services and personnel type work in their first job was slightly higher in 1970 (2 per cent of men and 8 per cent of women) than in 1960 (1 per cent of men and 6 per cent of women). A similar pattern exists for secretarial and clerical types of work . . . . (Williamson 1979b, p.1228)

Catto et al. (1981) suggest that the problem of 'filtering down' is particularly acute for social studies and arts graduates.

The UMS study of the early career movements of 1970 graduates found that men were more mobile than women in terms of occupation and type of work, but the reverse was the case for sector of employment. Over half the graduates who changed their jobs did so in the first two years, and a high proportion of women left for personal reasons. In a study of the retention of graduates in 264 firms, Hutt and Parsons (1981) discovered that half their graduate recruits had left these firms after five years, with most of the losses occurring during the first three years.

Among the reasons for choosing their first jobs, graduates placed particular emphasis on responsible and interesting work, a sufficient intellectual challenge, the opportunity to work with people and the constructive use of time. Although salary was often a secondary factor, engineers were especially responsive to a high starting salary and promotion assumed greater importance a few years after graduation, especially for men. Arts and social studies students were more disdainful of industry that their scientific and engineering colleagues (Burns 1980; Williamson 1981).

Among the agencies found most helpful in applying for and obtaining first jobs, 1970 graduates gave high ratings (in a general order of priority) to academic staff, friends and relatives, careers appointment services, newspaper or journal advertisements and employers' visits. Women, in particular, found contacts through an existing job very useful and Careers Appointments Services were especially popular in universities (Williamson 1981). A MORI study, commissioned by graduate employers and carried out in 1980, interviewed 1,085 final-year undergraduates and found that 80 per cent had made use of the university careers service before March in their final year (Burns 1980).

Of the 1970 UMS sample, the highest starting salaries were generally paid to engineering graduates, while arts graduates were usually the least well paid. On average, women obtained lower starting salaries than men, irrespective of degree subject, class of degree, type of institution, etc. (Williamson 1981).

In addition to lower starting salaries, women graduates face a variety of problems which can place them at a disadvantage in the labour market. Only a few of numerous examples can be cited here, ie: the priorities which are typically given to her partner's career (eg limitations on geographical area); the lack of opportunities for promotion and the unrepresentativeness of women in many employing organizations (eg, on the basis of the UMS research, Williamson (1981) concluded that, in contrast to male graduates, women have only half the chance of reaching managerial status in their early careers); the various socialization processes which lead many women to perceive certain areas of employment as unsuitable for their gender (eg there is some evidence to suggest that the percentage of unsuccessful applicants for posts in industry is the same for both sexes – hence the problem seems to be a short-fall in applications from women[7]).

Understanding the demand side of the market on the basis of employers' predictions of their future requirements is fraught with difficulties. Consequently, much of the literature infers demand trends from unemployment rates in the supply of graduates. Using this approach, it is apparent that rates in the late 1970s favoured graduates in engineering and science, with an emphasis on applied rather than pure knowledge. For the arts, and to a lesser extent the social studies graduates, the position deteriorated still further. Catto et al. (1981) conclude:

> The unemployment rates of recent graduates in these subject areas suggest that there has been a certain amount of slack and that proposals to expand the number of higher education places, especially in arts subjects and particularly at polytechnics, should be looked at very critically. (Catto et al., p.11)

Using an alternative definition of new graduate unemployment Tarsh (1982) presents evidence from the 1980 first destination statistics which confirms that the broad subject areas of arts and social sciences are generally associated with comparatively higher rates of unemployment. Taking the analysis a stage further, he demonstrates that within these broad subject categories there are variations in performance according to more detailed subject classifications. Within the category social studies, for example, men university graduates in geography, sociology and psychology were more likely to be unemployed than their counterparts in business studies, accountancy and economics. In the arts broad subject category, male unemployment ranged from 25 per cent in French to nearly 40 per cent in English and arts generally. A similar pattern of detailed subject based differences emerged for women graduates in social studies, but Tarsh continues:

> Within each subject women's unemployment rates were lower than men's. In aggregate their unemployment rate was slightly higher because they were more likely to have graduated in subjects where unemployment was high for men and women. The better employment performance of women graduates in each subject is puzzling. It may be that employers are more willing to hire women for non-graduate jobs and that women are more willing to take these so that they are better equipped to find some sort of employment. It has been suggested by careers advisers that, on the other hand, employers may perceive women as having more favourable personal qualities such as maturity and motivation to work. To some extent also women might be more willing to adapt to poor employment prospects by deferring entry to the labour force and undertaking further training, especially teacher training. (Tarsh 1982, pp.210–211)

These findings and interpretations are highly pertinent to college graduates, since it is widely accepted that the college student constituency includes a high proportion of women who not only take courses in the arts and social studies, but typically study the specific subjects within these broad categories with the highest rates of unemployment.

Among qualitative demands consistently made by employers are those for improvements in numeracy. especially among arts students, for an increase in the practical awareness of real-life problems and for an analytical capacity to solve them (Scott 1980; Hunter 1981).

Finally, a survey of the opinions of eighty-six 'milk-round' employers challenges the notion that university and polytechnic qualifications are of equal status and currency value (Bacon et al. 1979). The vast majority of employers thought that the universities produced better students both intellectually and socially. Polytechnics were viewed as producing second-rate graduates and a knowledge of industry was not felt to compensate for this deficiency. Interestingly, the most common reason given to account for the perceived differences was lower intake standards. From this, the researchers suppose a self-perpetuating cycle:

> . . . lower grade applicants become lower status graduates giving the polytechnics themselves a lesser reputation than universities, which therefore attract lower grade applicants, and so on. (Bacon et al. 1979, p.101)

The combined effects of the above trends[8] make it difficult to imagine a more unfavourable time for college students to be launched into the graduate employment market. They entered at a time when the highest ever output of new graduates coincided with a diminishing number of suitable vacancies. Declining opportunities for further study and training presented additional difficulties, which resulted in exasperating and increasing competition for scarce employment. Worse still, it is widely believed that the majority of college graduates fall within the two categories of graduates, women and arts/social studies graduates (particularly graduates from social studies other than economics – see Tarsh 1982), who are most susceptible to unemployment, or lack of demand or 'filtering down'.

Neither does it appear that this over-representation of graduates with special difficulties can be offset by a high ranking in any 'institutional pecking order'. If the lower intake standards attributed to polytechnics also apply to colleges, then it would seem likely, following Bacon et al. (1979), that employers will perceive college graduates as third-rate material, or, at best, equal second. Finally, in view of the acknowledged value of employers' visits and careers advisory services to university and polytechnic graduates, the absence, or only early development, of similar provisions in colleges may well constitute yet another handicap. It is against this wider background that the initial careers of non-teaching degree graduates from colleges of higher education must be viewed. In such adverse circumstances, most observers concede that it would be unrealistic to expect the 1979 cohort to excel in terms of first destination performance.

Summary

It has been argued in this opening chapter that, for a variety of reasons, the issue of higher education's contribution to economic and employment needs is of great importance. Reflecting this priority and in view of the absence of a similar study in the existing literature, the diversified degree graduates from colleges of higher education were held to be an interesting case in point. Having reviewed the historical background to the colleges' recent transformations, a number of specific concerns were subsumed under the general empirical question, 'What indications of the economic contribution of diversified degrees emerge from the portrayal of graduates' early careers?'

The discussion of these issues was thought to entail specific and general policy dimensions which were worthy of examination. Under the former, three areas were selected as being particularly significant issues for the colleges: (1) diversification through BEd or BA? (2) vocational or general diversification? (3) distinctive curricula features in diversified degree programmes? For the wider dimension, a review of the recent trends in the general graduate labour market was offered.

Notes

1 Throughout this book the abbreviation BA/BSc is used to refer to all 'occupationally unspecific' degrees, including the less common BHum and BCombined Studies.
2 The terms 'general arts' and 'liberal arts' are used interchangeably to denote the broad range of non-applied or non-technical degree subjects implied in the DES's (1972b) phrase 'the arts and human sciences' (p.44). When specifically referring to the subjects included in category 1 of the 'Subject Classification of College Degrees' (see Appendix B), the terms 'arts' or 'art-based' are adopted.
3 [ ] denote authors' editorial insertions.
4 Source: First Destinations of University Graduates (University Grants Committee).
5 Source: First Destinations of Polytechnic Students (Polytechnic Careers Advisers Statistics Working Party).
6 For differences between full-time and sandwich courses, and for fluctuations in the constituent element of the overall unemployment percentage (viz 'believed unemployed' and 'temporary employment') see the Department of Education and Science's Statistical Bulletin 2/80 (DES 1980).
7 See Williamson (1979a).
8 For a useful, more detailed discussion of recent trends in the graduate labour market, see Hunter (1981) and Tarsh (1982).

2

The 'Beyond Graduation' Inquiry

Research Methods and Context

Attempts have been made in the data collection and analysis for this study
to complement participants' written accounts of their experience, made in
response to 'open' questions, with the observed variations in the results for
similar but 'closed' questions, where the response categories had been
selected by the researchers. For example, graduates' own accounts of the
intellectual aspects of their work are set alongside the results for an
attitudinal item which had requested them to indicate within pre-coded
categories their 'satisfaction with the intellectual stimulation in jobs'. In this
way, the research makes use of both qualitative and quantitative data (Cook
and Reichardt 1979).

Adopting several of the techniques suggested by Spradley (1979), the
analysis of the qualitative material arising from the research has made
regular use of the construction of typologies. A useful commentary on the
techniques of typology construction is provided by Hammersley and
Atkinson (1983). On a number of occasions, the use of such techniques has
allowed the interpretative material to be subjected to some rudimentary
quantification. On other occasions, an indication of the quantifiable
dimension has been gained, as mentioned above, by setting the qualitative
accounts alongside the numerical frequencies of the corresponding
responses to the codable items. Participants' qualitative accounts of their
experiences and attitudes have also been used to illuminate their replies to
the closed and fixed-choice items in the questionnaire.

In analysing quantitative data from small-scale surveys, over-reliance on
tests of statistical significance can have stultifying and distorting effects on
the interpretation of the results. In an attempt to avoid such effects, the
commentary on the questionnaire results has concentrated on highlighting
a practical or commonsense significance rather than a simple statistical
significance. Similarly, it has emphasized general trends rather than
isolated occurrences of statistical significance or insignificance. In keeping
with this approach, any decision to treat a difference in frequencies as
significant involves the consideration of educational, sociological and
economic factors, rather than of purely statistical ones.

The empirical data were collected as part of a larger programme of
research conducted under the auspices of the Combined Colleges Research
Group (CCRG). This group, an association of four colleges and two
institutes of higher education, was formed in 1980 to fund and initiate
research into different facets of their institutions and roles in the higher
education sector.

As well as providing a valuable cross-section in terms of geographical
location and size of institution, the group, all of which were former colleges

of education, contained a useful variation in degrees of diversification – from one institution with very little diversification to another with over 60 per cent of its students on non-teaching degree programmes. It also spanned a wide spectrum of religious affiliations: on the basis of constituent colleges rather than institutions, it included three non-denominational, five Anglican, one Methodist, one Catholic and one Free Church college. On the other hand, the sample of the six CCRG institutions entailed slight biases towards university rather than CNAA (Council for National Academic Awards) validation (four of the former, two of the latter) and towards voluntary rather than LEA (local education authority) maintained status (four of the former, one of the latter and one an amalgamation of a voluntary and LEA college).

With a research team consisting of a senior research fellow, a research fellow and a research assistant, the programme of work undertaken has covered such topics as the characteristics of the student constituency upon entry to the colleges and their experience as undergraduates in this sector of higher education, and the subsequent careers followed by graduates after leaving their colleges. The present book is an account of research on the last of these topics and makes use of the findings of the early careers survey called 'Beyond Graduation'.

As an attempt to foster the opportunities for institutional self-study, the research adopted a cyclical model of research (Spradley 1979) in preference to the conventional linear model. Consequently, rather than basing the work on a single period for defining the research problem, leading to a single data collection stage, followed by an analysis published in one long report, the project has followed, as far as possible, an alternative sequence of stages: tentative formation of research questions, preliminary fieldwork, analysis, short report, re-specification of research questions, further fieldwork, and so on. This cyclical model has facilitated a regular interchange between fieldwork and analysis, as well as the production of a number of interim papers and reports which have formed the basis of consensual approaches to data interpretation. As an example, before interpreting the results of the 'Beyond Graduation' survey, substantial amounts of preliminary findings were disseminated to college staff and their interpretations of the material were collected during an extensive series of special interest discussion groups.

The research was designed and implemented in two stages:
1 An analysis of graduates' first destination statistics.
2 A postal survey of college graduates thirty months after leaving their colleges (the main stage) (the 'Beyond Graduation' survey).

The First Destinations Analysis

The bulk of this book is based on information derived from the questionnaire, 'Beyond Graduation'. Covering graduates' experiences and expectations in the two years after leaving college, this was administered to 1979 graduates from sixteen colleges of higher education, including the six CCRG institutions. However, a preliminary and complementary analysis of the first destinations of a wider cohort of 1979 graduates was also undertaken, for two reasons.

First, subsequent questionnaire responses can only be fully understood when seen against the background of the overall pattern of first destination trends for a larger number of graduates in a particular year group. Only by this means was it possible to place college graduates in a comparative context with university and polytechnic graduates, at least for the period covered by first destination surveys (six months after graduation). Due to limited resources, however, it was not feasible to extend the comparative dimensions by administering the 'Beyond Graduation' questionnaire to graduates from universities and polytechnics.

Secondly, in initial exploration of the questions posed in the previous chapter, the first destination statistics are a valuable source of information in their own right, despite the inherent limitations clearly set out by Williams (1973a). Concentration on the first destination returns of the 1979 graduates at this stage enabled any emerging issues to be extended and elaborated in the subsequent analysis of the questionnaire results.

This phase of the research is based on three sources of information:

1 Secondary sources within the available literature.
2 Biographical details collected, in preparation for the 'Beyond Graduation' Survey, from the registries of the sixteen colleges concerning each of their 1979 graduates in the survey sample (viz. details of gender, A level subjects and grades, degree awarded and classification, subjects studied at college, and first destination categories, when known).
3 The 1979 pilot survey of first destinations carried out by ACACHE.

These sources contain several weaknesses which should caution against making firm generalizations. For example, the second and third sources include only two institutions representative of those colleges which did not offer some element of teacher education, the proto-polytechnics. In the total, however, the colleges included in the second and third sources provided a reasonably sound cross-section of colleges of higher education: two proto-polytechnics, six combination colleges and ten former colleges of education. Ten of these institutions were validated by universities, six by CNAA, and three had courses validated by both. All the proto-polytechnic and combination colleges were LEA maintained, as were four of the former colleges of education. (Further details on the colleges included in the second source are presented in the following section.) It should be noted that this study is not concerned with the total output surveyed by ACACHE in 3 above. It ignores, for example, BEds, PGCEs (Postgraduate Certificate of Education), HNDs (Higher National Diploma) and Diplomates, and concentrates only on first degree graduates with non-teaching Bachelors degrees.

The 'Beyond Graduation' Survey

Concentrating on college graduates with diversified degrees, the main purpose of the 'Beyond Graduation' survey was to document their experiences and attitudes after leaving college. Broadly speaking, the survey sought to provide an empirical basis for continuing the exploration of links between employment and higher education as supplied by the colleges. To do this, as noted in the previous chapter, there was an obvious need to extend the available knowledge on graduates' early careers beyond that of the first destination statistics collated in annual reports. Consequently, the information collected through the 'Beyond Graduation' survey was intended both to provide details on the external indices of graduates' careers thirty months after graduation, and to record their personal accounts of college curricula, occupations entered and long-term career prospects.

Within the external indices area, topics of particular interest included the categories and levels of employment obtained, the connections between careers and subjects studied, patterns of occupational mobility, job descriptions, and methods used in searching for employment. In selecting the more attitudinal items, priority was given to levels of satisfaction with jobs and career, perceptions of courses vis-à-vis marketability and occupational performance, attitudes to career choice and prospects, and accounts of the problems and opportunities experienced in the immediate years following graduation. Additionally, key biographical details (eg gender, classification of degree, A levels, parental occupations, etc.) were considered to be essential to any analysis of the relationship between graduates' higher education and their subsequent careers.

This postal questionnaire (Appendix A) was designed to reflect and cover the areas of interest presented above. Two sources of information were particularly influential in shaping it: the interview material collected from college lecturers and existing instruments used in previous surveys, especially Kelsall et al. (1970) and Williamson (1981). In addition, preliminary drafts of the questionnaire were circulated to some college staff and to a small number of graduates; many of their comments and suggestions were incorporated in the final version.

To save valuable space within the questionnaire, some information was derived from alternative sources. College registries and careers departments, for instance, were asked to provide data on A level subjects together with grades, degree programmes and classification, subjects studied and last known addresses. The questionnaire sought the remaining information through a mixture of closed and open-ended items, the latter being mainly concerned with details of career routes and evaluations of college courses and current employment. Unless they wished to indicate their willingness to participate in follow-up interviews, graduates were not asked to supply their names[1].

Practical considerations and the life expectancy of the project necessitated that the subjects of the 'Beyond Graduation' survey should be the 1979 graduates. Although this group had the disadvantage of being the colleges' first significant output from diversified degree courses, which meant that the information relating to their initial destinations was at times incomplete, it offered the advantage of providing details of early career patterns over a reasonable period of time, namely thirty months following graduation. A survey of the 1980 graduates, the only feasible alternative, would have been limited to eighteen months, a period which was thought to be too short to give an adequate picture of emerging careers.

Two different samples of 1979 college graduates received the questionnaire: those of the Combined Colleges Research Group and of the Association of Careers Advisers in Colleges of Higher Education. The first consisted of all non-teaching degree graduates from the four CCRG member institutions with a 1979 diversified degree output (ie BA/BSc/ BHum). The overall target sample for this distribution was 357. All the colleges in this sample were former colleges of education: three were voluntary and university validated, one was an amalgamation, with courses validated both by the CNAA and a local university.

The ACACHE sample, consisting of a percentage of non-BEd graduates from a wider group of colleges and institutes of higher education, provided comparative data for the CCRG sample. At the end of 1979, ACACHE collected first destination details of 1,052 non-teaching degree graduates from seventeen colleges and institutes of higher education. Towards the end of 1981, the research team and ACACHE agreed to administer the 'Beyond Graduation' questionnaire to a sample of these. Fifteen of the original seventeen institutions were invited to participate (the remaining two has already been covered by the CCRG sample described above) and twelve agreed to do so, providing a total target population for the ACACHE distribution of 805 1979 graduates.

In the ACACHE distribution two of the institutions were 'proto-polytechnics' and accounted for 416 graduates; six were 'combination colleges' and accounted for 270 graduates; four were former colleges of education and accounted for 119 graduates. The two proto-polytechnics were CNAA validated and LEA maintained. Of the six combination colleges, all of which were LEA maintained, three were CNAA validated, two university validated and one had courses validated by both. Of the four former colleges of education, three were LEA maintained and one voluntary, one of each was validated by the CNAA and by universities, and two by both.

When selecting a sampling procedure for the ACACHE group, two objectives were particularly important: (a) it should include sufficient numbers from former colleges of education to provide a comparative data set for the four CCRG institutions, all of which were former colleges of education; (b) it should include a reasonable representation of graduates from the other two types of college. Having considered a variety of different procedures, it was decided that a broadly proportionate random sample of 100 graduates should be taken from each of the three college types. Within the ACACHE sample, this provided the potential for a sizeable representation of graduates from former colleges of education and a useful, if not quite so strong, representation of graduates from the remaining types. The total size of the target sample for the ACACHE distribution amounted to 298.

The first destinations survey by ACACHE of 1,052 graduates supplemented by 260 covered by the CCRG only, constitute the only available data on the total population of 1979 college graduates with non-teaching degrees. Table 2.1 shows, however, why a sample taken from the composite CCRG and ACACHE numbers cannot be unreservedly representative of the entire group. Relative to the percentages of the total known population in each type of college, the target sample for the former colleges of education is over-representative, while that of the remaining types, especially the proto-polytechnics, is clearly under-representative.

Within each type of college, on the other hand, the representativeness of the sample deserves greater credence, especially for the former colleges of education. In this type, three-quarters of the known population were

	Total Known Population		Target Sample (TS)		Response Rates as % of TS
	N	(%)	N	(%)	
Former Colleges of Education	626	(48)	457	(70)	54%
Combination Colleges	270	(20)	98	(15)	42%
Proto-polytechnics	416	(32)	100	(15)	39%
ALL COLLEGES	1312	(100)	655	(100)	50%

Table 2.1
Composite survey sample and response rates.

covered by the survey and there are no grounds to suggest that the one quarter not included differs in terms of gender, age, size and status of college, validating bodies and so on. It should be noted, however, that the majority of the 1979 known population of diversified degree graduates was from voluntary, university validated institutions, and the composite sample thus reflects this bias. Although the target samples for the remaining types are smaller, as one in three and one in four random selections from colleges which appear typical of their type, they do provide the basis for a reasonable, if cautious, degree of generalization. Of course, all the above points require confirmation in the light of the rate of responses received for each type of college.

Between September 1981 and March 1982, copies of 'Beyond Graduation' were administered to both samples. Some of the questionnaires were sent directly to graduates' last known addresses, but, more often than not, questionnaires sent to parental addresses for redirection were found to be a more reliable method of establishing contact. Questionnaires (see Appendix A) were accompanied by Freepost return labels and covering letters. To avoid exposing recipients to extraneous and irregular biases, it was decided not to use covering letters signed by members of the college careers service. Similarly, the practice of contacting graduates through professional registers – a method which the UMS study (Williamson 1981) found particularly useful – was rejected. Apart from appearing less applicable to the careers of college graduates, it was thought that this method could bias the responses in favour of the most successful graduates. One reminder letter with a further copy of the questionnaire was sent to initial non-respondents. In addition, more recent information on the whereabouts of non-respondents was sought from those who volunteered for a follow-up interview. Unfortunately, this 'snowballing' exercise, found useful by Kelsall et al. (1970) but not by the UMS study (Williamson 1981), had a negligible impact on the overall response rate.

Given such difficulties in reaching former students, particularly in view of the high level of graduates' geographical mobility at this stage in their careers, the incidence of 'non-contact' is probably much greater than the 7 per cent of questionnaires returned 'not known at this address'. As a result, the composite response rate of 50 per cent is considered satisfactory for this type of postal questionnaire. By way of comparison, it closely matches the 53 per cent achieved in the Williamson (1981) survey of university and polytechnic graduates. Although the latter was administered after a longer period following graduation, it used techniques of contacting graduates which were methodologically questionable and inappropriate to the college sample.

For the former colleges of education, checks showed that the distribution of respondents throughout the colleges closely parallels the distribution of the graduate population from each college. It was also revealed that the respondents from the combination colleges similarly represent the college constituency of the original population, but for the proto-polytechnics there was a more significant discrepancy. As a result, the case for using the response group to make generalizations relating to the 1979 graduates from former colleges of education remains sound. However, it should be stressed that, because of their less representative samples and response rates, a similar claim cannot be made for the two remaining types of college. It is intended that the use of the data collected from these latter types should be restricted to the illustration of tentative comparisons.

In order to confirm the above conclusion, it is necessary to ensure that the respondents are a fair representation of the appropriate population and that no grounds exist for believing that respondents systematically differ from non-respondents. To this end, in addition to the college variations discussed above, direct response bias checks were carried out for the following variables: gender, degree programme and classification, total A level score, discipline areas studied at college, and careers advisers' reports on first destinations.

For the former colleges of education, there was little evidence of differential response rates between men and women, types of programmes, degree classifications, discipline areas and A level scores. However, in common with respondents from other college types, graduates classified by careers advisers as 'unknown' were less likely than those otherwise classified to return completed questionnaires. Although not a feature of all colleges, this is perhaps not a surprising result, since it indicates both increased difficulties in contacting those graduates whose initial circumstances were unknown and a tendency for those unwilling to participate in first destination surveys to adopt the same approach to subsequent surveys. Nevertheless, this need not be viewed as an overriding bias, since several previous analyses have been conducted on the assumption that 'unknown graduates' tend to be evenly distributed among the remaining categories (eg Tarsh 1982) and Williams (1973a) has concluded 'that no assumption can be made that a particularly high proportion of the unknown category are unemployed' (p.26). If anything, it may well be a marginal advantage in the colleges' favour for this group to be under-represented: 'unknown' graduates who responded to the present survey tended to perform slightly lower than average on a number of key employment indicators. This, of course, says nothing about 'unknown' graduates who remain unknown.

Within the combination colleges, graduates in the arts discipline area and those who followed a Bachelor of Arts degree programme were reluctant to respond, while within the proto-polytechnics, social studies graduates and graduates with upper second class Honours tended to be slightly under-represented.

On the whole, it is considered that the response bias checks are very satisfactory and broadly speaking confirm the conclusions reached earlier. In the case of the former colleges of education, detailed analyses can proceed with a high degree of confidence.

Many of the questionnaire items were pre-coded, others were coded upon receipt of the completed returns, often by means of existing frames, eg the occupational classifications used in the Qualified Manpower Follow-up Survey (see Williamson 1981), the subject categories presented in Appendix B, and a modified version of the first destination classifications used by careers staff in all three sectors of higher education. Having punched all the coded data on to cards, these were submitted to a computer and an SPSS system file was created. Reports containing the preliminary frequencies of the coded data, as well as copies of the open-ended comments, were circulated to all colleges involved in the survey. Discussions aimed at exploring initial interpretations of the preliminary findings were held at most of the CCRG colleges and these have proved a valuable source of ideas for further analysis and commentary. The presentation and interpretation of the results of the 'Beyond Graduation' survey are set out in Chapters 4 to 7.

Summary

In the data collection and analysis attempts had been made to juxtapose interpretative qualitative accounts with the quantitative responses to pre- and post-coded indices based on the researchers' constructs. Having described the context and style in which the empirical work was carried out, the research design, comprising two main phases, was outlined. With regard to the postal survey, as a result of carrying out response bias checks and examinations of the samples involved, it was concluded that the replies from respondents from former colleges of education could be taken as representative of the wider group of 1979 graduates from this type of institution. The responses from the sample of the other two types of colleges of higher education should be used for illustrative purposes only.

Notes

1 Unfortunately, because of limited resources, it subsequently proved impossible to carry out these interviews.

3

First Destinations of the Third Kind

In studying the early careers of college graduates, the bulk of this book is based on information derived from the 'Beyond Graduation' survey. In order to locate college graduates in a broader context, however, a preliminary and comparative analysis of the first destinations of a wider cohort of 1979 graduates was also undertaken.

It was noted in Chapter 1 that the colleges produced their first appreciable output of diversified degree graduates in a period of economic recession and at a time when the more enduring processes of 'certificate inflation' and 'filtering down' were reaching crisis proportions (Dore 1978). In 1979 the highest ever output of first degree graduates from all sectors coincided with a declining number of suitable vacancies, and graduate unemployment was comparatively high. The colleges were further constrained by the legacy of their teacher training past: a disproportionate number of women students and of liberal arts graduates, lower A level grade applicants, traditionally inferior institutional status, and only elementary careers services, all of which combined to weaken the position of college graduates. In such a climate, it was thought that expectations of the career performances of college graduates needed to be realistic.

Comparing First Destinations

In considering how well college graduates actually performed, it must always be remembered that, in the case of the colleges, unlike that of the universities and polytechnics, the available data permits only very tentative observations about only a sample of the total output. This sample was not selected randomly. In effect, each college selected itself on the basis of administrative capacity and willingness to participate in the first destination surveys organized by ACACHE. Meanwhile, there is no available record at present of the total number of 1979 college graduates. The DES provide figures for the total output of the public sector, but do not disaggregate for the colleges. An ACACHE survey of the 1979 college graduates included 1,052 graduates with non-teaching Bachelors degrees and the preliminary data collection for the 'Beyond Graduation' survey added a further 260. And since there is no evidence to suggest that the total college output will exceed 2,000, it may be assumed, with a reasonable degree of confidence, that the analysis presented in this chapter is based upon a sample of at least 50 per cent of that.

Table 3.1 shows the first destinations of 1979 graduates from universities, polytechnics and colleges. Some important points of comparison begin to emerge. Although 1979 was the first time most colleges carried out first destination surveys, they managed to restrict the percentage of 'unknown graduates' to a level which bears favourable comparison with that of the universities and which is considerably lower than that of the polytechnics. This may be due in part to the relatively small and more integrated nature of the typical college campus. In view of the special and additional employment difficulties facing college graduates, it is interesting to note that the overall unemployment rate of college graduates, although higher than that of university graduates, is of the same order as that of graduates from polytechnics.

However, three other noticeable differences may be less comforting for the colleges. First, in comparison to university and polytechnic graduates, a smaller percentage of college graduates went on to research or further academic study. Secondly, a comparatively lower proportion of college graduates entered permanent home employment. Thirdly, a significantly greater share of college graduates took up teacher training as their first destination – double the rate of university graduates, and treble the rate of polytechnic graduates.

Percentage of first degree graduates (men and women, full-time sandwich) of total known destinations.[a]

	Universities	Polytechnics	Colleges (All types)
	%	%	%
Research/Academic Study – Home	12.0	7.0	3.4
Research/Academic Study – Overseas	0.8	0.3	0.2
First Degree Course – Home	0	0.1	1.4
Graduateship of Professional Body	0	0.5	0.5
Teacher Training	9.9	6.2	22.2
Social Work Training	0.3	0.1	0.3
Law Society Examinations	2.3	4.4	2.9
Other Training	5.2	2.6	5.0
Overseas Graduates returning Home	4.6	6.0	2.5
Already in Employment	1.4	1.4	4.3
Not Available for Employment	2.5	1.8	1.3
Permanent Employment – Home	46.8	52.2	36.3
Temporary Employment – Home	5.7	8.3	8.5
Permanent Employment – Overseas	1.4	1.0	2.5
Temporary Employment – Overseas	1.8	0.9	0.8
Believed Unemployed at 31 December	5.4	8.0	7.9
TOTAL KNOWN GRADUATES (100%)	52,441	12,436	924
Unemployed[b]	11.1	16.3	16.5
% Unknown of Total Graduates	10.5	22.2	12.2

Notes
a Includes all UK universities, polytechnics in England and Wales, and the 18 colleges and institutes of HE in the ACACHE pilot survey, excluding education and medicine graduates.
b 'Believed unemployed at 31 Dec.' plus 'temporary home employment'.
Source
UGC Annually; PCA Annually; ACACHE 1979.

Table 3.1
First destinations of 1979 graduates from different sectors of higher education.

Subsequent analyses revealed that this latter problem is particularly prevalent in those colleges which diversified from a teacher training base. There, almost one in three graduates entered teacher training courses, compared to one in ten graduates from universities or from colleges which were not former colleges of education. The proportion proceeding to PGCE courses from colleges formed by an amalgamation of teacher education and non-teacher education traditions was approximately one in four. Such variations demonstrate the need to distinguish between findings relating to the college sector as a whole and findings relating to particular types of colleges. Whether or not this comparatively high proportion of graduates entering teacher training courses from former colleges of education is problematic largely depends on the extent to which the colleges see themselves as offering diversified courses merely as alternative paths into teaching, or as deliberate preparations for a wider range of career outlets. The determination with which the colleges implement their answers to this question seems likely to be the single most important influence on the first destinations of their future graduates.

Analysis of the employment areas entered by graduates who obtained permanent home employment revealed that, when compared with university and polytechnic graduates, a much smaller proportion of college graduates (all types) entered industry. Correspondingly, a larger proportion of college graduates found employment in the public service sector, especially in the 'Local Government/Hospital Service' category. Relative to other types of college, the former colleges of education had particularly low numbers entering industry, and high numbers entering public service. Again, in comparison to the universities and polytechnics, the colleges (all types) had a larger share of their graduates finding employment in the 'All Others' category (especially in 'Publishers, Cultural, Entertainment' and 'Others'), and slightly more in commerce where the sub-category 'Other Commerce' is particularly high. This relatively high concentration in the miscellaneous categories suggests that a significant proportion of college graduates is entering employment areas with no tradition of graduate entry. Whether or not this amounts to 'filtering down' depends on the type and level of work performed.

Table 3.2 shows the proportions entering different types of work categories as a percentage of the totals who found permanent home employment. It should be emphasized that these categories cannot, in themselves, substantiate the existence of 'filtering down', but they can provide a rough indication of its likelihood. College graduates, particularly graduates from former colleges of education, are noticeably under-represented in such type of work categories as 'Scientific R,D&D, 'Environmental Planning', 'Production Operation and Maintenance', and 'Financial Work'.

In contrast, one interpretation which might be drawn from the table is that college graduates are highly represented, relative to university and polytechnic graduates, in the following kinds of work:

1 Buying, marketing, selling
2 Secretarial, clerical and non-specialist adminstration
3 Health and social welfare
4 General traineeships (to a lesser extent)[1]

Percentage of total entrants to permanent home employment in various type of work categories.

	Colleges %	Polytechnics %	Universities %
General Traineeships	7.5 ⎫ 17.9	4.0 ⎫ 8.5	9.1
General Management & Administration	10.4 ⎭	4.5 ⎭	
Scientific Research, Design & Development	0.9	10.4	15.3
Environmental Planning	1.2	15.5	6.1
Scientific Analysis	1.8	3.5	4.1
Production Operation and Maintenance	1.2	10.7	7.4
Buying, Marketing, Selling	18.2	8.3	8.4
Services to Management	6.3	7.2	9.7
Financial	9.0	11.8	18.2
Legal	0.9	0.6	3.9
Information, Advisory, Non-scientific Research	2.7 ⎫ 7.5	1.5 ⎫ 4.7	3.3
Library, Museum, Archive	4.8 ⎭	3.2 ⎭	
Personnel	0.9 ⎫ 8.4	1.4 ⎫ 5.9	7.6
Health, Social Welfare	7.5 ⎭	4.4 ⎭	
Teaching, Lecturing	4.5	1.0	1.7
Creative, Entertainment	10.7 ⎫ 21.8	8.4 ⎫ 11.8	5.2
Secretarial, Clerical	7.8 ⎭	1.9 ⎭	
Others	3.3	1.5	
TOTAL ENTRANTS (100%)	335	6,396	24,542

Notes
a Includes all UK universities, polytechnics in England and Wales and the 18 colleges and institutes of HE which participated in the ACACHE pilot survey – excluding education and medicine graduates.

Source
UGC Annually; PCA Annually; ACACHE 1979

Table 3.2
Type of work categories for 1979 graduates from different sectors of higher education.[a]

It does seem probable that the comparatively high numbers entering these types of work could well be associated with signs that college graduates are 'filtering down' in the labour market. Williamson (1979b) cites clerical and social welfare work as areas indicative of 'filtering down', and many of the jobs within the category 'Buying, Marketing, Selling' : eg sales representatives or trainee managers in chain stores – could be entered until quite recently on the merits of A levels only. However, recognition of the likelihood of 'filtering down' is not synonymous with the conclusion that college graduates are failing to make a positive contribution to the economy, or that very little demand exists for them. Their unemployment was no higher than that experienced by polytechnic graduates, although it should be recognized that, relative to other sectors, the college unemployment figure was improved by high numbers going into teacher training rather than permanent employment. However, it is still feasible that particular kinds of employers may have specific demands for college graduates and further research may be needed to address two questions relating to this: (i) How do these particular employers explain and articulate their recruitment of college graduates? (ii) Does higher education from a college improve the quality of work performed in the jobs associated with 'filtering down'? This latter question will be discussed in greater detail in Chapter 5.

Gender Differences

Information on the whole of the 1979 sample (1,217 graduates) supports the earlier assertion that the majority of college graduates were women: the proportion of women to men in all types of colleges was three to two. However, this overall ratio conceals variations between different types of colleges which qualify the general conclusion. While former colleges of education had a ratio of two women to every man, those colleges without teacher education, the proto-polytechnics, had an equal share of male and female graduates. Combination colleges had a ratio of three women to two men.

Turning to a comparison of the first destinations entered by each sex, the review of recent trends in graduate employment suggested that a slightly higher share of female graduates would fall into the overall unemployment category than male.

This turned out to be the case for university and polytechnic graduates, but not for college graduates. A slightly higher percentage of women university graduates (12 per cent) than men university graduates (10 per cent) were unemployed. For polytechnic graduates, the difference was much larger: 21 per cent compared to 14 per cent. In contrast to 22 per cent unemployment for men college graduates (the highest rate for either sex in any of the three sectors), only 13 per cent of women college graduates were unemployed. However, this relatively low unemployment rate for women college graduates is not accounted for by a corresponding higher rate of entry into permanent home employment. Female college graduates had the lowest rate of entry into permanent home employment of either sex in all three sectors (37 per cent) – lower than male college graduates, if the unusually large difference in the 'already in employment' category is given due consideration.

The comparatively low proportion of women college graduates in employment and unemployment is better explained by their high proportions in teacher training, which they entered at a rate almost twice that of their male colleagues and considerably higher than that of female graduates from other sectors of higher education. It would seem then that, whereas a sizeable number of men college graduates appeared to accept temporary work or unemployment rather than enter teacher training, a significant group of women college graduates opted for teacher training in preference to temporary work or unemployment. This observation seems to be particularly true of students in former colleges of education; in the proto-polytechnics, a greater share of women than men entered teacher training, but the proportions unemployed[2] were more equally matched.

If colleges consider it desirable to check the flow into teacher training, then in addition to assisting those graduates, male and female, who have no intention of teaching, they also need to devote more resources to influencing undergraduate attitudes to career opportunities other than teaching, especially among women. In the absence of any such influence, it seems probable that traditional values and practices will ensure that the diversified programmes will be perceived and implemented mainly as alternative, more flexible, routes into teaching.

The distribution of male and female college graduates among different areas of unemployment resembles the variations between different genders of university and polytechnic graduates. Roughly the same proportions of male and female college graduates entered commerce and 'All Others'; a greater proportion of women found work in the public service and education sectors; and a larger share of men was employed within industry.

Of the key type of work categories entered by college graduates, 'Buying, Marketing, Selling' had approximately the same proportions of each sex, as did 'Health, Social Welfare'. Not surprisingly, 'Secretarial, Clerical Work' absorbed many more women than men. 'Teaching, Lecturing' and 'Library, Museum, Archive' showed similar trends, but more men were to be found within 'Services to Management' and 'Financial'.

Subject Differences

Before discussing the implications for curriculum development, there is clearly a need to study the associations between graduates' early careers and the courses they studied at college. If, for example, comparisons could be based upon the first destination statistics for a specific discipline, instead of those for an undiscriminated total, an inferior aggregate unemployment rate could be shown to overlie a superior rate in a particular area. Expressing the example in question form: despite an inferior overall rate of unemployment, are college arts graduates less likely to be unemployed than university arts graduates? Moreover, if a significantly greater proportion of college graduates studied arts subjects than did graduates in other sectors, then the approach illustrated in this example represents, for some purposes at least, a more valid and appropriate form of comparison than composite-based ones. Therefore, for some purposes, in order to avoid comparing apples with oranges, there exists a strong need for colleges to examine, and hence collect information on, the first destinations of their graduates in relation to the subjects they studied.

Unfortunately, attempts to implement subject-specific comparisons soon encounter intractable problems which inevitably compromise the outcome. Basically, most of the difficulties can be traced to the comparatively low number of college graduates, especially in certain disciplines, coupled with a wide variety of permutations in combined subjects. It is thus difficult to devise a method of subject classification which is truly appropriate to the course content of the colleges' curricula, which allows some comparison with other sectors of higher education, and which, at the same time, produces a reasonable number of graduates in each subject category. The latter problem is particularly awkward for the 1979 graduates since, in many cases, the necessary data were not available for a sufficient number of graduates to reduce the impact of 'colleges' as an intervening variable, eg if a particular discipline area contains graduates from a very small number of colleges, are the early career patterns of these graduates attributable to the influence of 'college attended' or 'subject studied'?

Notwithstanding these unavoidable weaknesses, a method of subject classification has been adopted which permits some degree of sensible comparison with other sectors. This method, set out in full in Appendix B, puts college degree courses into five categories: 'Arts', 'Social Studies', 'Arts and Social Studies', 'Science', and 'Other Combinations'. Although 'Arts' and 'Social Studies' are broadly comparable with corresponding discipline areas in university and polytechnic first destination statistics, 'Science' requires greater caution because it includes home economics in the colleges. The remaining two categories, 'Arts and Social Studies' and 'Other Combinations', preclude all forms of cross-sector analysis.

Using information from the ACACHE pilot survey, the non-CCRG colleges participating in the 'Beyond Graduation' project, and three of the six CCRG member institutions, it has proved possible to classify the discipline area and first destinations of 874 of the 1,217 graduates included in this analysis (approximately 72 per cent). It revealed that the majority of the sample (57 per cent) undertook courses, or combinations of courses, completely within the arts area. (The corresponding percentages for 1979 university and polytechnic graduates were 23 and 21 per cent respectively.) Adding to this the fact that a further 12 per cent of college graduates studied arts and social studies combinations, and only 9 per cent graduated from the science area, the data can be taken as confirmation of the view that 1979 college graduates were predominantly arts-based. Moreover, a more pronounced concentration of arts graduates was found to exist in the former colleges of education and combination colleges than in the proto-polytechnics, where a comparatively greater proportion of social studies graduates was evident. The following discussion is concerned with the initial destinations of the college graduates in this sample who studied for degrees exclusively in the arts area (ie the 59 per cent majority group).

Table 3.3 compares the first destinations of 1979 college arts graduates whose circumstances were known with those of 1979 arts graduates from universities and polytechnics.

A review of the first destinations of college arts graduates in relation to those of university and polytechnic arts graduates constitutes the most promising form of cross-sector comparison so far presented for the colleges. College arts graduates achieved an entry into permanent home employment (34 per cent) which was higher than that for the universities (31 per cent), and only slightly lower than that for the polytechnics (37 per cent). College arts graduates experienced an unemployment rate (20 per cent) lower than the polytechnic rate (28 per cent), although higher than the university proportion (16 per cent). In addition, the share of arts graduates from colleges embarking on teacher training courses almost matched the proportion taking the same route from universities.

From the colleges' standpoint, the form of comparison presented in Table 3.3 below provides a clearer picture than the composite-based comparison presented in Table 3.1 and clearly demonstrates the value of classifying and collating first destination details according to the main discipline categories.

However, it must be acknowledged that, for this particular year group at least, the colleges attained this encouraging comparison because of the

Percentage of first degree arts[a] graduates (male and female) in each sector of higher education whose whereabouts were known.[b]

	College	University (Groups 8 & 9)	Polytechnic (Languages, Arts & Music etc.)
	%	%	%
Research/Academic Study – Home	4.9	8.0	8.4
Research/Academic Study – Overseas	0.3	1.1	0.6
First Degree Course – Home	0.3	0	0.1
Graduateship of Professional Body	0.5	0	0.3
Teacher Training	23.8	20.2	14.1
Social Work Training	0	0.4	0
Law Society Examinations	0.3	0.8	0.1
Other Training	4.9	10.6	4.1
Overseas Graduates returning Home	2.8	1.4	1.0
Already in Employment	0.3	1.0	0.1
Not Available for employment	2.8	3.5	3.1
Permanent Employment – Home	33.6	31.4	37.1
Temporary Employment – Home	11.3	9.0	14.2
Permanent Employment – Overseas	4.4	1.7	1.5
Temporary Employment – Overseas	0.8	3.8	1.6
Unemployed at 31 December	9.2	7.2	13.7
TOTAL KNOWN GRADUATES (100%)	390	13,297	2,777
Unemployed[c]	20.5	16.2	27.9
% Unknown of Total Graduates	21.2	12.5	29.7

Notes
a See Appendix B for method of subject classification and text for details of college sample.
b The relatively low numbers involved emphasize the need for caution when drawing comparisons.
c 'believed unemployed at 31 December' plus 'temporary home employment'.

Table 3.3
First destinations of 1979 arts graduates from different sectors of higher education.

destinations achieved by arts graduates from proto-polytechnics, and in spite of the comparatively poor performance of arts graduates from former colleges of education. For example, whereas arts graduates from proto-polytechnics found permanent jobs at a higher rate than those from universities and polytechnics, arts graduates from colleges which diversified from a teacher education base displayed the lowest of all proportions entering permanent home employment (Table 3.4). Similarly, although the latter type of colleges had a slightly lower proportion of unemployed arts graduates[2], this result was almost certainly due to the very high percentage taking up teacher training courses (41 per cent). In addition, these problems take on an increased significance when it is recalled that the former colleges of education tended to produce a particularly high preponderance of arts-based graduates.

To conclude this section, it appears that the inclusion of discipline areas in the analysis of first destinations certainly unfolds a more favourable picture for the colleges as a whole. However, a breakdown of arts graduates by different type of college suggests that the former colleges of education

Percentage of first degree arts[a] graduates (male and female) in each type of college whose whereabouts were known.

	Former Colleges of Education	Proto-polytechnics	Combination Colleges
Research/Academic Study – Home	2.2	7.7	4.2
Research/Academic Study – Overseas	0	0.6	0
First Degree Course – Home	0.7	0	0
Graduateship of Professional Body	0	1.3	0
Teacher Training	41.3	12.2	17.7
Social Work Training	0	0	0
Law Society Examinations	0.7	0	0
Other Training	8.0	3.8	2.1
Overseas Graduates returning Home	0	3.8	5.2
Already in Employment	0	0.6	0
Not Available for Employment	4.3	1.9	2.1
Permanent Employment – Home	28.3	39.1	32.3
Temporary Employment – Home	9.4	9.6	16.7
Permanent Employment – Overseas	0.7	9.6	1.0
Temporary Employment – Overseas	0	1.9	0
Unemployed at 31 December	4.3	7.7	18.8
TOTAL KNOWN GRADUATES (100%)	138	156	96
Unemployed[c]	13.8	17.3	35.4
% Unknown of Total Graduates	18.8	17.5	29.4

Notes
See Table 3.3.

Table 3.4
First destinations of 1979 arts graduates from different types of colleges of higher education (Breakdown of 'College' column in Table 3.3).[a]

confronted particular problems in extending and diversifying the career prospects of arts-based graduates.

Differences in Entry Qualifications

A further argument maintains that any comparison of first destinations should incorporate an analysis of differences in the entry qualifications, and by inference the academic standards, of graduates from the various sectors: ie variations in the output of an establishment must be studied in relation to variations in the input. Applied to college graduates, it is claimed that because the currency value of a college degree is higher than that of mediocre A levels, the career opportunities of those with relatively low entry qualifications are considerably enhanced, though not to a level commensurate with university graduates, who generally start with higher entry qualifications.

At present, the information required to examine this and similar arguments is not available. Practically, all that can be undertaken here is a brief consideration of the view that the 1979 graduates of former colleges of education were generally of a lower academic standard, as indicated by their GCE A levels upon entry, than graduates from universities. To this end, we compared the A levels of 357 students who graduated in 1979 from four CCRG colleges with those of a sample of 7,051 undergraduates entering universities in the academic year 1976.

Whereas 75 per cent of the university sample possessed three or more A levels, only 42 per cent of the college sample did so. Similarly, 52 per cent of the university sample had A level scores of nine points or over (scored on three subjects) in contrast to 9 per cent of the college sample. At the lower end of the spectrum, 4 per cent of the university sample, compared to 32 per cent of the college sample, had scores of between four and two points (scored on two subjects).

Furthermore, it should be stressed that scores for A level subjects not usually accepted for university entrance were excluded from the university sample but were included in the college sample. The findings tend to support the first premise in the argument presented above: namely, so far as 1979 graduates were concerned, that the former colleges of education attracted students with lower academic qualifications than those entering universities.

Over-reliance on the differential entry-standards argument – either as a line of defence or as a positive admissions policy which deliberately discriminates in favour of those with low or no A levels (see Gibbs and Cree 1982) – entails some considerable risks for the colleges. For instance, questions need to be asked about the effects a low level intake policy could have upon employers' perceptions of the merit of a college degree. It should be recalled that Bacon et al. (1979) discovered that one of employers' main reasons for perceiving university qualifications to be of a higher value than polytechnic ones was the lower intake standards operating in the polytechnics. Given the existence of similar standards in colleges, it seems highly probable that colleges will find themselves in the same, if not a more acute, 'down market' self-perpetuating cycle like that which confronts the polytechnics.

Additionally, in order to implement an admissions policy based on the recruitment of lowly qualified entrants, it would appear necessary for the colleges to substantiate two important claims: first, that the careers-currency value of a college degree is indeed higher than that of mediocre A levels – a point which cannot be presumed, especially in view of the likelihood of some filtering down by college graduates; and second, that students of a comparable academic standard do not attain greater enhancement of career opportunities by attending a university – a point which is of special importance in view of the demographic trends which may well lead to a far greater proportion of the lower qualified being offered places at universities.

Summary

On the basis of the review of the literature on the graduate labour market presented in Chapter 1, it has been argued that the entry of college graduates into the labour market for the highly qualified needs to be understood in the context and trends of the graduate employment market as a whole. In recent years, this market has become extremely competitive and certain parts of the highly qualified pool – namely, liberal arts graduates, female graduates and graduates from low status institutions – have faced particular problems. Unfortunately for the colleges, there are clear indications that the output from former colleges of education largely consists of these categories of less employable graduates.

From a comparison of 1979 composite outputs from different sectors of higher education, it was noted that the polytechnics displayed unemployment rates similar to those of the former colleges of education, although the latter had significantly smaller percentages entering permanent occupations and further academic study. In contrast, a higher proportion of graduates from former colleges of education entered PGCE training – a route which a large and disproportionate number of women college graduates seem to favour. Very few graduates from this type of college found employment in industry and, relative to graduates from other sectors, they were highly represented in areas lacking a tradition of graduate entry – perhaps suggesting a greater propensity for filtering down to lower status occupations. Restricting the comparison to graduates in the arts improved the position for the college sector as a whole, but did little to ameliorate the overall picture of the relatively poor performance of graduates from former colleges of education.

First destination statistics provide a useful basis for a preliminary impression of graduates' early career trends, particularly in so far as they afford the opportunity for drawing comparisons between different sectors of higher education. However, they suffer from a number of important limitations. For example, they are restricted to information collected up to a maximum of six months after graduation; clearly, in order to assess more enduring career benefits, details over a longer period of time are essential. Information on the nature of employment entered is, of necessity, very rudimentary and no analyses of such variables as length of contracts, salaries, and range of occupations applied for, are possible. Moreover, the data obtained through first destination surveys are limited to external behavioural indices, with no attempts being made to collect subjective and phenomenological accounts of early careers and employment experience. Finally, there also exists an understandable tendency in all institutions to present their first destination statistics in the best possible light. It was to overcome such deficiencies as these that the 'Beyond Graduation' survey was designed and implemented.

Notes

1 Creative and Entertainment could have been included, but this figure is only slightly higher than the percentage for polytechnics, and the vast majority of college graduates in this category are from the combination colleges with a tradition in the Fine and Graphic Arts.
2 ie 'Temporary home employment' *plus* 'believed to be unemployed on 31 December' of the graduating year.

4

Early Career Patterns

Using the survey responses of the sample described in Chapter 2, we now set out to portray the career patterns of 1979 college graduates who obtained first degrees other than the BEd. The present chapter concentrates largely on external indices of career patterns and employment trends but includes some subjective accounts of employment areas; Chapter 5 will pay more attention to the subjective and attitudinal aspects of graduates' careers while also examining the interrelations between levels of satisfaction and objective circumstances. In broad terms, the present chapter addresses the question, 'Into what circumstances, and areas of employment, have college graduates progressed?' while Chapter 5 considers, 'To what extent were college graduates satisfied with these circumstances?'

For reasons given in Chapter 3, the interpretations presented here are predominantly concerned with graduates from colleges which have diversified solely from a teacher training base. Hence, for the sake of brevity the term 'college' is reserved throughout this chapter for the former colleges of education. Specific references will be made whenever the two

	SOURCE OF INFORMATION			
	College Careers Adviser	'Beyond Graduation' Questionnaire		
	31/12/79 %	31/12/79 %	31/12/80 %	31/12/81 %
Research/Academic Study	1	0.5	1	1
Teacher Training	30	36	5	3
Social Work Training	0	0	0.5	0.5
Law Society Exams	0.5	0.5	0.5	0
Other Training	7	7	2	3
Not Available for Employment	2	1	2	4
Permanent Home Employment	31	33	68	73
Temporary Home Employment	2	9	9	3
Temporary Overseas Employment	0	2	2	1
Unemployed	3	11	10	11
Unknown	23.5	0	0.5	0.5
TOTAL RESPONDENTS (100%)	247	247	247	247

Note
Unless stated to the contrary, all tables in Chapters 4 and 5 display results as percentages of the survey respondents.

Table 4.1
Primary classification details of 1979 non-BEd respondents from former colleges of education at different stages in their early careers.

other types of colleges are in question – the combination colleges or the proto-polytechnics.

By way of tracing the graduates' overall progression since leaving college, Tables 4.1–3 give details of the circumstances of respondents from each of the three types of college and the proportions in each of the main careers classifications at three different points in time: 31 December in 1979, 1980 and 1981. In addition, column 1 gives the graduates' first destinations as recorded by their careers advisers. The remaining columns are based on information from the 'Beyond Graduation' questionnaire.

	SOURCE OF INFORMATION			
	College Careers Adviser	'Beyond Graduation' Questionnaire		
	31/12/79 %	31/12/79 %	31/12/80 %	31/12/81 %
Research/Academic Study	0	0	0	3
Teacher Training	22	17	5	2
Law Society Exams	0	0	0	3
Other Training	2	5	0	0
Not Available for Employment	5	7	7	7
Permanent Home Employment	32	42	49	51
Temporary Home Employment	7	12	12	7
Unemployed	10	17	27	27
Unknown	22	0	0	0
TOTAL RESPONDENTS (100%)	41	41	41	41

Table 4.2
Primary classification details of 1979 non-BEd respondents from combination colleges at different stages in their early careers.

	SOURCE OF INFORMATION			
	College Careers Adviser	'Beyond Graduation' Questionnaire		
	31/12/79 %	31/12/79 %	31/12/80 %	31/12/81 %
Research/Academic Study	3	0	0	5
Teacher Training	13	13	3	0
Law Society Exams	0	5	0	0
Other Training	13	10	5	5
Overseas Students returning Home	0	3	3	3
Permanent Home Employment	43	54	79	77
Temporary Home Employment	3	5	5	3
Unemployed	5	10	5	7
Unknown	20	0	0	0
TOTAL RESPONDENTS (100%)	39	39	39	39

Table 4.3
Primary classification details of 1979 non-BEd respondents from proto-polytechnics at different stages in their early careers.

Studying for Higher Degrees

Some college prospectuses cite research and further academic study as a potential career outlet for diversified degree graduates. The evidence suggests that this claim may reflect a 'stars syndrome', whereby the advanced academic achievement of exceptional graduates ('one of our former students is doing research for a PhD in 19th Century Foreign Policy') gains greater saliency in the minds of college staff than the very low statistical probability of college graduates entering this area.

Table 4.1 indicates that a negligible number of college respondents advanced their academic studies to higher degree level. No more than 1 per cent in any one of the three years since graduating had undertaken full-time further academic study. Put another way, during the thirty months since leaving college, only four of the 247 respondents had, at any time, followed a course leading to a higher degree. All four pursued their courses at institutions other than those from which they had graduated. Although some initially felt their higher degree courses would entail employment benefits, there were no immediate signs of increased employability, and indeed, their expectations on completing their courses were often quite low:

(Q.20ii)[1] MSc – useful for certain jobs but my course was very specific and would only open doors into a limited number of jobs, which were very rare in appearing.

(Q.21) MA – I expect to join the dole queue.

However, a longer time scale is almost certainly required to assess the impact of taking a higher degree.

Not Available for Employment

Although small at the end of the graduating year, the proportion of college respondents not available for full-time employment rose slightly, but steadily, and amounted to 4 per cent by the end of 1981. Only two respondents had been unavailable for the entire thirty months since leaving college. One had started a family immediately after graduation; the other, although virtually unemployed for long periods, saw herself as a self-employed potter and casual arts worker. Rather than applying for a single full-time job, she preferred 'to have several quite different work styles'. In addition, of the nine who were unavailable for employment at the end of 1981, five had given up their jobs (none of which were teaching posts) in order to concentrate on motherhood and domestic work.

As Tables 4.2 and 4.3 indicate, the percentage of respondents not available for employment was only slightly higher for the combination colleges, but was non-existent for the proto-polytechnics. The marginally higher proportions for the combination colleges may reflect a greater share of fine arts graduates, several of whom attempted to preserve a self-employed 'artist' identity. One such graduate said:

(Q.21) I went to art college. I now have a part-time typing/ secretarial job in order to earn money, but this has nothing to do with my 'career'. I consider myself an artist – a sort of unpaid research worker, working for him/herself.

---

1 See Appendix A for the questionnaire eliciting these responses.

Temporary Employment

At the end of the graduating year, 9 per cent of college respondents were temporarily employed. This proportion remained stable during 1980 and then fell to 4 per cent by the end of 1981. It would, however, be incorrect to interpret such a trend as the experience of a single group of graduates who had continuous difficulties escaping the temporary employment category. Closer examination of the data reveals considerable differences in the constituencies of each of the three year groups of temporary workers.

Of the twenty-three who were in temporary employment at the end of the graduating year, the majority (seventeen) occupied posts which were in effect permanent, but which the respondents, at least at the time of completing the questionnaire, *perceived* to be temporary. The remaining six were in posts which were fixed to limited periods, irrespective of how they were perceived by their incumbents. Most explained these temporary posts, whether perceived or actual, as 'fill-ins, while looking for more permanent appointments', though a few saw them as a means of testing their suitability for training in such professions as social work, teaching and nursing. Respondents' comments illustrate two variants of this latter approach to temporary work; one, now a teacher, advised would-be PGCE entrants to:

> (Q.21) Take a year (at least) off if they have not already done so, before entering teaching – get other employment or travel, or voluntary work – anything to broaden experience, and to remove self from teaching scene.

With a slightly different intention in mind, a nurse recommended would-be student nurses to:

> (Q.21) Either gain some experience working during vacations in a hospital or work as a nursing assistant for a few months before committing yourself to a further 3-year course in training.

Nevertheless, the majority of temporary workers at the end of 1979 were not in posts related to professional employment, but in such occupations as clerical worker, receptionist or shop assistant. Most eventually found permanent employment or further training, though only one obtained permanent and higher level work within the organization which initially employed her for a temporary job. (Unfortunately, she subsequently found the permanent post frustrating and lacking in promotion prospects.) The average duration for remaining in temporary posts beyond 31 December 1979 was approximately eight months and only three out of the twenty-three were still working in temporary employment a year later.

In sharp contrast to the previous year, the vast majority of the 1980 group of temporary workers were not in permanent positions perceived as temporary. Eighteen out of the twenty-two 1980 temporary workers occupied short-term, fixed-period jobs, sixteen of which were, in one way or another, concerned with teaching. Of the twenty-two, seventeen had studied for a PGCE in the academic year following graduation and a further two were 'trying out' teaching pending entry to PGCE courses in September 1980. A year later, at the end of 1981, of the sixteen respondents in temporary teaching posts in December 1980, five were in permanent teaching appointments, two were following PGCE courses, but the remaining nine were either unemployed, not available for employment or still in temporary posts. Only one of the five who obtained permanent teaching appointments did so in the school at which she first worked as a temporary teacher.

By the end of 1980 there were signs that some of the six temporary workers in non-teaching jobs, including some who had completed a PGCE course, were beginning to recognize that jobs initially perceived as short-term might have to be accepted as permanent. Perhaps the following graduate honestly expresses what several respondents, acting with the benefits of hindsight, never clearly stated, namely that the jobs they recorded on the questionnaire as permanent were originally intended to be temporary:

(Q.21) As a graduate in a non-graduate job [clerical assistant] within a large organization . . . I fear I may throw out the final statistics as I am a 'failure' as far as degree relates to job. Having left the College of Education [where she unsuccessfully studied for a PGCE] I got a job to give me time to work out what to do as I couldn't teach. The temporary job then turned into a permanent one as I found I was happy in an undemanding job with no responsibility attached. I'm afraid I am quite happy with 'a job till I have children' which is an attitude modern girl graduates are supposed to abhor.

Although numerically smaller, those in temporary employment at the end of 1981 faced greater problems than temporary workers of earlier years. Eight of the nine 1981 group of temporary workers had completed PGCE courses, but had failed to secure the permanent teaching post to which almost all of them aspired. Most of the nine were in short-term teaching posts and four were in similar temporary positions a year earlier. With respect to non-teaching jobs, in view of the probability that the longer one remains in permanent posts the less likely it is to be considered temporary, it is perhaps not surprising that by the end of 1981, few respondents were to be found in perceived temporary posts. One respondent, however, despite having spent twenty-seven months in residential houseparent posts, continued to describe her employment as temporary.

Comparing temporary employment in the three types of colleges, once again Tables 4.2 and 4.3 suggest that the problems seem most acute for the combination colleges. This latter type had the highest rates of temporary employment in each of the three years; the proto-polytechnics had the lowest.

Unemployment

The proportion of college respondents unable to find employment, despite being available for it, remained at the 11 per cent mark throughout the period covered by the survey. Of the twenty-six who were unemployed at the end of 1979, six continued to be unemployed for the entire period under study; eight eventually obtained permanent work but in rather low status jobs (eg as clerical assistants, van drivers or sales assistants); four acquired positions more commensurate with graduate status (eg as graphic designers or trainee journalists); five accepted temporary jobs; two entered teacher training courses; and one got a grant to train as a social worker. The experiences of this group suggest that there is a fairly high probability that graduates identified as unemployed at the end of the graduating year will continue to encounter career problems in the following years.

Unlike the trend for temporary employment, unemployment at the end of 1980 did not include a substantial influx of graduates who had completed a PGCE course in the academic year following graduation. Only eight of the twenty-three unemployed in December 1980 had taken PGCE courses and half of the remaining fifteen were unemployed a year earlier. The unemployed group at the end of 1981 consisted of eleven PGCE and sixteen non-PGCE graduates. Although, at the end of 1981, the proportion of unemployed PGCE graduates was only slightly smaller than the proportion of non-PGCE graduates, the former graduates had an average total unemployment time of only nine months compared with fifteen months for non-PGCE graduates. It seems that by taking a PGCE course the 1979 college graduates could significantly reduce the length of time spent in unemployment.

With the benefits of hindsight, some of the longer-term unemployed laid the blame for their predicament at the door of the liberal education values associated with their degree courses. A graduate in English and art, who had been unemployed for twenty-seven months, stated:

(Q.20i) My degree course was not vocational and did not help me get a job. Such courses should be abolished or radically altered. Today, it is unrealistic to enrich a student's 'personal qualities' and then leave him/her on the dole. Degrees are now so common that they have lost any 'prestige' that might have been useful in getting a job.

In a similar vein, another graduate, unemployed for a total of twelve months, wrote:

(Q.20i) . . . Taking Drama, TV/English very seriously at college and then at the end of my college career being advised that theatre etc. was a no-go area for people from our type of college and that I should work for the Post Office or something – does rather seem to undercut the validity of the last 4 years.

A graduate in geography/education and community studies, also unemployed for twelve months, believed the nature of her degree to be a cause of her unemployment:

(Q.20i) . . . the only thing my degree courses did for me were to extend my horizons, interests and experiences and put 'letters after my name'. My degree course was far too broad-based to allow me to compete against university graduates who had specialized in branches of my subject; and for more general graduate entry jobs my degree wasn't of a high enough standard.

Another unemployed graduate, however, did not overlook the fact that she freely chose such courses:

(Q.20i) My degree courses were, by and large, irrelevant to any job I have had or am likely to have – this is not to criticize the courses – it was me, after all, who chose them.

Teacher Training

The single most popular career outlet for the 1979 college respondents was teacher training. Having obtained their first degrees, 36 per cent of the college cohort entered PGCE courses in the following academic year; a further 5 per cent and 3 per cent respectively did likewise in 1980 and 1981.

With a total of 44 per cent of their graduates having completed postgraduate teacher training, the former colleges of education had substantially higher proportions entering PGCE courses than combination colleges and proto-polytechnics, the latter closely matching the rates in university and polytechnic first destinations.

Neither should the 44 per cent who embarked upon PGCE courses be taken to represent the upper limits of college graduates' orientations towards teaching. As Table 4.4 illustrates, a further 15 per cent of respondents would either have liked to have entered teaching ('thwarted teachers') or still intended to do so, circumstances permitting, ('aspiring teachers'). As a result, an overall 59 per cent were either involved in teaching or expressed positive orientations towards it. The same table also reveals that only a third of the respondents declared no connections with teaching and were permanently employed in full-time alternative occupations.

	%		%
Teaching Oriented	59	Completed a PGCE course	44
		Thwarted or Aspiring Teachers	15
Non-Teaching Oriented	41	Not Employed	8
		Permanent Home Employment	33
TOTAL RESPONDENTS (100%)	247		247

Table 4.4
Teaching orientations of 1979 non-BEd respondents from former colleges of education at 31 December 1981.

Although a subsequent section will consider the extent of mobility between occupations, it may be noted here that many of the 1980 and 1981 entrants to PGCE courses appeared to be taking up teacher training because of the shortage of suitable alternative employment. The following comments are typical of several later entrants to PGCE courses:

(Q.11) I wanted a more demanding job than the one above [Employment Assistant in careers office] and teaching seemed to be the type of challenge I was looking for.

(Q.11) Decided [a PGCE course] may lead to professional employment as teacher – disillusioned with general job situation.

(Q.11) [In contrast to previous work as Higher Clerical Officer with a regional health authority] I wanted a job where I would be fully occupied, life was not predictable, and was stimulating.

So extensive was the proportion of respondents who entered PGCE courses that one of the most meaningful ways of describing graduates' early careers is to visualize them as two broad streams: one which undertook teacher training and one which did not.

Taking this approach, additional analyses contrasted the latest known career circumstances of PGCE and non-PGCE respondents. Although a slightly higher share of non-PGCE graduates was unemployed and not available for employment, 76 per cent of them, compared to 69 per cent of PGCE respondents, were in permanent employment. The lower percentage of PGCE respondents in employment is perhaps not surprising in view of the fact that they had spent one year less in the labour market than most of the non-PGCE graduates. In addition, 7 per cent of the PGCE group were still in the process of completing their training and the same proportion were employed in temporary posts, while still applying for permanent appointments. There are thus firm grounds for believing that by the end of the following year the proportion of PGCE respondents in permanent employment would match, and probably surpass, that of the non-PGCE group.

Closer examination of differences between these two streams can be taken a step further by considering the rates and areas of employment entered by the respondents. However, before turning to the topic of employment trends, it is worth pausing to consider the entry of graduates into training for occupations other than teaching.

Training for Other Occupations

As with teacher training, the highest participation in training for other occupations occurred at the end of the graduating year and then declined to lower levels in subsequent years. Accordingly, whereas in December 1979, 8 per cent of college respondents were undertaking other training (including law and social work), only 3 per cent were doing so by the end of 1980 and 1981 (Table 4.1).

Apart from the teaching profession, the most prevalent form of occupational training was in secretarial work. Thirteen out of the nineteen who were in non-teacher training at the end of 1979 completed secretarial and personal assistant courses. By the end of 1981, almost all of the respondents who had completed such courses, which usually lasted about six to ten months, were to be found in full-time secretarial work. One or two respondents clearly appreciated the experience of these courses:

(Q.20ii) The bi-lingual secretarial course helped to improve my French tremendously and develop my skills.

Most, however, expressed serious reservations about training for this type of employment. The following were typical:

(Q.21) Intensive one-year personal assistant course invaluable for present employment. However in retrospect and considering future prospects in this field I would not advise this type of course for a graduate – not intellectually stimulating or demanding of initiative .... [I would warn present students] not to be taken in by prospect of position as 'graduate secretary' – few posts available worthy of graduate candidate's educational background – almost exclusively in London. Salary low even in comparison with teaching.

(Q.21) Secretarial work – I think it is best to undertake a full academic year of secretarial training and get the best skill qualifications possible as the better secretarial jobs generally ask for these, and employers can pick and choose at the moment. Even with a degree and good skill qualifications it is still a battle to get a decent job. There seems to be quite a high turnover of secretaries generally, so getting some sort of a job is, comparatively, not difficult. However, because secretarial work is 'women's work' it is often underrated and underpaid. I think you have to be lucky to be able to move up or sideways from secretarial work – I hoped it would be a spring-board into something else eventually, but I can see that it may take a long time.

(Q.21) As my present position [a legal secretary] is not strictly a graduate post I am not sure if this is applicable. However, if it is, I would not advise anyone graduating in a similar discipline [English/ history] to embark on a secretarial course as the way to a senior, non-secretarial position, as in my experience and that of my colleagues, there is very small scope for this. One tends to end up merely as a secretary which is boring, subordinate and frustrating, although adequately paid. On the other hand, if one does acquire these skills there is always employment available which is advantageous in the present economic climate although not in the long term.

Whereas the proportion of graduates in secretarial training started high and then declined during the following years, the proportion training for nursing started low and increased slightly so that by the end of 1981 they accounted for five of the eight in non-teacher training. However, the training period for graduates in SRN nursing is usually two or three years, so nursing respondents generally appear in more than one of the year-ending percentages for training. Altogether, six of the 247 college respondents undertook nurse training at some time since leaving college. Opinions on the life of a student SRN nurse were evenly balanced: some clearly disliked the demands made on them by a working environment which differed in many respects from the cultural climate of a college:

(Q.21) [For nurses] long term prospects might be better with a degree but initial training is difficult to put up with due to 'subservient' side of the job.

(Q.11) I wished to work as a nurse. The reasons I left were that my training was extremely unsatisfactory and attitudes to myself were unfavourable.

Others, perhaps more strongly motivated, appeared to have been more successful in making the necessary adjustment:

(Q.21) I think that nursing is an unusual career choice for graduates, especially with the new nursing degree courses. There are some courses of two years for graduates of any profession, but I chose the three-year SRN as there seems to be so much to learn! Nursing is very often dismissed as a career, but I think that any undergraduate who is interested in working with people, and isn't afraid of going back to the 'bottom of the pile' after three years of college, should consider nursing – at least, people thinking of teaching, social work, etc. I am almost certain that I would not have enjoyed nursing at 18 years of age, as I lacked the ability to talk to people and see things from their point of view – college gave me a chance to mature enough to do this and nursing is an ideal job for me as I can use my love of communicating every day.

In addition to secretarial work and nursing, respondents who undertook other training included one in each of the following fields: the ministry, vocational guidance, hotel and catering, social work and legal training.

Extending the nurses' comments concerning the 'culture shock' of demanding training courses, the sole trainee solicitor complained of the mis-match between the rigours of his occupational training and the academic quality of his college experience:

(Q.21) [Prospective trainee solicitors should] be prepared to work to a degree which can make you 'crack' if not totally committed to the end product. Having undergone no pressure at college, I was thrust into a world of exams with a high failure rate and exacting standards. The Law Society Exams have a 50% pass mark. There are 8 exams – fail one – fail them all. Over 50% of graduates taking the exam failed last year.... The courses which I undertook at college [English/ history] were on the face of it more than adequate. However, the general standard of many students reduced the style of teaching to little above A level standard. There was a total lack of pressure academically which could have led to a state of academic lethargy. In my final year (3), I had approximately three to four lectures per week, very little set work and end of semester examinations which were held in a most casual and arbitrary style. Therefore, courses provided *no* incentive to achieve anything above a moderate standard.

The above comments raise questions of whether or not more should be done, not only to prepare undergraduates for the anticipated problems of postgraduate 'culture shock', but also to increase their awareness of possible differences between liberal 'educational' experiences and vocational 'training' ones.

Permanent Employment

At the end of 1979, one-third of college respondents were in full-time permanent employment. At the end of 1980, as a consequence of a substantial pool of graduates finding full-time work upon completion of training courses, mainly in teaching, the proportion of respondents in permanent employment had doubled to two-thirds. A year later, in December 1981, the latest known proportion in permanent employment had reached 73 per cent. Although, on the basis of Table 4.5, there are sound grounds for predicting that the most recently trained PGCE graduates would increase the number of employed in 1982, it must also be noted that the probable increase in the numbers 'not available for employment' would offset these additions to the overall employment rate.

Due to the absence of any appropriate previous or comparative information, it is difficult to evaluate the adequacy of the latest known employment rate of 73 per cent. Williamson's UMS study (1981), the most recent early careers survey of university and polytechnic graduates, was based on the 1970-1977 graduate labour market, which, for reasons presented earlier, cannot be legitimately compared with that of the late 70s and early 80s. Moreover, the UMS survey focused on graduates' employment seven years after graduation, in contrast to the thirty-month period covered by this study. Virtually all that are available, despite their obvious limitations, are the tentative comparisons drawn by this present study between the employment rates for the two other college types.

Taking this approach, Table 4.2 shows that in contrast to the 73 per cent for former college of education graduates, only 51 per cent of combination college respondents were in permanent employment at the end of 1981. On the other hand, Table 4.3 indicates that 77 per cent was the corresponding proportion for proto-polytechnic respondents. Given that this latter type of college was the closest to the first destination employment rates for university and polytechnic graduates, and assuming that first destination variations in employment rates persisted over the period covered by the survey, then it may be estimated that, at the end of 1981, university and polytechnic graduates would have had employment rates of around 80 to 85 per cent respectively. Interestingly, these percentages matched the rates some college commentators hoped that college graduates would have achieved by the end of 1981. It would appear, therefore, that while the latest known employment rate for former college of education respondents should certainly not be considered a discreditable one, neither does it give rise to a great deal of satisfaction. Although a tolerable percentage, it does suggest that difficulties were encountered by college respondents in their search for permanent employment, irrespective of how graduates from other institutions fared.

The first destination statistics presented in Chapter 3 demonstrated that very few college graduates had entered permanent employment in the industrial sector and most were employed in public service and commerce. Following the subsequent entry of many PGCE graduates into full-time teaching appointments, at the end of 1981, the proportion in industry was even smaller and the majority were to be found in education and public service.

Table 4.5 shows that, of the 180 college respondents permanently employed at the end of 1981, 39 per cent were employed in education, predominantly in schools; roughly a quarter worked in public service, mainly in local government and hospitals; another quarter were employed in industry and commerce with approximately equal proportions in each category; and a further 11 per cent were to be found in the employment area known as 'All Others'.

Similar proportions of combination college respondents were employed in public service and industry and commerce, though fewer were located in education (14 per cent) and substantially more in the 'Publishers, Cultural, Entertainment' category (33 per cent). In marked contrast to the two other college types, over half of the proto-polytechnic respondents who were permanently employed worked in industry and commerce. Also, rather surprisingly for this type of college, 28 per cent of their graduates were employed in education. This unexpectedly high proportion of proto-polytechnic respondents involved in teaching is also evident in Table 4.6, which gives details of the kinds of work carried out by those in permanent employment at the end of 1981.

Given the preponderance of college graduates who embarked on postgraduate teacher training, it is not surprising that Table 4.6 should demonstrate that teaching was the main type of work engaged in at the end of 1981. Thirty-six per cent of college respondents in permanent employment were teachers. By comparison, the proto-polytechnic respondents had a higher than expected corresponding proportion of 24 per cent. This seems to be due to the fact that the teacher trained proto-polytechnic

	Former Colleges of Education	Combination Colleges	Proto-polytechnics
	%	%	%
Civil/Diplomatic Service	8	5	4
HM Forces	0	0	3
Local Government/Hospital Service	15	18	10
ALL PUBLIC SERVICE	(23)	(23)	(17)
Schools	35	9	21
FE Colleges	2	0	4
Polytechnics	1	5	0
Universities	1	0	3
ALL EDUCATION	(39)	(14)	(28)
Agriculture/Forestry	1	0	0
Oil, Chemical & Allied Industries	2	0	7
Engineering & Allied Industries	2	5	7
Other Manufacturing	6	5	17
Building/Civil Engineering	0	0	0
Public Utility/Transport	3	5	4
Accountancy	2	0	0
Banking/Insurance	2	5	3
Other Commerce	9	5	14
ALL INDUSTRY/COMMERCE	(27)	(25)	(52)
Solicitors	1	0	0
Publishers, Cultural, Entertainment	4	33	3
Others	6	5	0
ALL OTHERS	(11)	(38)	(3)
TOTAL RESPONDENTS	180	29	21

Table 4.5
Employment categories of 1979 non-BEd respondents who were in permanent employment at 31 December 1981.

respondents found full-time teaching appointments at a higher rate than did their college counterparts: all six of the former were employed in permanent teaching posts at the end of 1981, while only sixty-three out of 108 of the latter were likewise employed – although, as noted earlier, a further sixteen were either still in training or temporary employment and it was felt that by the end of 1982, many of these would have found permanent employment in teaching.

Turning to occupations other than teaching, it was suggested in Chapter 3 that the major type of work categories entered by college graduates – relative, at least, to university and polytechnic graduates – were, in descending order of significance: 'Secretarial, Clerical Work', 'General Administration', 'Buying, Marketing, Selling', and to a lesser extent 'Health, Social Welfare'. It was argued that, following the pattern of existing literature, these areas of work were considered to be highly susceptible to the process of 'filtering down' – when graduates enter occupations lacking a tradition of graduate entry or status.

	Former Colleges of Education	Combination Colleges	Proto- polytechnics
	%	%	%
General Traineeship	0	0	0
Non-Specialist Administration	10	5	10
Scientific R,D & D.	1	0	0
Environmental Planning	1	0	7
Scientific Analysis	2	0	0
Production Operation and Maintenance	1	0	0
Buying, Marketing, Selling	9	14	31
Services to Management	1	5	4
Financial	4	5	10
Legal	1	0	0
Creative, Entertainment	2	19	0
Information, Advisory, Non-scientific Research	4	0	7
Library, Museum, Archive	1	5	4
Personnel	2	0	0
Health, Social Welfare	6	9	0
Teaching	36	19	24
Secretarial, Clerical	18	14	3
Others	1	5	0
TOTAL RESPONDENTS (100%)	180	29	21

Table 4.6
Type of work categories of 1979 non-BEd respondents who were in permanent employment at 31 December 1981.

It is very noticeable in Table 4.6 that the type of work categories identified in Chapter 3 as the most significant at the end of 1979 are precisely those which emerge as the most prevalent at the end of 1981, namely: 'Secretarial, Clerical Work' (18 per cent), 'General Administration' (10 per cent), 'Buying, Marketing, Selling' (9 per cent), and 'Health, Social Welfare' (6 per cent). Correspondingly, those types of work which appeared in Chapter 4 as almost 'no-go' areas for college graduates (eg 'Scientific R,D&D', 'Environmental Planning', 'Production Operation and Maintenance', 'Services to Management', 'Legal', 'Creative, Entertainment', 'Personnel', etc.) remained as such for the duration of the period covered by the survey.

These findings seemed particularly important so, in order to scrutinize them more rigorously, the data were subjected to an alternative method of coding types of work: an occupational classification used by the 1971 Qualified Manpower Follow-up Survey and presented in Williamson (1981). The results undoubtedly verified the conclusions reached above. Apart from teaching (36 per cent), the major occupations of college respondents who were permanently employed at the end of 1981 were as clerical workers (22 per cent), general administrators (7 per cent), retail management (4 per cent), sales representatives (3 per cent), and social or welfare work (4 per cent).

Overall then, the survey findings on the employment areas entered by college graduates substantially confirm the interpretations made in Chapter 3. Any hopes that the early signs of considerable 'filtering down' would disappear as graduates' careers progressed seem to have been ill-founded.

Moreover, the results indicate that during the period covered by the survey, a large proportion of respondents had been unable to develop their careers through entry to occupations more compatible with their graduate standing.

One immediate qualification that must be made to the above interpretation, however, is that not all college graduates were equally vulnerable to the problem of 'filtering down'. Of the two streams depicted earlier, namely PGCE and non-PGCE college graduates, the former showed few signs of having to move down market in search of jobs. For example, at the end of 1981, although 15 per cent of PGCE college graduates appeared to have entered non-graduate areas of work similar to those who did not follow a PGCE course, 85 per cent of the PGCE stream were employed as teachers.

Thus, it may be said that by taking a teacher training course, college graduates can substantially reduce their chances of encountering 'filtering down' and the often demoralizing effects of underemployment. Similar advantages emerge for the PGCE stream in relation to two topics to which we now turn, occupational status and salaries.

Occupational Status

An unavoidable shortcoming of the argument presented above is that in spite of the validity of the reasoning followed, instances of 'filtering down' are dependent upon inferences being drawn from the relative proportions in each of the type of work categories. What is required is a direct method of checking that the areas of work typically open to college graduates are in fact largely associated with occupations lacking a tradition of graduate entry and status. Hence, in order to extend the discussion beyond the inferential and indirect approach, a rudimentary attempt has been made to classify graduates' occupational status according to the researcher's appraisal of respondents' replies. Additionally, for the purposes of subsequent analyses (see Chapters 6 and 7), the capacity to identify high and low status employees constituted a further reason for carrying out such a classification, albeit a fairly basic one. Existing and more sophisticated instruments for ranking occupational status were rejected, usually on the grounds that they tended to be rather dated, based on foreign occupational structures and insensitive to the specific characteristics of the graduate labour market involved.

The occupational status classifications adopted here were based on three criteria:

1 Respondents' comments volunteering their own perceptions of the status of their work (eg 'I am a graduate in a non-graduate job' or 'I did not need my degree to enter this area of work').

2 Indications of suitable graduate entry occupations as contained in the coding frame for the Qualified Manpower Follow-up Survey (see Williamson 1981).

3 In the event of 1 and 2 above proving insufficient, the researcher's assessment of the normal qualification requirements for the occupation concerned.

Details of respondents' employment circumstances on 31 December 1981 were then used to assign them to one of the following categories:

1 Not employed – all respondents who were not in full-time permanent employment.
2 Low status – respondents in posts which would normally require O levels or less.
3 Medium status – respondents in posts which would normally require A levels.
4 Graduate status – respondents in posts with a tradition of graduate entry.

Examples of the kinds of occupations in each status category are offered throughout the following interpretation of the results.

Covering each of the three types of college, Table 4.7 presents the results of the analysis. The first row shows that the colleges and the proto-polytechnics had similar proportions who were not in employment (27 and 25 per cent respectively), but the combination colleges had the much larger proportion of 49 per cent.

	Former Colleges of Education		Combination Colleges		Proto-polytechnics	
	%		%		%	
Not employed	27		49		25	
Low status employees	7		2		0	
Medium status employees	27		27		8	
Graduate status employees:		(39)		(22)		(67)
Teachers	26		5		18	
Non-teachers	13		17		49	
TOTAL RESPONDENTS (100%)	247		41		39	

Table 4.7
Occupational status of 1979 non-BEd respondents according to their employment circumstances at 31 December 1981.

Seven per cent of college respondents were employed in low status occupations, a slightly higher rate than the other two types of colleges. The majority of these seventeen low status workers were to be found in the types of work categories 'Secretarial, Clerical Work' and 'Buying, Marketing, Selling'. Most of those in the former category worked as typists or general office clerks and one, a clerical worker with the DHSS, typically reported:

(Q.21) I would advise anyone about to enter the Civil Service to enter at the highest level possible for their qualifications. I have entered at a level which only requires O levels and to gain promotion I will have to take examinations and Boards. If I had applied at the outset for a higher level I could have made a direct entry.

Most of the low status workers in 'Buying, Marketing, Selling' were sales assistants in shops or furniture sale rooms and two had been appointed as assistant managers of small retailers. One sales assistant expressed the common complaints:

(Q.20i) . . . anyone with a reasonable level of intelligence could do my present job – I did not need my degree.

Another salesperson, although typical in so far as he felt his work was not as intellectually stimulating as he hoped a graduate's job would be, was atypical in his perceptions of the tensions he felt between the demeaning status ascribed to his job and the potential scope that he believed existed in his work in an ironmongery shop:

(Q.21) No matter what knowledge or skill you have in a particular field it has little importance to the average tradesperson who will still quite often treat you as being the lowest of the low. By comparison though, there are certain rewards gained through dealing with customers and their problems that can give rewards far greater than I can express in a few short words. So this leaves me in a constant state of confusion about my opinions of my job. I dislike it as a result of the stereotype 'shop assistant' – non-helpful, not interested, not very well informed image (which happens to be the opposite of my particular role in my shop) against the rewards of problem-solving on behalf of the customer.

Other low status occupations included a van driver, a postal officer, library assistants and general accounts clerks.

At the other end of the scale, while 26 per cent of college respondents had achieved graduate status by working within the teaching profession, only 13 per cent of all college respondents had attained graduate status in occupations other than teaching. This finding highlights the extent of the difficulties faced by college graduates when trying to find appointments commensurate with graduate status entry yet unrelated to the teaching profession. By comparison, the corresponding proportions with non-teaching graduate status occupations from combination colleges and proto-polytechnics were 17 and 49 per cent respectively.

A quite remarkable feature of the 13 per cent of college respondents in graduate status work is that nearly all were to be found in type of work categories not typically obtained by college graduates, ie those in type of work categories with percentages under 6 per cent in Table 4.6, except for 'Information, Advisory, Non-scientific Research', which included more medium status respondents. Conversely, only three of the thirty-one graduate status workers were located in either 'Secretarial, Clerical' or 'General Administration' and none were to be found in 'Buying, Marketing, Selling'. Consequently, areas of work with high proportions of college graduates were not associated with graduate status, but areas of work with low involvement of college graduates were. This finding strongly suggests that considerable credence can be given to the 'filtering down' inferences drawn from the type of work categories discussed in the previous section.

It also indicates the kinds of jobs college graduates may have to compete for if they want to take a greater share of the available graduate status employment in areas other than teaching. Such jobs (in descending order of frequency) were as accountants, executive officers in the civil service, journalists, computer programmers, social workers, graphic designers and personnel officers. For graduates from the other two college types, the occupational categories 'Secretarial, Clerical' and 'General Administration' were associated with low status employment, but the category 'Buying, Marketing, Selling' contained several proto-polytechnic graduates who were working as sales executives and as such were awarded high status classification.

In between the two extremes of the status scale, 27 per cent of college respondents held occupations which were classified as medium status. This proportion was the same for combination college respondents, but lower for proto-polytechnic respondents, 8 per cent of whom were assigned to the medium status level.

Just over half of the sixty-seven college respondents in the medium status category were to be found in either 'Secretarial, Clerical' or 'General Administration'. Of these, the most common occupations were as secretaries, civil service clerical officers (as distinct from civil service executive officers, who were given graduate status ranking), administrative assistants in health and local government institutions, and general administrative personnel in sports and leisure centres. In contrast to the proto-polytechnic respondents' orientations towards sales executive jobs, typical occupations among the eleven college respondents in the 'Buying, Marketing, Selling' area of work included assistant or departmental manageresses in large stores, branch managers in smaller retail outlets and various sales representatives. A further five medium status workers were located in the 'Health, Social Welfare' category and included three residential care officers, a policeman and an assistant home help organizer.

Overall then, three-quarters of those employed in medium status occupations were to be found in the type of work categories most commonly entered by college graduates. Once again, these findings confirm earlier inferential interpretations which suggested that, in the case of college graduates, the most frequently entered type of work areas were indicative of a substantial degree of moving down the labour market to work of a lower status than that normally accepted by first degree graduates.

Given the finding that 27 per cent of college respondents were able to find graduate status by entering the teaching profession, it is not difficult to appreciate why, when compared to the alternatives, teaching remains a very attractive proposition for many college graduates. The status rewards derived from teaching are clearly demonstrated by the finding that 59 per cent of the PGCE stream compared to 23 per cent of the non-PGCE stream had attained graduate status, while, conversely, 9 per cent of the former compared to 53 per cent of the latter were in medium or low status occupations. Moreover, as we shall see in the following section, status was not the only benefit which college graduates found difficult to obtain in occupations other than teaching.

Latest Known Salaries

Approximately 78 per cent of all non-BEd respondents who were in permanent employment at the end of 1981 provided details of their gross monthly income. These details were then grouped into the seven categories presented in Table 4.8.

From this table, it is clear that a larger proportion of proto-polytechnic respondents commanded higher salaries than respondents from other types of colleges. The modal income group, that is, the income category with the highest number of cases, was £500–600 a month for proto-polytechnic respondents; they had the highest proportion in the £600–700 bracket and none earned less than £300 per month. This largely reflected the number of well-paid sales executives among their ranks. In contrast, the college respondents were highly concentrated in a lower modal group of

£400–500 a month, had larger proportions in the lower income brackets and fewer in the higher ones. The combination college respondents displayed an even lower model income, £300–400 a month.

Gross monthly income	Former Colleges of Education	Combination Colleges	Proto-polytechnics
£	%	%	%
Under 200	1	0	0
201 – 300	11	17	0
301 – 400	23	35	9
401 – 500	47	12	17
501 – 600	13	12	39
601 – 700	4	18	26
Above 700	1	6	9
TOTAL RESPONDENTS (100%)	137	17	23
No. of permanently employed respondents who did not provide salary details	43	4	6

Table 4.8
Salaries held by 1979 non-BEd respondents who were permanently employed at
31 December 1981.

Looking in more detail at the salaries of college respondents, it is noticeable that, although half of those permanently employed at the end of 1981 had secured salaries of between £400–500 a month, only a small number had more than this and over a third had less. Furthermore, supplementary analyses confirmed that the main reasons for college respondents showing up well in the middle of the salary range are the moderate but sound salaries procured by the substantial numbers working as teachers. Whereas 77 per cent of the PGCE stream earned between £400–600 per month, approaching half of the non-PGCE stream were working for less than £400 a month. Put another way, while the average mean monthly salary for the PGCE stream was £459, the same for the non-PGCE stream was £407. Consequently, a comparison of the salaries achieved by PGCE and non-PGCE respondents suggests that the comparative financial benefits and security to be gained by entering teaching may act as an additional inducement towards that profession.

This conclusion is reinforced by an examination of the latest known income attained by college respondents in each of the main types of work entered by these graduates. In contrast to other occupations, teachers had the lowest proportions in the £400–600 range, although they had slightly fewer reaching the highest salary brackets. In addition, it should also be remembered that these differential amounts had been secured in spite of the fact that teaching respondents had spent a full year less in employment than most of the respondents in other occupations. Clerical work, which after teaching was the main occupational area for college graduates, had the highest percentage of respondents with lower range salaries: two-thirds of clerical workers earned less than £400 a month.

Internal Promotion and Upgrading of Work

Faced with a declining number of vacancies in jobs conventionally associated with graduate entry, many graduates were advised to seek lower status work in the hope that, having gained 'a foot in the door', internal promotion to positions more appropriate to a graduate's intelligence and standing would quickly follow. It was advocated that, once ensconced within an employing organization, the graduate could court promotion by displaying more initiative and skills than could the non-graduate counterpart. Similarly, according to a related argument, it has been suggested that it is not the case that jobs associated with 'filtering down' always demean the graduates; sometimes the graduates, with their higher intellectual capabilities, upgrade the quality and skills requirements of the jobs performed. In this sense, 'upgrading of work' denotes the alleged increase in the actual quality of the skills required by a job and not, as is sometimes the meaning intended, the rise in the level of qualification demanded by an occupation. The widespread existence of this latter phenomena is not disputed, as the survey findings clearly demonstrate. What is being questioned is the claim that there are frequent instances of graduates gaining recognition for extending the skill requirements of less demanding work.

In order to subject these opinions to some empirical investigation, the survey findings have been scanned for instances of job upgrading and internal promotion. For these purposes 'internal promotion' has been defined as the upward movement, within the same employing organization, between posts which were qualitatively different in terms of supervisory levels, status or skill requirements. Respondents who entered employment as trainees in an occupation in which they subsequently qualified were excluded as examples of internal promotion, though respondents who entered in one occupational capacity and then were promoted to train for another were included. Focusing only on college respondents in non-teaching occupations, it should be recalled that the analysis is limited to a period of thirty months after graduation – some proponents of the viewpoints just advanced may want to argue that a longer time scale is required before early indications of the extent of internal promotions and job upgrading can be adequately assessed.

Of the thirty-one respondents in graduate status non-teaching jobs at the end of 1981, five (16 per cent) advanced to these positions through internal promotion routes. They included two residential social workers who were promoted to supervisory levels, a student accountant promoted from a receptionist, a computer systems analyst from an accounts clerk, and an accounts executive from an executive assistant. At the time of completing the questionnaire, the two residential social workers had occupied their new posts for two and three months, the computer analyst for nine months, and the student accountant and accounts executive for twenty months each.

In stressing the importance of getting on to the first step, one of the residential social workers clearly subscribed to the 'foot in the door' technique: 'il n'y a que le premier pas qui coûte'. The other, however, signalled a problem that was encountered by numerous college respondents – how do you gain entry to lower status jobs and then proceed successfully to higher positions when so many employers, and their existing staff, view you as threats to themselves and as over-educated for the job in question?

(Q.21) Heads of small residential establishments may be suspicious and reluctant to employ graduates who are better qualified than themselves.

As we shall see in a later chapter, some graduates, in an effort to resolve such problems, resorted to concealing the fact that they possessed a degree and others sought boring temporary jobs in order to demonstrate to potential employers their ability to carry out monotonous work without becoming frustrated by the lack of opportunities and intellectual challenges.

With a more optimistic outlook, the receptionist who was promoted to a computer analyst encouraged prospective entrants to this field to seek out employers who would be willing to place them on training courses leading to further qualifications. Few of her peers, however, were able to find such opportunities. Out of the eighty-four respondents in non-graduate status employment at the end of 1981, only thirteen (15 per cent) had or were studying for qualifications in connection with, and while working in, their current job. Studying for these qualifications was normally on a part-time or day release basis and the most frequently sought were the Institute of Personnel Management examinations, for which three respondents were preparing.

Of the sixty-seven in medium status occupations on 31 December 1981, eight (12 per cent) had reached their latest known appointments through internal promotion: five were in 'General Administration', two in 'Buying, Marketing, Selling', and one in 'Secretarial, Clerical'. Three of the eight remained quite positive about their promotion experiences and future prospects. A publisher's respresentative, for example, was still optimistic, if somewhat guarded in tone:

(Q.21) Publishing is a highly competitive business and, particularly in the present economic climate, one in which suitable vacancies and then movement for promotions are thin on the ground . . . . Although I was advised not to enter publishing as a secretary, I do know of several who have successfully made the transition from secretarial to editorial roles – this may still be a possibility for those seeking a place in publishing.

Likewise, a clerk typist in a social services department was also fairly hopeful:

(Q.11) [My move from typist to clerk typist] represents a genuine promotion – work more varied and interesting. Also can be a way in to unqualified social work posts – [my] ultimate ambition. Also lots more money.

On the other hand, five of the eight were, to varying degrees, disillusioned with their experiences of internal promotion. For instance, an administrative assistant in a polytechnic (promoted from a clerical assistant) described the frequently mentioned problem of working in 'dead-end jobs or departments':

(Q.21) I would advise any students not to get into a job where there are no prospects of advancement. Faculty-based admin. assistants, in this institution anyway, cannot advance in their career unless they leave the faculties.

Similarly, other administrative workers were frustrated by their new posts:

(Q.21, a research writer in a publishing firm) The salary is good but the job satisfaction is minimal. It is very repetitive – mainly checking printed matter and transferring information from cards to printer's slips. There is no chance of a career there – for a student leaving college I would advise him to do a postgraduate course to achieve a relevant qualification for a career.

(Q21, a general administrative assistant in a health authority) [Students interested in my current area of employment] should be prepared for a job which is much more tedious than their time at college, and also for some suspicion, from colleagues but more especially superiors, of people with degrees.

Finally, a promoted assistant staff manager in a large chain store had decided that the benefits of the firm's well-established promotion structure could not compensate for the job's drawbacks:

(Q.21) I would advise any student to consider carefully the commitment involved in entering the retail industry, in particular, the long hours, no overtime payments and a fairly low salary in the training stage. The turnover of trainees in the retail industry is very high, because many of the above are not considered carefully enough! The problem of mobility within a variety chain store also causes trainees to resign. It is very easy to agree to moving around the country in theory, but in practice, given a week or two weeks notice to move 200 miles is not quite as easy!!

As a result, she had set her sights on a new career as a teacher of mentally-handicapped children.

In addition to those for whom the experience of promotion fell short of initial expectations, it must be noted that overall there were fewer respondents who had achieved promotion than respondents who volunteered comments on the lack of promotion opportunities. Secretaries, in particular, often expressed their frustration with the many obstacles which thwarted their attempts to use this area of work as a springboard into more rewarding jobs. One comment to this effect has already been presented in an earlier section (p.51), another succinctly summarized some of the weaknesses in the upgrading of work and the 'foot in the door' arguments:

(Q.21) Secretarial posts are easy to obtain, considering the level of unemployment and the difficulty of finding a job which demands a graduate's level of education. However, I would not advise people to enter secretarial work as the positions I have experienced have been mundane and soul destroying. Also, it is very difficult to avoid the inertia connected to secretarial posts; once esconced in typing and filing, it is very difficult to break this image created in employers' minds.

Clerical workers, especially in civil service departments, also felt disheartened by demeaning and restrictive work situations. Again, an illustration of this was offered earlier (p.57), but the following comments from civil service clerical workers were also typical:

(Q.21) [advice to prospective entrants to civil service clerical work . . .] Don't! Unless you are the type to enjoy working for a department of the civil service (DHSS) which is grossly inefficient. You should also have the ability not to mind any initiative exercised by you being squashed by petty bureaucratic rules. There is no room for commonsense in this area of employment.

(Q.21) Try somewhere else!! Actually, it may not be as bad as an executive officer, but if you have to take a clerical officer post you have very little hope of promotion but are expected always to give a high standard of work with little thanks. In gaining a degree I had hoped for something better, however it is a secure job which is something in this day and age.

For a final illustration of blocked promotion aspirations, several respondents urged prospective entrants to be sceptical of employers' offers and promises of organized career development schemes:

(Q.21, a transport administration trainee) From my own experience I cannot recommend too strongly to graduates that they do not accept glossy graduate recruitment literature as being an accurate reflection of career development within an organization. During interviews graduates should meticulously examine the offer of employment being made to them by asking a comprehensive catalogue of detailed questions. In short some recruitment literature can be deceitful to say the least. An advertised course of training in the field of bus operations management with [my employers] has in reality turned out to be a clerical merry-go-round rotating every three months around various administrative departments.

(Q.21) Don't become too enthusiastic with the pretence of graduate training schemes or career development. Having now returned to college [to study for a PGCE after working as a higher clerical officer in an area health authority] I have met many who have left work as it was boring, not stimulating, [poor] pay and holidays, limited conversation.

Overall then, on the grounds of the evidence derived from the survey, it would seem imprudent to invest too much faith in either the 'foot in the door' strategy or the upgrading of work argument, especially the latter. Although the evidence suggests that certain employing organizations offer better promotion prospects than others and that some isolated individuals have successfully advanced through internal promotion routes (eg the receptionist who progressed to a computer analyst), these appear to be the exceptions which prove a more general rule. Only a small fraction of all college respondents had progressed to graduate or medium status employment through internal promotion and several of these had subsequently become disenchanted by their experiences. Constituting an additional barrier, it was found that only a small proportion of respondents were involved in studying for further qualifications.

The open-ended responses have highlighted a whole series of reasons why trusting to internal promotion and job upgrading strategies could be beguiling. These included being over-educated for lower status jobs and promotion, the suspicions of many employers and their non-graduate staff, becoming ensconced in 'dead-end' departments and tedious occupations, unacceptable demands in such areas as the retail trade, the unfulfilled expectations of career development schemes, the lack of opportunities for displaying initiative, the drift into inertia as a result of prolonged exposure to demeaning work, and the immense difficulties of breaking the menial worker mould once cast and stereotyped. The latter difficulties make the chances of upgrading work particularly improbable. Significantly, not a single case of this type was reported in the respondents' replies. Perhaps the closest example was the worker in the ironmongery shop, who was endeavouring to construct an image of himself similar to a technical sales adviser, despite having to accommodate himself to the conventional perceptions of his prescribed role as a shop assistant. Unfortunately, there was no evidence to indicate that he had succeeded in gaining acceptance for his own upgraded perspective on the occupation.

Occupational Mobility

Although the size of the sample, in relation at least to the range of the occupations entered, is insufficient to extract any detailed observations of graduates' occupational mobility, a number of general points concerning the occupational movements of the group as a whole may still be made.

Only 12 per cent of the 247 college respondents held a post on 1 October 1979 in which they stayed for the remaining period covered by the survey. Inversely, the same result emerges from the perspective of latest known occupations: by 31 December 1981, only 13 per cent of all college respondents were in posts which they had occupied for twenty-five to twenty-seven months. This finding carried serious implications for the work of college careers services, since it appears that in simple terms of supporting graduates' search for permanent work during the graduating year, the services' sphere of long-term influence is restricted to a very small proportion of their total output. This may point to the need for careers services to mediate enduring influences through other means than fairly immediate 'job-fixing'.

Of the forty-four respondents who had moved out of their first jobs, the majority did so within a year, particularly within the latter half of the year. Apart from those who had remained in the same job for the full period covered by the survey, the categories with the highest frequencies for length of time in latest known jobs were sixteen to eighteen months (fifty-six respondents) and four to six months (twenty-eight respondents). This clearly indicates that the two peak periods for entering latest known jobs were the late summer months of 1980 and 1981 – times at which the substantial numbers of PGCE graduates were taking up their full-time appointments.

The trend is also revealed in Table 4.9, which shows the raw numbers of respondents in each of the type of work categories at four different stages of their early careers: 1 October 1979 and the three year-endings, 1979, 1980 and 1981. (It should be noted that this table refers to type of work areas and not to particular jobs, so that the movement of a respondent who had changed jobs but not type of work categories would not be detectable here. An analysis of individual mobility within type of work categories was carried out, but the numbers of cases in each of the outflow and inflow groupings were so small that few significant patterns were apparent.)

Table 4.9 shows that on 1 October 1979 the total number of college respondents in permanent employment was seventy-three and by the end of the year it was still only eight-two. A year later, however, following the main PGCE output, the number had doubled to 170, then it rose only slightly again to 180 by the close of the following year. As could be expected, the numbers in 'Teaching, Lecturing', which were negligible in 1979, increased dramatically to fifty-seven in 1980 and continued to climb

	1/10/79	31/12/79	31/12/80	31/12/81
	N	N	N	N
General Administration	13	13	16	18
Scientific R,D & D	2	3	2	2
Environmental Planning	1	1	1	1
Scientific Analysis	1	1	2	3
Production Operation & Maint.	0	0	0	1
Buying, Marketing, Selling	16	16	17	16
Services to Management	1	1	2	3
Financial	5	5	9	7
Legal	0	0	0	1
Creative, Entertainment	4	3	5	5
Information, Advisory, Non-Sc. Research	4	5	6	7
Library, Museum, Archive	2	1	1	2
Personnel	1	2	8	4
Health, Social Welfare	6	6	6	11
Teaching, Lecturing	1	3	57	65
Secretarial, Clerical	11	16	33	33
Others	5	6	5	1
TOTAL RESPONDENTS IN PERMANENT WORK	73	82	170	180

Table 4.9
Types of work entered by 1979 non-BEd respondents from former colleges of education at different stages after graduation.

to sixty-five a year later. Thus, of all the occupational areas, teaching showed the largest growth, not only between 1979 and 1980, but also between 1980 and 1981. Over the period December 1979 to December 1981, 'Health, Social Welfare' increased from six to eleven, 'Buying, Marketing, Selling' remained stable at around sixteen, 'General Administration' rose slightly from thirteen to eighteen and 'Secretarial, Clerical work', the second most prevalent inflow occupation, doubled from sixteen to thirty-three. Overall then, at the close of 1981 there were more graduates employed in the three main areas associated with lower status work than at any time since graduation. Once again, therefore, the results confound hopes that the preponderance of graduates in non-teaching and lower status work would decline as a result of occupational mobility.

5

Early Career Reactions

By and large, the preceding chapter concentrated on describing and interpreting quantifiable indicators of graduates' early career patterns. The main focus was placed upon trends in training, employment rates, types of work entered and levels of occupation achieved. Turning more directly to the 'subjective' items contained in the questionnaire, this chapter highlights college respondents' perceptions of their career experiences, particularly their levels of satisfaction with latest known jobs and career prospects. Maintaining a predominantly descriptive approach, it sets out to engage such questions as 'To what extent were college graduates satisfied with their employment circumstances?' and 'What is the nature of the relationship between occupational status and subjective accounts of job satisfaction?'

Rather than asking the all-embracing but non-probing question, 'Are you satisfied with your job/career?', the questionnaire used a variety of closed and open-ended items, each of which addressed a particular but related component of the respondents' likely, overall attitude. A closed item, for example, invited them to indicate their agreement or disagreement with a number of attitudinal statements, one of which dealt with the extent to which they found their latest work intellectually satisfying.

Intellectual Satisfaction

Faced with the statement, 'My present (or most recent) work is not as intellectually stimulating as I hoped a graduate's job would be', respondents were requested to indicate their agreement or disagreement with it according to a five point scale which, for ease of presentation, was subsequently collapsed to three: Agree, Neutral and Disagree.

The proportion of total college respondents agreeing with the statement (42 per cent) was roughly the same as that disagreeing with it (40 per cent), but Table 5.1 shows that once the sample was broken down into a PGCE and a non-PGCE stream, considerably more intellectual dissatisfaction emerged among those who did not complete a PGCE course than among those who did. Half of the non-PGCE stream, compared to one third-of the teacher trainers, were intellectually dissatisfied with their latest known jobs. Conversely, in contrast to 46 per cent of the PGCE stream, only 35 per cent of the non-PGCE stream could say they were satisfied with the intellectual demands of their work.

This finding suggests that college graduates encountered difficulties in finding intellectually satisfying work outside the teaching profession. Such an interpretation receives substantial support from a consideration of the different levels of intellectual satisfaction in each of the main type of work categories entered by college graduates.

'My present (or most recent) work is not as intellectually stimulating as I hoped a graduate's job would be.'

	All	PGCE stream	Non-PGCE stream
	%	%	%
Agree	42	32	50
Neutral	18	22	15
Disagree	40	46	35
TOTAL RESPONDENTS (100%)	247	108	139

Table 5.1
1979 non-BEd college respondents' intellectual satisfaction in latest job.

In comparison to only 25 per cent of teachers, 73 per cent of clerical workers, together with 61 per cent of general administrators and 50 per cent in 'Buying, Marketing, Selling' were disappointed by the lack of intellectual stimulation in their work. Similarly, while 57 per cent of teachers were able to disagree with the statement, thereby indicating their satisfaction with the levels of intellect demanded in their jobs, only 15 per cent of clerical workers, 33 per cent of general administrators and 31 per cent in 'Buying, Marketing, Selling' could do likewise. In comparison to teaching, therefore, the three main types of non-teaching work taken up by college graduates were commonly associated with an increase in intellectual frustration and underemployment.

An additional finding of some interest is that, although only eleven respondents were to be found in 'Health, Social Welfare' at the end of 1981, their levels of intellectual satisfaction were similar to those of teaching respondents. Although not shown in the table, because of the small numbers involved, another type of work category with a high rate of intellectual satisfaction was 'Financial', where all seven employees were clearly contented with the high degree of intellectual demands made upon them.

Table 5.2 demonstrates the strength of the correspondence between occupational status and levels of intellectual satisfaction in latest known jobs. Of those in low status jobs, while 76 per cent were intellectually dissatisfied with their work, only 7 per cent were satisfied. Alternatively, of those in graduate status jobs, only 22 per cent were disappointed with the intellectual requirements of their work, while 60 per cent expressed satisfaction.

Consequently, given the high statistical significance of this result, graduates in high status occupations were more likely to experience intellectual satisfaction in their work than graduates in low or medium status occupations, who were correspondingly more likely to have encountered intellectual dissatisfaction and frustration. Further analyses revealed that a similar correspondence did not exist between latest known salaries and levels of intellectual satisfaction.

When examining the nature of the intellectual satisfaction and dissatisfaction experienced by graduates, it is noticeable that the dissatisfied rather than the satisfied made greater use of the open-ended items to elaborate on their problems. Of the many teachers who disagreed with the statement,

'My present (or most recent) work is not as intellectually stimulating as I hoped a graduate's job would be.'

	Low	Medium	Graduate
	%	%	%
Agree	76	61	22
Neutral	18	10	18
Disagree	6	29	60
TOTAL RESPONDENTS (100%)	17	67	96

Table 5.2
1979 non-BEd college respondents: occupational status by intellectual satisfaction with latest job.

only five proceeded to offer such descriptions of their satisfaction as, 'teaching music gave me an opportunity to develop my interest in this area', 'teaching makes heavy mental demands' and 'teachers need to keep learning all the time'. By way of illustrating their contentment with the mental demands of their jobs, a small number of respondents in other occupations used such phrases as 'demanding', 'challenging', 'need a lively mind', 'need to be independent and take initiatives', and 'need a knowledge of all the company's operations'. Reminiscent of an earlier quotation from a trainee solicitor, accountancy was one occupation which was invariably associated with high levels of intellectual capabilities and stamina. Two extracts illustrate the mental pressures of this type of work and training.

(Q.21) One has to know that chartered accountancy is the career for them. One cannot just drift into accountancy because there seems nothing better to do. It is a career which should be thoroughly examined – perhaps even as far as taking an intermediate course to prepare oneself. Student accountants are told that they will have *no* social life as compared with college or university. It is true – the pressure of studying and exams far outweighs previous experience at college or university.

(Q.21) People must also realize the amount of work involved in obtaining a professional qualification. To give some idea of the standards, the average pass rate for the Chartered Accountants professional exams is currently 20 per cent and the majority of students are now graduates. If you are to qualify you must be prepared to commit yourself totally to studying for three years.

In marked contrast to those who found satisfaction in meeting considerable mental demands, one or two respondents intimated that they found some intellectual satisfaction in what many would consider were routine menial jobs:

(Q.21, a clerk in a magistrates office) The work is interesting and varied and, at the moment, relatively secure. However, when the 'fixed penalty' system is introduced for many minor traffic offences, this will reduce the work of a magistrate's court considerably. Anyone wishing to make a career in this field would be advised to take a degree in law, and then, within the framework of an office, go on to become a barrister or solicitor. However, even without this, it is possible to qualify as a court clerk, by studying for the relevant diploma, also while working in an office. I could do this if I wish, but have declined to do so. I'm qute happy to do an interesting job which ends at 5pm with no strains and leaving my evenings free.

This view, however, was rare; most of those in fairly routine jobs expressed considerable dissatisfaction with the underemployment associated with the lack of intellectual stimulation at work.

Of those who both assented to the statement and offered some open-ended indications of their reasons for feeling intellectually deprived at work, only three were teachers. Displaying tendencies to equate 'intellectual' with 'academic' development, two of these teachers warned against expecting the profession to be a facilitator of personal intellectual growth:

(Q.21) Don't look upon teaching as an extension to your own intellectual development. It could be many years before you come anywhere near the dizzy heights of degree work.

(Q.21) One should be more interested in the teaching of one's subject, particularly at lower levels, than in the actual subject area itself. It can be very difficult, for example, to adjust oneself to the demands of children who are musically semi-illiterate after one has achieved a high standard at undergraduate level.

Although an educational social worker complained that his work contained 'no academic content or satisfaction', the majority of the open-ended comments that described aspects of intellectual underemployment were volunteered by respondents in clerical and general administration jobs. They frequently perceived their work to be 'tedious', 'boring', 'unstimulating', 'mundane', 'repetitive', 'not requiring educated people with minds of their own', 'minimum intelligence is required', and 'O level ability is not even required'. Several, more lengthy quotations, clearly recording the mentally demeaning work being experienced by some respondents, were also included in Chapter 4. To close this section, three further extracts are indicative of the underemployment experienced by many of those who did not enter the teaching profession:

(Q.21, a secretary in the manufacturing industry) Perhaps the most important point to make about secretarial work is that even in the current employment situation there are still many secretarial vacancies available providing you are not too restricted regarding the area in which you are prepared to work. However, allowing for the odd exceptions where secretarial work might be combined with another area of employment, this area of employment rarely justifies the need for degree level education and so quickly becomes boring and routine. Having chosen this area it is difficult to risk leaving it to move into a totally different and more intellectually demanding field.

(Q.21, an executive officer) The Civil Service offers a relatively stable, secure work environment. It does *not* offer good promotional prospects and offers very little chance of creative thinking. Do not become a civil servant unless you are prepared to fall neatly into the niche which is carved for you.

(Q.21, an assistant houseparent) I have found that many young girls apply for child-care without any understanding of the nature of the work. I was the most qualified of the staff. It is very easy to let your brain lie dormant as it is often unstimulated. This will depend largely on the organization and the home which you choose to work for. It is my opinion that [my previous employers] offered the educated person more in the way of job satisfaction by understanding the needs of children. The job I am at present in offers no stimulation at all. I find I am largely a domestic and am not given time to discuss any of the children's behaviour or how this could be modified.

The Currency of the Degree

As a broad measure of the extent of satisfaction with the employment currency of their degrees, graduates were asked to respond to the statement, 'Given the current level of unemployment, I am satisfied with the range of jobs my particular degree has allowed me to consider'. Exactly half of all college respondents endorsed the statement, just over a quarter rejected it and just under a quarter remained neutral (see Table 5.3).

'Given the current level of unemployment, I am satisfied with the range of jobs my particular degree has allowed me to consider.'

	All	PGCE stream	Non-PGCE stream
	%	%	%
Agree	50	62	40
Neutral	22	18	26
Disagree	28	20	34
TOTAL RESPONDENTS (100%)	247	108	139

Table 5.3
1979 non-BEd college respondents: satisfaction with currency of degree.

Nevertheless, as with many other items discussed earlier, these overall proportions were not uniformly distributed between the two main streams of college graduates. Whereas only one in five of the PGCE stream were dissatisfied with the currency of their degrees, as many as one in three of the non-PGCE stream were. Conversely, in contrast to 62 per cent of the PGCE stream, only 40 per cent of the non-PGCE stream expressed satisfaction with the currency of their degree — the majority were either neutral or in disagreement with the statement.

Corroborating this, further analyses revealed that the vast majority of teachers were content with the employability range of their degrees — only 5 per cent of them disagreed with the statement — and there were higher proportions in both the neutral and disagree categories, but employees in the other main type of work areas were considerably less satisfied. In addition, therefore, to the problems of finding non-teaching work of graduate status which offered some scope for intellectual stimulation, a substantial proportion of college graduates were also disenchanted by the currency value of their degrees.

A similar interpretation can be placed on the responses to the statement, 'On reflection, I now think my future job prospects would have been as good without a degree'. This was a further attempt to gauge respondents' evaluations of the employment currency of their degrees, and Table 5.4 demonstrates that the overall majority (72 per cent) disagreed with it.

'On reflection I now think my future job prospects would have been as good without a degree.'

	All	PGCE stream	Non-PGCE stream
	%	%	%
Agree	22	7	33
Neutral	6	2	10
Disagree	72	91	57
TOTAL RESPONDENTS (100%)	247	108	139

Table 5.4
1979 non-BEd college respondents: satisfaction with degree as enhancement of job prospects beyond A level currency.

However, the table also shows that the 22 per cent who endorsed the statement were mainly those respondents who had not taken a PGCE course. One in three of such respondents considered that their future job prospects would have been as good without a degree; the corresponding proportion for the PGCE stream was 7 per cent.

As with earlier statements, while teaching respondents were almost unanimous in rejecting the attribution of such a low currency value to their degrees, respondents in other areas of employment, notably in clerical and general administration work, were more reluctant to do likewise.

It may also be noted that, although the attitudes to both statements on degree currency were strongly correlated with attitudes to intellectual satisfaction and occupational status, there was no such clear correspondence between attitudes to degree currency and latest known salary or employment circumstances. For example, those who were disappointed by their degree currency were more likely to be intellectually dissatisfied at work, and in low or medium status jobs, but not necessarily more likely to be low paid or unemployed.

A further statement which has some bearing on the relative currency value of degrees, 'I think I would have obtained a better job if I had gone to university', did not produce the differential response common to other attitude statements. Fifty-six per cent of all college respondents, with equal proportions from PGCE and non-PGCE streams, disagreed with the view that they would have improved their career prospects if they had attended a university rather than a college.

Of course, follow-up interviews would be necessary to ascertain their reasons for disagreeing with the statement: were they based on the belief that university graduates as a whole had no additional advantages in the search for employment or were their perceptions of their own abilities such as to make it improbable that they as individuals would not have received careers enhancement by attending a university? Approximately one-fifth of all respondents felt that a university degree would have extended their job prospects, while just over a quarter gave a neutral response. This comparatively high proportion of neutral responses may reflect the fact that some graduates attended PGCE university courses and others insisted that the colleges they attended were actually universities.

In conjunction with the answers to the above attitude statements, the contents of the open-ended responses were analysed for their levels of satisfaction with the currency of college degrees. Attention has been focused here on comments on the level and range of employment prospects permitted by the degrees, but not on the relevance of degree courses to occupational requirements, which will be discussed in detail in the following chapter. As with intellectual satisfaction in the previous section, those who were dissatisfied with the currency of their degrees expressed their opinions more frequently and more forcefully than those who appeared to be satisfied.

Turning first of all to those who showed some satisfaction with degree currency, it was clear that most of the teachers took it to be almost self-evident that they were satisfied with the employment benefits associated with their degrees simply because their degrees had gained them entry to a popular, largely graduate, profession. Four or five teachers went on to state their conviction that a BA degree followed by a PGCE possessed greater currency than a BEd degree. Thirty-two non-teaching respondents offered comments, which, in one way or another, acknowledged that they had obtained employment as a result of possessing a degree. The following short extracts illustrate the kind of responses they gave:

(Q.20i, a residential social worker) When I obtained my present post I was told that being a graduate got me the job, as they felt that 'I had something to offer'.

(Q.20i, a computer programmer) [My degree courses] had no relevance at all to my present job. However, I had no idea that I would be doing this job when I started college. However, I would not have been able to get my job unless I'd had a degree.

(Q.20i, a housewife who resigned from an executive officer post) I could not have got into the Civil Service at executive officer level without my degree, as non-graduates are seldom offered even clerical officer posts in the Inland Revenue in the present climate of unemployment.

(Q.20i, a clerical officer) I think that having a degree helped me obtain employment, but simply because of the employment situation, in that employers were demanding higher qualifications than they would have done, say, five years ago.

Very rarely, however, did respondents suggest that they were content with the currency of their degrees on the grounds that it provided a range of possible employment options. The following response was highly exceptional:

(Q.20i, an assistant retail manager) Degree course followed was a General Ordinary course, therefore allowing me to study four different subjects − giving great variety and also knowledge to the areas covered. The variation and broad span of knowledge enabled me to consider a vast range of careers and also helped considerably in coping with work that involves constant variation and instant decision making. However the course followed being general rules out jobs requiring specialist knowledge.

In moving on to consider comments from respondents who had reservations about the currency value of their degrees, it was evident that very few teachers fell into the category. A handful of teachers believed that their career prospects could have been improved by taking an Honours degree and one felt that the lack of opportunity to teach his subject at O and A level standard could be due to the perceived status of his degree. In the absence of any other open-ended comments to the contrary, however, it may be concluded that most teachers were content with the currency value of their degrees.

With respect to non-teaching graduates, for every respondent who commented that employment had been obtained as a result of possessing a degree, there was another respondent who stated that their entry into employment had not required a degree. Moreover, respondents who volunteered open-ended statements which indicated dissatisfaction with degree currency were more likely to comment upon its general currency than those who were correspondingly satisfied.

Non-teaching respondents provided numerous comments to illustrate how the limited currency value of their degrees had led to the acceptance of non-graduate entry jobs: 'didn't need a degree for this job', 'O levels not even needed', 'my eighteen-year-old friends with just A levels are doing better than me in this line of work', and so on. Among these, even respondents in fairly reasonable, medium-status jobs appeared to be disillusioned by the fact that they could have entered their employment with qualifications of a lower standard.

(Q.20i, an assistant development chemist) The courses I took [biology and rural science] gave me no real grounding in any particular aspect of either subject, and I soon found out that my degree was regarded as an 'educationalist's experiment' by prospective employers . . . .

(Q.21) I don't feel capable of answering this as I am not employed as a graduate, and those that are are finding it difficult due to increased competition, and the fact that many people now accept a position because it is a job which they may not be offered elsewhere.

(Q.20i, a cartographic draughtswoman) My degree course has so far done very little to help me obtain or prepare for work. I could have entered my present job at the age of sixteen with four O levels. It would have possibly been more useful had my degree course been an Honours course in three years – as are most degrees at university.

Others also registered frustration that their degree had not allowed them to compete with university graduates. One of the extracts from an unemployed graduate quoted earlier commented to this effect, as did the following respondent:

(Q.20i, a clerk) All the applications I made were to people who wanted a graduate. However, I would have had a better chance if I'd got a better class of degree or if it was a university degree.

A further type of comment showed up graduates' perceptions and experiences of the continuing fall in the currency value and status of a degree. An earlier quotation (see 'Unemployment') in Chapter 4 contained the observation that degrees seemed to be losing much of the prestige value they once possessed. Two more respondents made a similar point:

(Q.20i, a clerical officer in the Civil Service) The mere fact that I have a degree helps – though the job I now have I could have qualified for on my O level passes alone!! I found out quite early on that the fact you have a degree no longer means you walk into a top job!! – more's the pity!

(Q.20i, a quality control assistant) [My degree courses] have not, as yet, been useful in obtaining employment. A degree is useful in indicating to a prospective employer a certain level of general ability, although in the current employment situation most employers seem to prefer applicants with lower or no qualifications. I studied for a degree for personal satisfaction only, rather than to enter a particular career, although I would have thought that having a degree would carry more weight with employers than it appears to at the moment.

The down-grading of the employment currency of degrees has undoubtedly resulted in the growing phenomena of 'overqualified' graduates. Once again, examples of this have been presented earlier, but a further extract may serve to highlight some of the difficulties:

(Q.20i, a clerical officer in the Civil Service) I found that a lot of employers once they see you have a degree expect you to be ambitious, which I am not. I only wanted a job which was steady, ample money and not too demanding and I had a job convincing employers that I would be content with that sort of job. They expected that I would get bored and move off quickly. They also pointed out that the salary they would offer would not be one in line with my qualifications. In the end I started to play down my degree and for the clerical assistant post I even left it off the application form thinking that they would give me an interview as a courtesy to someone who could be bothered to apply for such a job with a degree, but not really want me (one employer told me this was why I had got an interview) – can be a foot in the door though. In the end I worked as a barmaid where they didn't ask about any qualifications and I think this helped get my present job as it showed I was willing to work at anything.

Overall then, the attitude statements showed that, while the majority of teachers were satisfied with the currency value of their degrees, a significant proportion of graduates working in other occupations were not. Furthermore, the open-ended comments tended to support this interpretation and revealed that their reasons for feeling discontented with their degree currency included working in jobs which required only O or A level qualifications, competing with graduates who possessed superior types of degrees, confronting a labour market in which the prestige value of degrees was falling, and encountering employers who frequently considered graduates to be over-qualified and probably over-ambitious.

Opportunities for Career Development

A separate item in the questionnaire (Q.13) invited respondents to select one statement from seven which best matched their feelings about the extent to which their latest job was compatible with their long-term career aspirations. Without taking too much for granted, the replies can be interpreted as indications of the levels of commitment, and perhaps, by inference, the levels of satisfaction, in a long-term perspective attached to the career opportunities afforded by their latest jobs. However, since commitment to a career cannot always be taken to imply satisfaction with the current stage of that career, a degree of caution is warranted when drawing such inferences.

Table 5.5 shows that just over a quarter of all college respondents were unable to answer the question because, for one reason or another, they were not in full-time permanent employment at the time of completing the questionnaire. Just under a quarter saw their career developing with their current employing organization and the same proportion expected their career to progress to a similar job but with a different employer. Adding these latter two groups together, 46 per cent of college respondents appeared to be committed to a career with their latest employer or occupation. On the other hand, just over a quarter of respondents, for a variety of reasons, did not envisage their latest employer or occupation as satisfactory long-term career possibilities. Consequently, taking those not in employment into consideration, in contrast to the 46 per cent who were fairly committed to a career, 54 per cent were either not employed or were uncommitted to their latest known line of work.

	All	PGCE stream	Non-PGCE stream
	%	%	%
Long-term career developing with this organization (1)	23	23	23
Stay about 3 years, then move to same job but different employer (2)	23	27	21
Stay 3 years then move to different kind of job (3)	6	4	7
Doing job for experience until something better turns up (4)	12	9	14
Dislike this job and trying to find another one (5)	5	4	5
Dislike this job but will stay here since no others available (6)	4	2	5
Not applicable because not in full-time employment (7)	27	31	25
TOTAL RESPONDENTS	247	108	139

Table 5.5
1979 non-BEd college respondents: attitudes to latest known jobs and career development.

Table 5.5 also shows that, while each of the two main streams had equal proportions of respondents who were committed to their employing organizations (23 per cent), a slightly higher share of the PGCE stream than the non-PGCE stream were committed to their occupations − 27 per cent for the former, 21 per cent for the latter. Correspondingly, only 19 per cent of the PGCEs, compared to 31 per cent of the non-PGCEs, were uncommitted to either employer or occupation.

Greater differences between teachers and non-teachers were more apparent when the answers to this question were considered in the light of the respondents' type of work category. Of those whose latest known occupation was teaching, 80 per cent saw their future career development remaining in the context of their employer or occupation. In sharp contrast, of those employed as clerical workers, the second most frequently entered type of work area, the proportion with either type of career commitment was 33 per cent. Two-thirds, therefore, were not able to see any career development in their clerical jobs. Respondents in 'General Administration' and 'Buying, Marketing, Selling' had roughly the same proportions as teachers who were optimistic of a career with their employing organizations, but had considerably smaller proportions who were inclined to consider their present occupations to have long-term career prospects. As a result, the three main non-teaching occupational areas had correspondingly higher percentages registering their dissatisfaction with the lack of career prospects in their jobs. The only slight exceptions to this trend were among the 'Health, Social Welfare' workers, who demonstrated a particularly strong attachment to their employing institutions. Overall though, the results substantiate the familiar pattern: outside of teaching, significant numbers of college graduates faced real difficulties in finding occupations and employers in which they could invest a commitment to long-term career development. It may be added that the responses indicating commitment to an employer or occupation were frequently associated with high occupational status, positive attitudes to intellectual demands at work and satisfaction with the currency value of their degrees.

Graduates' Accounts of their Latest Jobs

The following summary highlights much of the material presented in this chapter about respondents' experiences in their latest known employment.

Numerous respondents clearly felt that teaching was a rewarding and enjoyable occupation, even though many stressed that the work involved made very heavy demands on their time and energies:

(Q.21) . . . Teaching is not the job for those who like to rest on their laurels. It is *very* demanding and it often goes without rewards. There is also a great amount of administrative work that students are not aware of.

(Q.21) . . . The first year is hell but it's much better in the second year. Extremely tiring — days when you feel like chucking it all in *but* it does have rewards - children can be very lovely as well as being little horrors . . . . Rigidity and formality of school can be irritating. Holidays a perk but you *do* need them. Stress is a big factor . . . .

Expressing similar points, many respondents had found that very little spare time was left and, as a result, they often considered that teaching should not be entered simply because there was nothing else to do:

(Q.21) Make sure that you know that teaching is what you want to do. It is unfair to many people if you are not going to give your best. Teaching is *not* an easy option. It can be very hard work (physical and mental) and involves more 'home' work than you think — preparation, displaying, marking, meetings and further training.

(Q.21) Be ready to give up an exciting social life and spend many nights marking or preparing lessons!! Only go into teaching if you are strong-willed and able to put in a certain amount of dedication....By the way, I *do* enjoy my job but I am now just beginning to discover the pitfalls!

Finally, several teaching respondents alluded to the current depressed state of education in this country and perceived it to be undermining their motivation and enthusiasm for the job:

(Q.21) Beware of the severe effect of education cuts and the unemployment situation. Pupils and staff are suffering from lack of morale − pupils' frustrations at home and job-wise are often aired in the classroom. Education cuts and redeployment and compulsory redundancy are leading to a sense of disillusionment. Beware of the present job situation − teachers are far too used to a feeling of total security in their job and this is no longer true.

Overall though, despite this climate and the pressures of work, teaching emerges as an exacting but satisfying occupation for the many college graduates who entered it.

The same cannot be said for the other main areas of work entered by these graduates. In contrast to the teachers, the vast majority of clerical workers were almost invariably frustrated by the undemanding and monotonous nature of their work. Of the thirty-three respondents working in a clerical capacity, only one − the clerk in a magistrate's office, cited earlier − stated that she found her work interesting, though even she conceded that she had no aspirations to seek any more demanding tasks. As several earlier quotations have repeatedly shown, secretaries frequently complained that their work was under-valued, boring, mundane, unworthy of degree level education, soul-destroying and lacking in opportunities for genuine promotions. Civil Service clerical workers were particularly disheartened by the extent of underemployment in their employing organizations. Some protested about the 'dead hand of bureaucracy' and the 'squashing of initiatives'. One respondent wanted to alert present graduates to the fact that even the clerical duties in the fairly glamorous work environments of the theatre and the media are often repetitive and routine:

(Q.21, a secretary in a theatre) . . . Theatre administration can be just as tedious as any other job; there's a lot of routine work and it helps if you're a shorthand/typist like me . . . . Production secretaries work very long hours and the pay is bad, but be careful of working for love, it leaves you open to exploitation.

Similar problems were reported by employees in 'General Administration', though of the eighteen respondents in this category there were proportionally fewer expressions of job dissatisfaction and, on the whole, they tended to be less severe. Moreover, one or two respondents were clearly appreciative of the challenges entailed in their type of administrative work:

(Q.11, an accounts executive) This job is exactly what, if I had known it existed, I would have chosen to do as it allows me to unite my love of sport with a desire to be with people in an organizational capacity . . . .

(Q.21) You really need to enjoy working with people to do the job I am involved with at the moment. You need to be able to contend with a certain amount of rudeness and inefficiency from the clients. Organization and the ability to take the initiative are essential . . . . I should also say that I know that I was and am incredibly lucky to have found a job that I love so much in such a way . . . . I would still like to go into teaching at some stage although I am enjoying my present career too much at the moment to contemplate renouncing it. The experience that I now have of many different companies and business will be very useful whatever I choose to do in the future.

This type of work area also included a number of administrative and general managerial personnel in sports and leisure centres, though these respondents were not forthcoming in the open-ended comments and hence gave little indication whether or not they were satisfied with their jobs. One warned graduates contemplating this area of work to consider carefully the 'unpleasant side of man management' and the 'unsociable hours' involved in the work.

As depicted in earlier quotations, general office administrators were more decidedly dissatisfied, such as the administrative assistant in a local health authority who found her work very tedious and a faculty assistant who was frustrated by the lack of promotion prospects. Similarly, administrative assistants in a Youth Opportunities Scheme and a health centre both recorded low opinions of the status and value of their work. In expressing disenchantment with his situation, a trainee transport administrator drew attention to the difficulties of finding a sympathetic ear to listen to his grievances:

(Q.21) ... An advertised course of training in the field of bus operations management has in reality turned out to be a clerical merry-go round rotating every three months around various administrative departments. All graduates should ascertain from employers the practical dividents from so-called 'professional' examinations; personally, my studies for the 'Chartered Institute of Transport' have not been acknowledged in any real sense by [my employers] despite having won a prize for the best overall performance in the second year examinations this summer. Finally I would warn all graduates to be prepared to cope with a dose of hyper-boredom if they become employed by any large organization. My deep feelings of discontent are not appreciated by my 'development' or 'career' adviser within [the organization] despite the fact that she is a relatively recent graduate herself; so graduates should not be surprised if they find that people who they would naturally feel would be aware of their plight in reality turn a deaf ear, and, instead of assisting, merely inform you of 'how lucky you are to have a job'. What was it that Disraeli said about getting to the top of the greasy pole?

Overall, although 'general administration' workers did not display the almost unanimous disappointment expressed by clerical workers, they provided more open-ended indications of dissatisfaction than satisfaction, notwithstanding the enthusiastic extracts offered earlier.

The general impression gained from the open-ended comments of employees in the 'Buying, Marketing, Selling' category resembles that gained from 'general administration' workers: namely, a few respondents expressing positive attitudes to their work but a slightly greater number suggesting they were less than happy. An assistant retail manager, quoted earlier, saw his work as 'enjoyable and rewarding', as did the following sales representative:

(Q.21) The job is very demanding and competitive. It requires great self-motivation and determination and is not a job for people who do not enjoy pressure. It is very important to choose a company who are prepared to train you. It is only through being a competent salesman that you can hope to move into management. It is a popular misconception that there is complete freedom in selling. It is a very disciplined profession. However, there are numerous rewards and you can see the results of your efforts.

From the opposite perspective, there were more retail workers whose jobs did not bring these type of rewards. Disillusioned by the lack of intellectual stimulation in their work, they often complained that their degrees were neither required by, nor relevant to, their latest jobs. For example, one respondent, an assistant manager in a garden centre, was aggrieved by the lack of opportunities:

(Q.21) Listen very carefully at the interview for aspects which may be glossed over very quickly. Take particular notice of such words as 'we would expect', 'possibly in the future', 'should the need arise' and 'circumstances permitting'. In my experience these words provide bait for the job but hide unfulfilled promises . . . . Don't believe everything they tell you.

For a further example, a deputy manageress in a large chain store experienced the many drawbacks of her work with little reward to compensate for them:

(Q.21) Be prepared to give a lot more than will be given to you, ie working the odd extra couple of hours here and there 'for the love of the job.' And also be prepared for the extremely long hours – including Saturday morning. I think that for those who are willing to be mobile (ie move every twelve months) life can be extremely lonely.

As could be predicted from the responses to the attitudinal statements, open-ended comments provided by workers in the 'Health, Social Welfare' category showed a tendency to a similar degree of job satisfaction as that displayed by teachers. There were a number of complaints – lack of academic involvement and career structure – but most of respondents seemed to be enjoying their work, however tiring and demanding. The following two illustrate this experience:

(Q.21, a residential social worker) The work of a residential social worker is challenging, interesting and vocational. People from many different backgrounds and with widely differing life experiences can find satisfaction and stimulation within the work, each is employed largely on character rather than qualifications. The work tends to be time-consuming and presents unsociable hours, which can lead to various problems outside the work. I would suggest that anyone seeking to find this kind of employment firstly considers at what stage their own personal and emotional development has reached because the children who come into care are increasingly difficult and demanding, and require a relatively stable and mature personality to work with them. Also try to assess how much you really are prepared to work among angry, confused, sometimes maladjusted teenagers and what you can hope to offer them in terms of compensation. If all this hasn't put you off then get stuck in because it's a great job.

(Q.21, a policeman) I would tell [prospective entrants to this career] that it is a very rewarding job and that popular opinion of what the job is like, is very different from the one they would find themselves in. The hardest part of the job is training but this is designed to weed out the half-hearted applicants. In my opinion no one should drop out of the job at this time as you learn to be a policeman on the streets not in the training school.

The problem with this category of work appears not to be the underemployment characteristic of the other three non-teaching areas of work predominantly entered by college graduates, but the shortage of vacancies in a very popular range of occupations.

Summary

Since detailed summaries of the findings presented above are provided in Chapter 8, they need not be duplicated here. At this point, suffice it to say that Chapters 4 and 5 have offered an interpretation of the main descriptive results to emerge from the 'Beyond Graduation' survey of the early careers of the 1979 diversified degree graduates from colleges of higher education. Thus far, no attempt has been made to relate graduates' career experiences to biographical and institutional variables. This task is undertaken in the following two chapters.

6

Careers and Biographical Factors

Interpretation of the data derived from the 'Beyond Graduation' survey has so far in this study treated non-teaching degree graduates from former colleges of education as an undifferentiated, homogeneous group. In order to extend the analysis, the present chapter and the following one break the group down into various sub-groupings so that the early careers of different kinds of graduates can be examined and contrasted. Variations in, for example, employment patterns, occupational status and levels of satisfaction are related to differences in such key variables as gender, age, courses studied and college attended. While this chapter focuses on variations related to differences in ascriptive and biographical qualities, Chapter 7 highlights those associated with institutional factors. Throughout, the analysis is restricted to the 1979 diversified degree respondents from former colleges of education only.

Gender

Of the 247 non-teaching degree graduates who responded to the questionnaire, 177 were female and seventy were male – a similar proportionate ratio (72 per cent:28 per cent) to the one reported in Chapter 3 for the total known population of 1979 college graduates (67 per cent : 33 per cent). Corroborating the indications from the first destination returns (see Chapter 3), a slightly higher proportion of women (46 per cent) had followed a PGCE course than men (37 per cent).

At the time of completing the questionnaire (31 December 1981), 74 per cent of women graduates, compared to 70 per cent of men, were in permanent employment (Table 6.1). Male graduates also experienced a higher rate of unemployment: 19 per cent compared to 8 per cent for women, although larger proportions of the latter were temporarily employed and not available for employment. However, given that a greater proportion of women were either permanently or temporarily employed and that the vast majority of women who were not available for employment were working as housewives, it is noteworthy that, in comparison to their male counterparts, a higher share of women graduates were engaged in some sort of productive activity. Correspondingly, approximately one in ten women, but as many as one in five men, were without any sort of work. It would seem that, unemployment, though not insignificant for women, was a greater problem for men college graduates.

Differences between the sexes also emerge when comparing the latest known type of work areas occupied by those in permanent employment on 31 December 1981. Further analyses revealed that 63 per cent of such female graduates were concentrated in just two of the available seventeen

	Male	Female
	%	%
Research/Academic Study	1	1
Teacher Training	6	2
Social Work Training	0	1
Other Training	1	3
Not Available for Employment	0	5
Permanent Home Employment	70	74
Temporary Home Employment	0	5
Temporary Overseas Employment	0	1
Unemployed	19	8
Unknown	3	0
TOTAL RESPONDENTS (100%)	70	177

Note

a All tables in Chapters 6 and 7 refer to 1979 non-BEd respondents from former colleges of education.

Table 6.1
Gender by latest employment circumstances at 31 December 1981.[a]

type of work categories − teaching and secretarial/clerical work − viz. almost two-thirds of women employees were working as teachers or secretarial/clerical workers. In contrast, with a smaller proportion in their two main categories (46 per cent) − teaching and non-specialist administration − male graduates were more widely dispersed across a greater range of categories.

Thus, although teaching was the main occupational area for both genders, clearly discernible patterns surfaced for each: while a larger share of women occupied teaching posts and as many as one in four entered secretarial and clerical work, a smaller proportion were to be found in alternative areas; correspondingly, while a smaller share of men were employed as teachers and the number in secretarial/clerical was negligible, a higher proportion remained unemployed or worked in alternative occupations. These alternative areas included 'Non-specialist Administration', 'Buying, Marketing, Selling', 'Creative, Entertainment', 'Financial' and 'Health, Social Welfare'.

Although scattered across a wider spectrum of non-teaching jobs, the question remains whether or not male graduates were more successful in obtaining entry to occupations with status levels commensurate with that of the teaching profession. Supplementary analyses suggested that, although only a small proportion of men graduates had found graduate status jobs outside of teaching, they apeared to be more successful in obtaining such jobs than their female peers. Women graduates were very poorly represented in non-teaching, graduate status occupations. Although roughly the same proportions of each gender had attained graduate status work (37 per cent of men; 39 per cent of women), women graduates did so largely as a result of entering the teaching profession (29 per cent), while men graduates had almost as many in alternative graduate status jobs (17 per cent) as in teaching (20 per cent). Consequently, in spite of showing a higher unemployment rate, a larger share of male respondents were able to find non-teaching, graduate status jobs, while more women graduates appeared to have evaded unemployment by entering either teaching or lower status secretarial work.

Turning to consider the influences of gender differences on other criterion variables, such is the nature of the contrasting patterns of occupational entry for each sex that at an aggregate level variations are often cancelled out. For example, the aggregate salary distribution for women graduates, who were virtually polarized into the two groups of relatively well-paid teachers and of low-paid clerical workers, closely matches the same for men graduates, who were not so polarized and had higher proportions in a wider range of occupations. The overall effect is that at each of the different salary levels little variation existed between the genders. For the same reasons, at an aggregate level, no significant differences were found to exist between men and women respondents' attitudes to the extent of intellectual stimulation in their latest work.

One item which did produce slight differences between the sexes was the attitudinal question concerning graduates' levels of satisfaction with the currency of their degrees. In comparison to women graduates, there was an increased tendency for men respondents to be less satisfied with the range of jobs their degrees had allowed them to consider. Compared to 24 per cent of females, 39 per cent of male respondents indicated dissatisfaction with their degree currency.

This finding is closely related to the higher rate of male unemployment and may also reflect a higher propensity among men to expect more from their 'careers' than women. Some support for this latter supposition is found in the responses to the question on career intentions associated with latest jobs. In comparison to 61 per cent of women graduates, 76 per cent of men graduates expressed commitment to a career with their employing organization or their chosen occupation. Correspondingly, a higher proportion of women graduates (19 per cent) than men (10 per cent) indicated that they were 'doing (their) job for experience until something better turns up'.

On the strength of the above evidence, it would appear that women college graduates were fairly successful at avoiding unemployment, entered teaching at a slightly higher rate than their male peers, frequently accepted clerical jobs with limited opportunities for satisfaction and career prospects, and were under-represented in occupational areas other than teaching or clerical work.

For male graduates, teaching also constituted the main career outlet but was proportionately less prevalent than for female graduates; secretarial and clerical work was almost completely eluded; unemployment was higher; a greater share obtained non-teaching graduate status work, though as high a proportion as women graduates were to be found in medium or low status jobs. Men respondents displayed slight tendencies towards greater dissatisfaction with their degree currency and greater commitment towards career development within their employing organization or occupation.

At an aggregate level, there were few variations between the sexes in salaries and intellectual satisfaction. However, as was seen in the previous chapter, occupational areas had a more direct influence on these two variables, and variations between the sexes in the distribution of salaries and intellectual satisfaction would thus appear to be more adequately accounted for by the different patterns of occupational area entered.

Opportunities for Women

As a result of the gender imbalance in the student constituency of colleges, a number of academic staff were of the opinion that if the colleges were to develop as specialist institutions they should increase career opportunities for women. In view of this, an item was included in the questionnaire similar to one in Kelsall et al.'s (1970) survey: namely, 'To what extent do you think your opportunities for appointments and promotion have been, (or are being) hampered because you are a woman?' The results are presented in Table 6.2.

'To what extent do you think your opportunities for appointments and promotion have been (or are being) hampered because you are a woman?

	All women	Single	Married
	%	%	%
Not at all	49	57	36
To some extent	36	26	52
Largely	7	6	9
Don't know	8	11	3
TOTAL RESPONDENTS (100%)	175	111	64

Table 6.2
Marital status by women's attitudes to restricted job opportunities.

Further analyses revealed that, although there was little correlation between the response to this item and graduates' latest known employment circumstances (eg unemployment, permanent employment, etc.), there was some association with certain types of latest known occupational areas. While 'Teaching' showed a distribution similar to the overall percentages, 'Secretarial, Clerical' had the lowest proportions of 'Not at all' responses (34 per cent) and 'Buying, Marketing, Selling' and 'Health, Social Welfare' achieved the highest of any 'Not at all' percentages (approximately 70 per cent in both cases). Corroborating the prevailing trend, the largest share expressing some recognition of limited opportunities were to be found in the 'Secretarial, Clerical' section.

Breaking down the overall percentages into the frequencies for single and married respondents, Table 6.2 clearly demonstrates that in comparison to single women, married women were far more likely to perceive themselves as having encountered some form of unequal and discriminatory treatment. For instance, 61 per cent of married women compared to 32 per cent of single women thought that their opportunities had been hampered either 'to some extent' or 'largely'. These findings provided some basis for believing that being married *and* being female can amount to a serious handicap in the graduate labour market.

The responses to an open-ended follow-up question, inviting women respondents to give further details of unequal treatment over employment opportunities, lent support to the view that it is married women who were particularly vulnerable in this respect. Of the forty-five women who volunteered further comments, twenty-six were concerned, in one way or another, with the restrictions placed on career prospects and job opportunities by their marital or motherhood roles. Several respondents, who were dispersed across the full range of occupational areas, emphasized that simply being female was not the chief reason for thwarted opportunities but being married or, worse still, being a mother or mother-to-be. The following were typical of many such comments:

(Q.19, a student nurse) Rather than being female, being married has made some difference − supposition that I would be leaving jobs to have children.

(Q.19, an assistant manager in a sports complex) Before I was married I was given equal opportunities to those which a man receives but after I was married this encouragement dwindled and now I am no longer given those privileges of a man.

(Q.19, a teacher) When you get to a certain age and you happen to be married, promotion seems to be determined on whether the interviewing panel think that you are likely to become pregnant or not. The choice seems to be a full-time career with promotion or a family.

(Q.19, a teacher) In the future I want a family, therefore will have to leave work − losing time and therefore promotion prospects. I am resigned to believing this is inevitable.

(Q.19, unemployed) As a married woman, employers are not prepared to take the risk of employing someone whom *they* consider is likely to start a family.

As implied in the last comment, several respondents had been offended by employers' questions and suspicions regarding their personal and familial intentions:

(Q.19, not available for employment) I found that I was sometimes asked questions which I considered to be impertinent at the interview stage, eg do you intend having a family?

(Q.19, unemployed) Employers (or prospective employers in interviews) always ask whether one is engaged, married or wanting a family soon. Some go so far as to ask how many years they may presume me to be available.

(Q.19, a student accountant) I have been asked when I am getting married, and then about having children. Even though I am getting married next year, I still *want* to work for a number of years. Why don't prospective employers believe this?

Another familiar case among married women was the tendency to suspend their own career in deference to that of their partners:

(Q.19, a secretary) I accepted that it was more important for my fiance to secure full-time employment first and so restricted the area in which I applied for posts. Present secretarial post has limited prospects − already near top of salary scale − difficult to transfer to administrative grades once have been labelled as a secretary.

(Q.19, not available for employment) My husband is a police constable and when only engaged to him I was asked if he would be moving with his job and if so would I move with him. These types of questions are typical, especially by women on the interview panel.

In addition to the twenty-six who perceived marital and motherhood roles to be the main source of unequal job opportunites, eleven respondents felt that their opportunties had been hampered by employers' tacit preferences for male applicants. The following extracts indicate the type of responses received from this group:

(Q.19, an assistant retail manageress) Recent opportunity for promotion within company to one of largest stores. One of four interviewees (three others male). Was informed I had been unsuccessful because manager thought the position involved could only be filled by a male. (NB Position mentioned was equivalent to job I was and am currently fulfilling.)

(Q.19, a retail branch manager) Within retailing, store management is regarded as a man's job and, although I am as committed to this type of career as much as any man, I have been rejected because of being a woman.

(Q.19, a teacher) There being far less men in [primary] teaching, authorities seem more eager to employ more men, to redress the balance in schools.

A handful of respondents attributed their experience of restricted opportunities to the male-dominated ethos which allegedly prevailed in their workplaces:

(Q.19, an assistant personnel officer) I work in a predominantly male organization with several 'old school' types at the top. Women were not employed by them at all until well on into this century. Changes are occurring, but only slowly.

(Q.19, a secretary) It really is, surprisingly, a male dominated industry — perfumery.

Finally, two or three respondents pointed to the negative stereotyping of women which provided employers with a set of rationalizations for not engaging or promoting them:

(Q.19, an executive officer in the Civil Service) I have the impression that certain employers feel women are a risk in that we are more 'emotional'.

(Q.19, an administrative assistant) I applied for one job, working for British Rail and I was the only female applicant and I felt that this affected their judgement because they *seemed* to be very worried that I wouldn't like getting dirty or travelling for most of the week.

To conclude this review of women respondents' descriptions of the kinds of unequal opportunities they faced, four main types of disadvantages have been identified: first, and by far the largest category, conflicting interests between employment commitments and familial responsibilities, real or imputed; secondly, prejudices for male candidates; thirdly, male-dominated work organizations; and finally, negative stereotyping of female qualities. It should be stressed, however, that in reality these types frequently overlapped and several comments incorporated elements of two or more of them. Furthermore, in setting out respondents' constructions about women's unequal opportunities, the possibility that the participants may be unaware of, or misguided about, the real underlying processes of discrimination must not be overlooked.

Marital Status

Any impression gained from the previous section that it was only women graduates, particularly married ones, who encountered career difficulties must be dispelled. In comparing the careers of single and married graduates, it often seems to be the case that, in many respects, single male graduates constituted the least successful group of graduates.

With female graduates showing only a slightly higher marital proportion than male graduates at the time of completing the questionnaire just over a third of college respondents were married. Of these, the majority (71 per cent) married after leaving college, whereas equal proportions of the remainder married either before starting, or while attending, college. Male graduates were slightly more likely to marry during their time at college; female graduates were marginally more likely to marry after college.

Contrasting the latest known career circumstances of single and married graduates, both groups had roughly the same proportions in permanent home employment, but a higher share of married respondents were not available for employment, while a higher share of single respondents were unemployed.

However, if gender is introduced into the analysis as an additional variable, some interesting differences emerge. Compared to 65 per cent of single male graduates, a substantial 85 per cent of married male graduates were in full-time permanent employment. Similarly, while there were no recorded cases of unemployed married men, as many as 27 per cent of single male respondents were unemployed.

Although it is tempting to view these disparities as reflecting the increased motivations and responsibilities associated with married life, an alternative direction of causality should not be ignored: namely that for many graduates permanent employment is almost a pre-condition of marriage. Neither should it be overlooked that graduates with particular personality types simultaneously seek work and relationships which are permanent and secure. Unfortunately, the survey data is insufficient to allow a more detailed investigation of these issues.

Turning to women respondents, single females had a significantly higher rate of permanent employment than single males – 78 and 65 per cent respectively – and that appreciably fewer single women were unemployed – 8 and 27 per cent respectively. Married women had the same unemployed proportion as single women, but showed a lower rate of permanent employment (68 per cent) due to the number of respondents who worked as housewives and mothers and were thus not available for employment (12 per cent).

Consequently, the results lend some support to the view that the employment rate of college graduates is partially attenuated by the poor performance of single male graduates and by married women's departure from permanent employment to domestic responsibilities. Alternatively, the employment rate was strengthened by the comparatively sound performance of married men and single women in finding permanent work.

Did married men and single women also experience superior rates of entry into graduate status occupations? In comparison with single respondents, a higher proportion of married graduates, male and female, were to be found in 'Teaching' and 'Health, Social Welfare'. In contrast, 'Secretarial, Clerical work' was predominantly occupied by single graduates, who were almost exclusively female. As a result of the larger shares in 'Teaching', proportionately more men and women married respondents attained graduate status posts (47 per cent compared to 35 per cent of single respondents), though not in non-teaching graduate status jobs, in which single men were marginally more successful and single women the least successful. Thus, to return to the question posed above, it would seem that married men achieved superior rates of graduate status job entry, but single women were not as successful as married women in this respect, due to the former's lower participation in 'Teaching' and higher involvement in 'Secretarial, Clerical Work'.

Briefly summarizing the employment performance of each of the four groups, it may be noted that single men had the lowest proportion in permanent employment, the worst unemployment, the lowest rate of entry to teaching, but marginally the highest participation in non-teaching graduate status jobs; single women had a high permanent employment rate, a reasonably low unemployment level, but the lowest proportion in non-teaching graduate status jobs, with a high concentration in the problematic clerical sphere; married women had a relatively low employment rate, which was almost entirely due to the proportion working as housewives, a reasonably low unemployment level, a high rate of entry into teaching jobs, but a fairly low participation in non-teaching graduate status jobs; married men had the best employment level, no unemployment, the highest entry into teaching and the second best participation in non-teaching graduate status jobs.

Further analysis also disclosed that proportionately more married than single men earned over £400 per month and that proportionately more married than single women were committed to a career with their employing organization or occupation. Of those who were permanently employed, single men were more likely to be dissatisfied with the currency value of their degrees. Finally, over and above the predictable point that the vast majority of housewives who were not available for employment were caring for children under the age of five, analysis of the effect of the number of children at home was invalidated by the scarcity of relevant cases.

Age

The question whether or not the career patterns of 'mature' graduates differ significantly from those of younger graduates, has attracted considerable interest. Unfortunately, because the number of 'mature' respondents was very small – only twenty-five of the 247 respondents were over twenty-one at the time they started college – definite or confident answers are not possible. However, in consideration of the interest shown, and in view of the fairly even distribution of 'mature' respondents across all participating institutions, some points, noteworthy if very tentative, were gleaned from the results. Overall, the findings tend to challenge the assumption that the comparatively low employment level of older graduates is due mainly to a higher proportion of married women not seeking permanent employment.

Notwithstanding the small size of the over twenty-one sample, two discrepancies between the over and under twenty-ones were apparent at the end of 1981: the older graduates displayed a lower proportion in permanent employment and a higher level of unemployment. Compared to one in ten of the younger graduates, one in four of the older respondents were unemployed. Furthermore, when the percentage of older graduates was disaggregated by gender and marital status, it was evident that all but one of the unemployed older graduates were single, and predominantly male. Similarly, 75 per cent of the younger group compared to 60 per cent of older students were in permanent employment

Contrary to some expectations, the results thus suggest that unemployment among older graduates may be more closely related to the problems of single men than those of married women. They also indicate that, unlike the improved employment rates connected with marriage, being an older graduate is not directly associated with higher levels of permanent employent. In addition, further analyses indicated no discernible differences between older and younger graduates with respect to type of work areas entered, the rate of embarking on PGCE courses, occupational status, and career intentions related to their latest jobs.

Occasionally, a few differences did emerge. Of those who were permanently employed, the over twenty-one group were slightly more likely to earn over £400 a month. As indicated in Table 6.3, older graduates were slightly more satisfied with the currency of their degrees, but considerably more dissatisfied than younger graduates with the intellectual content of their latest jobs.

(1) 'Given the current level of unemployment, I am satisfied with the range of jobs my particular degree has allowed me to consider.'
(2) 'My present (or most recent) work is not as intellectually stimulating as I hoped a graduate's job would be.'

	(1)		(2)	
	Under 21 %	Over 21 %	Under 21 %	Over 21 %
Agree	48	60	39	64
Neutral	22	24	20	8
Disagree	30	16	41	28
TOTAL RESPONDENTS (100%)	222	25	222	25

Table 6.3
Age by (1) satisfaction with degree currency and (2) intellectual satisfaction in latest job.

On examining the cases expressing this dissatisfaction, two kinds of 'mature' graduates figure highly: single males undertaking relatively menial jobs (eg van driver, postman) and women graduates working in secretarial or clerical posts. Such findings give rise to a number of questions worthy of further research: Are there significant numbers of mature students who are attracted to three-year degree courses because they were experiencing employment and occupational problems before attending college? If so, are they more likely to continue to confront similar problems on completion of their courses? Similarly, is the increased job dissatisfaction of older graduates precipitated by the additional disappointment of having to return to routine work after what is, for many mature students, an intellectually invigorating experience at college?

Finally, it has been suggested that older graduates may be more employable than younger ones because more of them have acquired vocational qualifications prior to commencing their degree courses. But there was little evidence to indicate that pre-college vocational qualifications were a major factor in extending the employability of older graduates. Of the fifteen older respondents in permanent employment at the end of 1981, only three reported that their earlier vocational qualifications were instrumental in obtaining their present work. Significantly, all three were working as secretaries. One emphasized the importance of possessing work-related qualifications 'to fall back on':

> (Q.21, a secretary) . . . The employment situation at present means that someone without a skill or a vocational training in business or hospital work, etc. cannot be sure of gaining, and holding on to, full-time employment. Even a simple skill like typing has enabled me to find employment on both a full-time basis and for as little as six weeks.

Other older respondents, especially teachers, valued the general benefits gained from having worked before attending college, even if employability had not been extended by pre-college qualifications. The following quotation was typical:

> (Q.20 viii, a teacher) [Work experience prior to attending college was] most useful preparation for life in general and in gaining a broader outlook on the needs of pupils in general. All teachers should undergo such a period of work outside of an academic environment in order to break the school-college-school cycle and give a more balanced viewpoint.

Although two respondents remarked on the general employment benefits of pre-college work experience, one reinforced the impression gained from the above quantitative findings: namely that there were few signs that older graduates as a whole found it easier than their younger colleagues to obtain graduate status work:

> (Q.20 viii, a van driver) Having worked before college, I knew what sort of thing was in store but it was just as difficult (if not more so) to find.

A Levels and Degree Results

Some careers advisers have expressed the suspicion that employers continue to use graduates' A level results as important criteria for occupational selection. In a related manner, questions have been raised concerning the possibility of positive correlations between A level results, degree classifications and employment indices. For there to be any widespread palpability in these hypotheses, it could be expected that graduates with higher A level scores would display more successful employment records than those with lower A level scores. The survey results provide little evidence to encourage either hypothesis.

Excluding those without any A level qualifications, the median A level score for college respondents was 4.5 (scored as follows: A=5, B=4, C=3,

D=2, E=1). Forty-five per cent of college respondents with A levels had total scores of four or below (these have been categorized as the 'below average group') and 55 per cent had scores of five or above (the 'above average group').

Having carried out comparative analyses of these two groups, no consistent and significant differences were apparent in career patterns, employment rates, occupational status, teacher training rates, types of work entered, and latest known salaries. The only significant variations suggested that the 'below average group' included proportionately more respondents who held fairly firm career orientations related to their latest known employment areas and who were more intellectually satisfied by the demands of their work than members of the 'above average group'.

A higher proportion of the 'above average group' obtained Honours rather than Ordinary degrees – 56 per cent, compared to 42 per cent of the 'below average group' (Table 6.4). Furthermore, contrary to expectations, a significantly higher share of the 'above average group' achieved good Honours classifications – 33 per cent gained a First or Upper Second (mainly the latter), compared to 5 per cent of the 'below average group'.

	Below average A levels	Above average A levels
	%	%
Honours Degrees	42	56
Ordinary Degrees	58	44
TOTAL RESPONDENTS (100%)	102	123

Table 6.4
A level groups by level of degrees.

On this evidence, it would seem that relative to their less well qualified peers college students with good A level scores have better chances of obtaining an Honours degree with higher classifications. However, these advantages do not appear to have been translated into enhanced opportunities for gaining graduate status employment – at least at an aggregate level. The overall results of comparisons between career patterns and degree levels (Honours/Ordinary), including degree classifications, were very similar to those for the A level groups: namely little significant variation in employment indices, and only a slight tendency for graduates with Ordinary degrees to be more committed to, and more intellectually satisfied by, their latest known job. The findings do not therefore suggest major career enhancements according to A level results and level or classification of degree, but there could be a case for arguing that larger samples and a greater range of intervening variables (eg degree subjects) are required to confirm this interpretation more confidently.

Social Class

Recent research has indicated a gradual decline in the proportion of students from working class backgrounds studying at the former colleges of education (Gibbs and Cree 1982). Such a trend inevitably reduces the extent to which this type of college can claim to be providing the avenue of occupational and social mobility it offered many working class students in the 1960s. Questions need to be asked, however, about the impact of diversification on the colleges' capacity to facilitate upward occupational mobility. In spite of the overall reduction in the proportion of working class students at colleges, do working class graduates with diversified degrees experience forms of occupational advancement? If so, is this upward mobility achieved through the traditional avenue of teaching or through entry to alternative professions?

Based on the Registrar General's classification of fathers' occupations and social classes (Office of Population Censuses and Surveys 1980), Table 6.5 shows the numbers of non-BEd respondents in each of the seven categories. By a large margin, the highest category was 'Intermediate' employees (one hundred and twenty respondents) and the lowest was 'Unskilled' employees (one respondent). Adopting the same method for collapsing these categories as Gibbs and Cree (1982), namely, grouping 'Professional', 'Intermediate' and 'Skilled Non-manual' workers as 'Middle Class' and 'Skilled Manual', 'Semi-skilled' and 'Unskilled' as 'Working Class', 76 per cent of the classifiable respondents were from middle class families, the remaining 26 per cent had working class origins.

	Frequency	Class Categories	Frequency	Gender	
				M	F
Professional	38				
Intermediate	120	Middle	175 (76%)	69%	79%
Skilled Non-manual	17				
Skilled Manual	45				
Semi-skilled	8	Working	54 (24%)	31%	21%
Unskilled	1				
Unclassified	18	(Excluded)			
TOTALS (100%)	247		229	62	167

Note
a Office of Population Censuses and Surveys (1980).

Table 6.5
Social class (father's occupation).[a]

These proportions were identical to the percentages for each social class of the 1980 *entrants* to the six institutions in the Combined Colleges Research Group (Gibbs and Cree 1982). Only one student in four was from a working class background – a proportion very similar to that for the 1979 entrants to British universities.

The same table also reveals that middle class respondents included a higher proportion of women graduates, while working class respondents had a correspondingly higher share of male graduates. Apart from a slight tendency for a higher share of Honours degree respondents to belong to the middle class category, few class-based variations were detectable in terms of A level scores, degree classifications, subject areas and marital status.

In a comparison of the latest known career circumstances of the two broad social groupings, while both classes demonstrated similar unemployment rates, 83 per cent of working class respondents were permanently employed, compared to only 71 per cent of middle class respondents. Consequently, because the latter exceed the former by more than two to one, they had the effect of depressing the overall level of permanent employment.

Furthermore, whereas 5 per cent of middle class respondents were not available for employment and 4 per cent were temporarily employed, not a single case from the working class group was to be found in either of these categories. Since all the respondents who were not available for employment were women, and in both classes women tended to marry and have children at similar rates, the reasons why middle class mothers were more likely to be unavailable for employment than their working class counterparts are not immediately obvious. Although the greater aggregate number of women in the middle class group create grounds for caution, possible explanations could be related to the differential influences of class-based cultural norms or of discrepancies in the material resources that allow the option of becoming totally unavailable for employment. Reminiscent of the earlier proposition that married male graduates appear to be more highly motivated to acquire and sustain permanent employment, perhaps some married women with working class origins are likely to be similarly pressured into continuing in some form of employment.

Returning to the questions raised in the opening paragraph, further analyses established that 44 per cent of working class respondents had advanced to positions of graduate status employment. The corresponding percentage for middle class respondents was 39 per cent. However, the vast majority of working class respondents (37 per cent) had achieved this level of occupational status by entering the teaching profession and only 7 per cent of this social class attained graduate status jobs in non-teaching occupations. In comparison to the middle class group (42 per cent), a higher share of working class respondents (52 per cent) undertook PGCE courses and a higher proportion of the latter actually gained employment as teachers. This result is particularly interesting and is somewhat contrary to expectations since the middle class group contains a higher share of women, who, as indicated earlier, were slightly more likely to take up teaching. The middle class group had a lower proportion employed as teachers but a higher share in non-teaching graduate status jobs − 15 per cent compared to 7 per cent of the working class group.

In addition then to the phenomena of a falling working class element in the colleges, the findings suggest that occupational mobility to graduate status professions as a result of taking a diversified degree was not within the experience of the majority of graduates from working class families. Moreover, the extent of mobility attained by this class of graduates remained highly reliant on the conventional avenue into the teaching profession.

Career 'Choice' or Career 'Accommodation'

In addition to considering the effect on careers of such factors as gender and social class, there is a related need to inquire how the low level of entry into graduate status jobs apart from teaching may have been influenced by students' own career aspirations and attitudes. Although lacking the kind of longitudinal evidence necessary to conduct a thorough examination of the personal development and decision-making associated with the transition from college to work, the remaining data to be derived from the questionnaire provides at least an introduction to the topic.

It should be stressed, however, that a major drawback of attempting to discuss attitudinal development without the benefits of longitudinal data, is the dependence on respondents' hindsight constructions of previously held aspirations and motivations. The reliability of their evidence is inevitably weakened by memories which are not infallible and by biographical accounts which are not immune from the tendency to reconstruct the past in the light of subsequent experience.

Given that the limited evidence only permits a preliminary exploration of the topic, it would be inappropriate to raise too many specific and detailed questions, but one general question seems particularly important:

To what extent do graduates' constructions of their biographies and decision-making approximate a career 'choice' model (sifting information, rational choice, aspirations to graduate status employment, appropriate applications, rejection/acceptance, etc.) or a career 'accommodation' model (reduced emphasis on choice, more a matter of adjusting to difficult external circumstances, hence comparatively low aspirations with a more adventitious experience of occupational entry)?

When the jobs obtained by respondents were set alongside the jobs applied for upon graduation but not obtained, apart from a slight increase in applications for more creative outlets (eg journalism, acting), the type of jobs unsuccessfully applied for closely resembled those actually obtained. On the basis of the career choice model, more applications indicating higher levels of aspiration and ambition could have been expected.

Approximately a quarter of the respondents thought that, at the point of leaving college, they had been undecided about their ultimate career goal; a third had had teaching as their career objective; the aspirations of the remaining group had closely matched the type of occupations predominantly entered, and the group included a small minority who had aspired to professions of a more creative nature than those typically entered by this type of graduate (Table 6.6). If the career choice/ambition model had been widely applicable, it would seem reasonable to have anticipated higher levels of aspiration at least in terms of expressed ultimate career objectives, if not in terms of actual job applications.

Table 6.6 also reveals that a substantial proportion of respondents considered that as undergraduates they were heavily committed to teaching as their ultimate career goal. With as many as 38 per cent suggesting that they were undecided about their career aims when entering college, 43 per cent stated that they aspired to teaching. Put another way, of those who had decided on a career goal upon commencing life as an undergraduate, 70 per cent had chosen the teaching profession. The 43 per cent with teaching ambitions on starting college had fallen slightly to 34 per cent upon completion of their studies.

This finding suggests that the high proportion of college entrants who pinned their hopes on becoming teachers is an important factor in

	When entering college	When graduating	Latest held
	%	%	%
Undecided	38	24	13
Teaching	43	34	38
Gen. Management and Admin.	0	5	6
Mother, Housewife	1	2	5
Author, Journalist	2	4	4
Social, Welfare Work	2	2	3
Librarian	0	1	2
Acting, Theatre Management	3	5	3
Higher Civil Servant	0	1	2
Personnel Manager	0	5	2
Retail Manager	0	3	2
Clerical	0	2	2
All Others	7	9	14
No response	4	3	4
TOTALS (100%)	247	247	247

Table 6.6
Respondents' perceptions of their career goals.

explaining the substantial number of college graduates who did eventually become teachers. Thus far at least, the pattern of career aspirations and job applications among teachers would seem consistent with the career choice/ambition model of occupational entry. However, for other careers this model is less appropriate.

In keeping with this interpretation, Table 6.7 demonstrates that, when leaving college, those who eventually found employment in non-teaching occupations experienced greater difficulties in making a decision about their careers than did those of their colleagues who were going into teaching. In Item 15 of the questionnaire, graduates were asked to select and rank five of ten categories according to the level of difficulty they presented in their job-hunting when leaving college. Table 6.7 shows the proportions of categories which were ranked either first or second; the inclusion of the lower order rankings produced no significant effect on the overall picture of the main difficulties faced by respondents.

While teaching respondents found 'Finding suitable vacancies' to be the major difficulty (29 per cent), followed by the problems of job-hunting techniques ('Application letters' and 'Interviews'), respondents employed in non-teaching jobs found 'Deciding what to do after college' (23 per cent) to be as great a problem as 'Finding suitable vacancies' (24 per cent). For this latter group, the techniques of job-hunting were relegated to positions of lower importance and the proportion of references to 'Knowing what I was good at' was higher than that for the teaching groups. Around 10 per cent of both groups ranked 'Obtaining relevant information' and 'Obtaining advice and counselling' as their first or second most difficult problems.

In the main, the variations in response to this item accord with the substantial number of open-ended comments that posed the overriding dilemma confronting diversified degree graduates, namely, what do you do if you don't want to teach? Among those seeking alternatives to teaching, there were few signs of 'vigilant information processing' (Janis and Mann 1977), anticipatory decision-making, or determined aspirations. The

	All	Teachers	Non-teachers	Not employed
Application letters	7	17	3	7
Finding suitable vacancies	29	36	24	31
Interviews	7	12	7	4
Deciding what to do after college	18	10	23	17
Obtaining relevant information	10	9	9	10
Knowing what I was good at	9	3	12	7
Obtaining advice and counselling	9	7	9	12
A levels	0	1	0	0
Selection tests	1	0	2	1
Others	3	2	3	4
None mentioned	7	3	8	7
TOTAL RESPONDENTS[a] (100%)	494	130	230	134

Note

a These totals refer to the total numbers of first and second ranked difficulties and not individual respondents.

Table 6.7
Job-hunting difficulties ranked either first or second.

overall impression gained was of hurried, eleventh-hour adjustments to a limited set of opportunities, which were frequently entered on the basis of chance, with little sense of personal control, and with the attitude that the levels of desirability of an outcome should be accommodated to match the perceived probabilities of achieving it (Dowie 1980). Testifying to its typicality, one college careers adviser referred to it as 'the headless chickens' approach.

Further evidence of the greater likelihood of the non-teaching group displaying characteristics associated with the accommodation model of occupational entry is supplied in Table 6.8. Responding to the statement, 'I did not give a great deal of thought to any particular career until my final year at college', a considerably larger proportion of the non-teaching employees, when compared to teaching respondents, indicated that they had deferred deliberations about specific careers until their final year. For example, compared to only 29 per cent of teachers, as many as 52 per cent of secretarial and clerical workers agreed with the statement.

'I did not give a great deal of thought to any particular career until my final year at college.'

	All	Teachers	Secretarial, Clerical	Gen. Man. and Admin.	Buying, Marketing, Selling
	%	%	%	%	%
Agree	43	29	52	39	44
Neutral	10	12	6	17	12
Disagree	47	59	42	44	44
TOTAL RESPONDENTS (100%)	247	65	33	18	16

Table 6.8
Timing of career deliberations by type of work areas.

Following on with a similar finding, Table 6.9 confirms the earlier
conclusion that, in contrast to the other main occupations, teachers were
more likely to contemplate their long-term career development in terms of
greater commitment to a particular occupation. While 49 per cent of
teachers were favourably disposed towards the statement, 'I think it is very
important that one should make a determined commitment to a career
rather than move from job to job', only 30 per cent of secretarial and
clerical workers were prepared to agree with it. Other non-teaching
employees were similarly disinclined to adopt any strong careerist perspective.

'I think it is very important that one should make a determined commitment to a career rather than move from job to job.'

	All	Teachers	Secretarial, Clerical	Gen. Man. and Admin.	Buying, Marketing, Selling
	%	%	%	%	%
Agree	38	49	30	28	38
Neutral	35	34	55	28	25
Disagree	27	17	15	44	37
TOTAL RESPONDENTS (100%)	247	65	33	18	16

Table 6.9
Attitudes to career commitment by type of work areas.

The lack among many non-teaching employees of much career ambition or
commitment to a particular occupation would seem to be more a reflection
of the perceived probability of finding suitable employment rather than of
any general or serious lack of motivation to carry out useful work within
society. Table 6.10 shows that only the small proportion of 12 per cent
agreed with the statement, 'All I want out of life is a steady, not too difficult
job with enough money to live comfortably'. Furthermore, the responses to
this item displayed no significant differences between men and women, or
between teaching and non-teaching respondents.

Finally, Table 6.11 indicates that the majority of college graduates
favoured work of a caring nature. Sixty-two per cent of the respondents
agreed with the statement, 'I prefer work which allows me to help and care
for other people'. Only 9 per cent disagreed with it. Women graduates
showed only a slightly higher tendency to prefer this type of work.

'All I want out of life is a steady, not too difficult job with enough money to live comfortably.'

	All	Male	Female
	%	%	%
Agree	12	13	11
Neutral	15	10	18
Disagree	73	77	71
TOTAL RESPONDENTS (100%)	247	70	177

Table 6.10
Attitudes to the level of occupational demands.

'I prefer work which allows me to help and care for other people.'

	All	Male	Female
	%	%	%
Agree	62	56	64
Neutral	29	33	28
Disagree	9	11	8
TOTAL RESPONDENTS (100%)	247	70	177

Table 6.11
Attitudes to caring work.

Summarizing the above, it appears that a careers choice and aspiration model of occupational entry was plausible for a sizeable share of graduates who proceeded to enter the teaching profession. Displaying an earlier consideration of a specific career than other graduates, a substantial proportion of teaching respondents indicated that they had aspired to their chosen profession both on entering college and on graduating. As a result, compared to other graduate employees, fewer teachers suggested that deciding what to do after college had been any particular problem. Even for this group, however, the ever present problem of finding suitable alternatives to teaching necessitates that the notions of 'choice' and 'aspiration' should be viewed as relative rather than absolute categories. Similarly, the possibility must remain open that, faced with few alternative employment opportunities on graduation, several teaching respondents retrospectively overestimated the degree to which they had had that profession as their chosen career goal when entering college.

Among the remaining respondents, although it is possible to identify individual cases of graduates who were successfully launched on routes towards their ultimate career goals (eg trainee accountants), few were applying or aspiring to posts outside a rather limited range of opportunities. With the exception of a relatively small number who wished to become actresses or self-employed writers, for the non-teaching respondents, jobs applied for and jobs aspired to closely resembled the modest range of jobs obtained. This group of graduates were less likely to have given early consideration to particular careers and were more likely to experience difficulties in deciding what to do upon graduation. Such characteristics correspond to explanations of occupational entry which emphasize its adventitious and accommodating nature.

On the basis of the timid personality traits allegedly associated with college entrants, some may argue that the above results demonstrate that many college graduates also displayed a lack of determined ambition and motivation in their job-hunting. In considering this argument, it should be recalled that the majority of graduates indicated a desire to find interesting and challenging work, especially of a caring and altruistic nature. While acknowledging the possible existence of a personality factor, it should also be remembered that the evidence is compatible with the view that graduates' levels of aspiration and motivation are strongly influenced by the state of the labour market, and by the quality of their information on available employment opportunties, as well as by their perception of the probability of their qualifications and abilities being good enough to allow them to compete.

7

Careers and Institutional Factors

Contrasting Four Colleges

Several colleges of higher education produced very small numbers of diversified degree graduates in 1979, so that contrasting the early careers of graduates from different colleges is difficult and necessarily requires the adoption of some methodological compromises. For instance, of the eight former colleges of education participating in the survey, four had fewer than thirty-five non-BEd graduates, and with a response rate of 54 per cent for this type of college it would be misleading to conduct a comparison of career trends among such small populations. However, the remaining four former colleges of education in the survey produced at least fifty non-teaching degree graduates in 1979 and some interesting points of contrast can be validly drawn from a comparison of the findings for each of these.

The comparison revealed that the main trends and interpretations presented earlier were visible as inherent characteristics, to a greater or lesser extent, in each of the four institutions. As a consequence, the case for establishing the institutional generality of the earlier interpretations is supported by the finding that the diversified degree graduates from the four colleges by and large share the same salient constituency features and career trends.

By way of illustration, it may be noted that the non-teaching degree output from each college was predominantly female, middle class and under twenty-one years old on entry. Thirty months after graduation, the graduates from each institution showed unemployment rates of around 10 per cent and approximately three in every four were permanently employed. By overwhelming margins, teaching was the main occupation entered by the four groups of graduates and each college also displayed similarly small proportions entering non-teaching graduate status occupational areas. For all colleges but one, the second most prevalent occupational outlet was secretarial and clerical work, none of the colleges had significant proportions entering the industrial sector, and generally less than one in five earned salaries of more than £500 per month. The extent to which graduates from each college were satisfied with the intellectual content of their work, and with the employment currency of their degrees, corresponded positively to the proportions each college had entering the teaching profession – the higher the share in teaching the greater the proportion of satisfied graduates. In view of the institutional similarities in terms of the general findings, good grounds exist for believing that the more detailed observations presented earlier also possess widespread significance and relevance.

Notwithstanding the above conclusion, the comparison did disclose some differences between the colleges, even though most tend to be differences of degree rather than of kind. A brief consideration of these differences represents a useful way of exploring factors which appear to have a bearing on graduates' careers, and which, as such, deserve fuller investigation in subsequent sections.

Of the four institutions in the comparison, College 1, a voluntary, university validated college in a moderately sized city in the north of England, contained the highest proportions of men graduates (41 per cent) and mature graduates (15 per cent), though they still showed a predominantly middle class bias (83 per cent).

The 1979 non-teaching degree output from College 1 consisted of graduates with BA Ordinary degrees in combinations of liberal arts subjects, and although no Honours degrees were taken, it is worth recalling at this point that, at an aggregate level, no significant employment-related differences between Ordinary and Honours degrees were detectable.

Thirty months after graduation, graduates from the college displayed the highest proportion in permanent employment (79 per cent) and the lowest proportion in unemployment (6 per cent). Although the college attained a rate of entry into graduate status occupations that paralleled that of other colleges (38 per cent), it did so by being heavily dependent upon entry into the teaching profession. Only 6 per cent of its graduates were employed in non-teaching graduate status occupations – the lowest for any college – and 38 per cent of its respondents were employed in medium status areas – the highest for any college. College 1 was the only institution for which 'Secretarial, Clerical' work was not the second most prevalent occupational outlet for its graduates, instead, it was 'Buying, Marketing, Selling'. The fairly reasonable levels of satisfaction indicated by its graduates reflect the substantial proportions of teachers in its output, and possibly an element of low aspiring graduates who seem content with medium status positions.

These features appear to be consistent with the proposition that College 1 represents an interesting case and bears important implications for several institutions of its type: namely that without the good fortune to be situated close to a local labour market relatively rich in opportunities for graduates, without more marketable and vocationally-related subject areas, and possibly without distinctive curricula features such as careers education schemes, fairly satisfactory proportions of this college's graduates will obtain employment but they will tend to be heavily concentrated in teaching or in occupational areas previously unaccustomed to graduate entry. The majority of graduates from this kind of college face two options: teaching, or occupational areas associated with being overqualified and underemployed.

College 2 has several affinities with College 1. Situated in, and close to, a city of an equivalent size, also in the north of England, College 2 is another voluntary, university validated college with a similar rather limited local market for graduate employment – at least, in comparison to the greater number of graduate opportunities available in London and the South East. (Out of all the 247 non-BEd respondents from former colleges of education, thirty-two obtained non-teaching graduate status jobs and half of these were located in and around London.)

Apart from an additional provision of some science courses, College 2 also offers a matching range of subject areas. In one respect, however, it clearly differs from College 1. In addition to providing the 1979 graduates with a careers advisory service, as did the first college, it also mounted a careers education scheme, which included a four-week off-campus work experience component. This provision was unique among the colleges in the survey and underscores the significance of the particular case of College 2.

Of the four institutions under comparison, College 2 contained the highest proportion of respondents from working class origins (34 per cent) and the highest with A levels in the below average category (54 per cent). It had very few mature graduates (3 per cent), only a quarter of all students obtained Honours degrees and of these only 9 per cent gained Firsts or Upper Seconds.

Thirty months after leaving college, a marginally higher share of graduates from this college were unemployed (11 per cent) than from elsewhere, although this group of respondents displayed a proportion in permanent employment commensurate with that of the two other colleges and higher than the fourth (77 per cent).

One of the most striking features of the career trends of graduates from College 2 was the relatively low proportions working within the teaching profession. Teaching remained the foremost occupational outlet, but, in comparison to other colleges, by a significantly reduced margin. In contrast to the average rate of entry into PGCE courses for the other colleges (approaching 50 per cent), 36 per cent of College 2 graduates embarked on teacher training courses. Likewise, while other colleges had between 41 and 57 per cent of their employed graduates working as teachers, College 2 had the smaller corresponding percentage of 26 per cent.

However, because the rate of entry into non-teaching graduate status work for College 2 (13 per cent) was no higher than that for the norm of the other colleges, the effect of reducing the involvement with teaching was to give the college the lowest overall proportion of respondents with graduate status positions (33 per cent). Conversely, related to its diminished dependence on careers in teaching, College 2 displayed the highest proportions in medium and low status occupations (44 per cent).

Moreover, apparently as a consequence of their high proportions in both non-graduate and non-teaching work, respondents from College 2 were the least well-paid of the colleges under comparison, were the least satisfied with the intellectual content of their work, and the least content with the employment currency provided by their degrees.

Being one of the first to diversify, College 2 provides early warnings to other institutions of the difficulties they and their graduates could face in the event of students being successfully diverted away from thinking of teaching as the automatic employment outlet. There seems little doubt that this college was successful in broadening the career orientations of its students away from a narrow pre-occupation with teaching, and that its career education package played an instrumental part in helping to achieve this. However, to some extent, it then paid the penalties for success: it faced the bigger problem of helping relatively more graduates to find appropriate alternative employment.

While the careers education scheme appears to have effected a widening of graduates' career awarenesses, it does not appear to have brought the suitable accompanying levels of employability. This college's relatively high level of unemployment and low levels of occupational status, salaries, and job satisfaction highlight the considerable obstacles colleges face when diversifying the range of career possibilities for non-teaching degree graduates. Indeed, there is an important need to contemplate the hypothesis that in 'warming up' students' career insights and expectations then failing to fulfil them, the college may unwittingly heighten graduates' sense of disappointment and dissatisfaction. Ironically, colleges where little effort is made to concentrate the minds of undergraduates on life beyond graduation may provoke less criticism and disillusionment, simply by not planting the notion in students' minds that careers is a problem for which the college authorities share joint responsibility.

College 3, a voluntary, university validated institute of higher education situated in London, clearly enjoys a more favourable local graduate labour market than the two provincial colleges just considered. Concentrating on degrees in subject combinations, it also appears to offer one or two allegedly more marketable courses (eg business studies). Unlike the previous two institutions, however, a properly organized college-based careers advisory service was not available until after the 1979 cohort had graduated. The respondents from College 3 were particularly strong in women (80 per cent) and middle class graduates (86 per cent). Very few of the college's graduates were mature students (6 per cent); all obtained Honours degrees and as many as a quarter of these gained Firsts or Upper Seconds. Although its graduates exhibited an unemployent rate compatible with that of other colleges (9 per cent), they showed the lowest of all proportions in permanent employment (68 per cent). This disparity is partly accounted for by the higher percentages in research/academic study and in temporary overseas employment (3 per cent in each).

Given that 51 per cent of its respondents proceeded to take PGCE courses – the highest percentage for any college – it is surprising that only 27 per cent of the cohort from College 3 were employed as teachers thirty months after graduation. Thus, graduates demonstrated a marked tendency to take teacher training courses without subsequently entering employment as teachers – just under half of its respondents who completed PGCE training were not working as teachers.

Matching the norm for all the colleges, 39 per cent of its respondents were to be found in graduate status occupations, though this percentage was heavily dependent on a continued commitment to the teaching profession, and despite its proximity to a broader range of graduate opportunities, the proportion in non-teaching graduate status jobs was no higher than that attained by graduates from the provincial colleges (12 per cent). Compared to the remaining three colleges, more College 3 graduates were in receipt of salaries over £500 a month but this is thought to be largely a function of London Weighting allowances.

Finally, and somewhat contrary to expectations derived from the occupational status distributions, this institution had the lowest proportion who were satisfied with their degree currency in terms of its occupational range (39 per cent), and the second highest proportion who were dissatisfied by the lack of intellectual demands in their work (39 per cent). Three factors are especially noteworthy in interpreting these levels of satisfaction: (i) the higher than average percentages of neutral responses owing to this group's larger than usual proportion not in employment; (ii) an impression gained when coding the questionnaire responses that some London-based teachers were more demoralized by their working environments than teachers elsewhere in the country; and (iii) a similar degree of strong dissatisfaction among non-teaching and non-graduate employees as expressed by College 2 respondents.

With regard to the quality of impact on graduates' careers, College 3 seems closer to College 1 than College 2. Whereas College 2 had started the process of broadening graduates' career horizons to a range appropriate to diversification but had by and large failed to enhance employability, College 3 appeared to have had little effect on either. It seemed to have made little impact either in diverting graduates' career intentions away from teaching (as shown by the large proportion entering PGCE courses) or in assisting them to enter graduate status occupations outside teaching (particularly in view of the opportunity to capitalize on a more favourable range of employment openings).

As with College 1, the consequence of following the College 3 approach is that the very substantial dependence on teaching as the major career outlet justifies adopting the so-called 'diversified' degree programes as unpremeditated and adventitious substitutions of one method of training teachers for another. Implemented as such, the main employment-related criteria for evaluating the 'diversified' courses must focus on how successfully they prepare students for teaching, in comparison, say, to the existing concurrent BEd programmes or the more innovatory teacher education programmes that have been proposed (eg the three cycle scheme recommended in the James Report, DES 1972a).

Although possessing fewer respondents, College 4 provides a number of qualities which deviate from those of the previous three. Situated in the south west of England, this college is controlled by a local education authority and validated by a university and by the CNAA. Located in a graduate employment market that would probably resemble that of College 2, its 1979 graduates completed BA and BSc Honours degrees in single subjects, music and home economics. The respondents were nearly all women (86 per cent), were almost invariably middle class (95 per cent) and included no mature students. Of all the colleges, this one contained the highest proportions in the above average A level group (71 per cent) and in the group with first or upper second class Honours (30 per cent).

Displaying average employment and unemployment rates, 48 per cent of this cohort proceeded to take PGCE courses, and, in sharp contrast to College 3 graduates, when they completed their courses almost all gained employment as teachers. With a substantially higher proportion of teachers among their ranks (43 per cent) and a share of non-teaching graduate employees fractionally higher than other colleges (14 per cent), College 4 possessed, by a significant margin, the largest proportion of respondents in graduate status occupations (57 per cent). As a derivative of this comparatively high proportion in graduate employment, the group expressed the greatest extent of satisfaction with their degree currency (72 per cent) and the lowest extent of dissatisfaction with the intellectual content of their work (29 per cent).

The career trends of College 4 graduates clearly evince the same kind of propulsion towards teacher training that characterized graduates from

College 1 and College 3. Nevertheless, the careers direction taken by College 4 graduates is manifestly related to the single subject studied at degree level. Whereas music graduates exhibited a very marked predilection for teaching, home economics graduates entered a greater variety of careers, and a promising proportion succeeded in entering occupations of a suitable status. The overall impact of this institution, however, followed the same pattern as two of the three colleges previously described: by a significant margin, the overriding employment outlet of the non-teaching degree courses was teaching.

In addition to the influence upon careers of the degree subjects taken by graduates, the above comparisons have exposed a number of other determining factors which could be examined in the light of the questionnaire findings: among them the geographical dispersion of suitable vacancies and the requisite mobility of graduates; courses taken; and careers education and advisory services. The remaining sections in this chapter examine the influence of such topics.

Geographical Mobility

To permit an analysis of the relation between employment trends and geographical mobility, graduates were asked (i) what was the furthest distance away from college and their parental or permanent home before starting college of the posts they applied for and (ii) what was the distance from college and their parental home of their current places of work (items 8 and 9 in the questionnaire).

At the time of leaving college, few significant differences were evident between sexes, A level groups or the two broad social classes in the proximity of posts applied for either to college or the parental home. Mature students, however, showed an increased tendency to apply for jobs closer to college and home, and married graduates were marginally less likely than single graduates to apply for posts over a hundred miles away from their permanent residences before starting college. Relative to Ordinary degree graduates, proportionately more Honours degree graduates applied for appointments nearer to home and college, but this result is definitely a reflection of the high share of Honours degree graduates from the London college, many of whom remained in the capital after graduation. With regard to the proximity of latest known workplaces to college and parental homes, in addition to reiterating the latter point about Honours graduates from the London college, proportionately more mature and married respondents stayed closer to their colleges, but only the former showed an increased tendency to be resident at or near to their pre-college homes.

In spite of the inevitably small numbers of cases in each group, the data strongly suggest that, whereas for provincial colleges such as College 1 and College 2 the more mobile graduates improved their chances of being permanently employed in graduate status occupations, for the London college, the reverse was the case: the least mobile group stood the better chances of reaping these benefits. Conversely, in the provincial colleges, proportionately more of the least mobile group were not employed and occupied in graduate status work, while in the London college, a relatively greater share of the more mobile graduates were without employment and were less evident in graduate level work.

These trends were particularly prevalent among non-teaching graduate status occupations, but the patterns of mobility required for teaching jobs bore a parallel, if less marked, resemblance to them. It is felt that these results go a long way towards vindicating the earlier assumption that the wider graduate opportunities in London are advantageous to College 3 graduates, even though comparatively few appear to have made the most of them. Similarly, the findings underline the need for provincial colleges to emphasize the benefits of geographical mobility; and here College 1 graduates appear not to have been as willing to travel so much as College 2 graduates. This factor may explain the difference in the proportions in non-teaching graduate employment between these two institutions.

College Courses and Services

Reflecting the importance of relating graduates' careers to the courses they studied, Chapter 3 contained a cross-sector analysis of the first destinations of graduates from five broad discipline areas: arts, social studies, arts & social studies, science, and other combinations. Owing to the many permutations of combined subjects involved, the low numbers of graduates in discipline areas other than the arts, and the small numbers of colleges offering some certain courses, it was acknowledged that the exercise was one of compromise and circumspection. Indeed, when comparing all types of colleges of higher education, the social studies category was completely eliminated from the interpretation, because the vast majority of graduates in this discipline were exclusive to the proto-polytechnics.

Nevertheless, in spite of such shortcomings, the analysis provided useful indications that, for the college of higher education sector as a whole, the arts clearly constituted the predominant discipline area. Arts graduates appeared to experience a slightly lower employment demand than graduates from other disciplines, and although contrasting college arts graduates with those from universities and polytechnics amounted to the most favourable form of comparison from the colleges' viewpoint, the proportion entering permanent home employment from former colleges of education was lower, and with a greater drift towards teaching, than that from the two other college types.

Developing the above, but not focusing on a within-group comparison of graduates from former colleges of education, each of the respondents was assigned to one of the five discipline classifications used in Chapter 3 (see Appendix B for classification frame). In extending this analysis, particular interest centred on whether discipline areas such as science and social studies demonstrated superior employment indices when only graduates from former college of education were included as opposed to graduates from all types of colleges as in the first destinations analysis.

Unfortunately, because the analysis is impeded by similar difficulties to those which beset the earlier attempt, eg low numbers in discipline areas other than the arts, the results obtained do not inspire high levels of confidence. Notwithstanding this, although one or two specific subjects appeared to be more marketable, the results, however tentative, offer little or no encouragement for the view that employability is enhanced by the colleges' non-arts disciplines. This finding suggests that the earlier indications of increased employability for science graduates was determined more by the college type attended than by discipline-based differences within the former colleges of education. With regard to the latter institutions, graduates' career experiences and patterns were generally common to all discipline areas, and where slight differences did occur, these were in such minority areas as to have negligible impact on the overall trends for the substantial majority of arts-based graduates, Thus, the features of graduates' careers depicted earlier are thought to be of a generic, college-based nature, unspecific to particular disciplines, but, of course, most evident among graduates in the arts.

Table 7.1 demonstrates that just over half of the respondents were awarded combined degrees with both subjects in the arts discipline area and at least a further quarter had one subject in the arts, reaffirming the very considerable bias towards the arts among college graduates. In contrast, only 7 and 8 per cent respectively studied two subjects in the social studies and science disciplines, the remaining 11 per cent being classified in the other combinations area (eg PE/any other subject, social studies/ science combinations).

	Colleges 1, 2, 3 and 4				Others	All
	1	2	3	4		
	%	%	%	%	%	%
Arts	41	51	44	62	70	51
Social Studies	0	3	19	0	6	7
Arts & Social Studies	21	24	33	0	12	22
Science	3	11	0	38	3	8
Other Combinations	35	11	4	0	9	11
TOTAL RESPONDENTS (100%)	34	90	69	21	33	247

Table 7.1
Discipline areas by college.

The same table also displays the discipline distributions for each of the main colleges involved: College 2 closely resembled the average distribution for all participating colleges; the apparently low share of arts graduates at College 1 is deceptive, due to the fact that three rather than two subjects were taken and, hence, more respondents with, say, two arts subjects combined with PE or a science were assigned to the other combinations area; College 3's distribution reflects the more extended provision of social studies rather than science courses; and College 4's output consisted of single subject degrees in music (arts) and home economics (science). Although not shown in the table, women were slightly over-represented in the arts and arts & social studies areas, and were correspondingly under-represented in social studies, science, and, particularly, in other combinaions.

Respondents who studied arts subjects were marginally more likely to proceed to PGCE courses, while those in science, and especially social studies, were less likely to do so. All discipline areas showed matching proportions who were not in employment thirty months after graduation (between 26 and 30 per cent), except graduates in the 'Other Combinations' category, in which, with only 18 per cent not in employment, respondents from College 1, the college with the highest share in permanent employment, were over-represented. Additional analyses confirmed that all five discipline areas were associated with similar unemployment rates.

The proportion of arts graduates employed as teachers (29 per cent), was higher than the corresponding proportion for science (20 per cent) and social studies graduates (5 per cent), while the share of social studies respondents in alternative graduate status jobs (28 per cent) was greater than the appropriate shares for arts (13 per cent) and science (15 per cent) graduates. Due allowance should be given, however, to the small numbers in the science and social studies categories, the latter of which included a number of graduates who, as explained below, studied education, having transferred from a BEd to a BA programme.

Overall, the results suggest that, because the influence of such a substantial majority of arts graduates is so great and the career outcomes of other disciplines lack an alternative and consistent distinctiveness, broad discipline areas, in the face of the overall college culture and curricula, do not appear to impart a major differential impact on graduates' careers. However, in order to trace a course-based influence on careers, it may be necessary to look in more detail at the trends and outcomes for particular subject offerings.

Although several subjects had insufficient graduates to permit a subject-based comparison of the early careers associated with them, it has proved possible to present details of graduates' latest known type of work areas for the seven most prevalent subjects studied: English, history, education, science/maths, religious studies, language & area studies, and geography.

With only relatively minor exceptions, the dominant pattern of occupational distribution depicted earlier was broadly similar for each subject: the principal occupational outlet was teaching, followed by secretarial, administrative and retail work. Education, for which secretarial work constituted the main occupational outcome, was the most noticeable deviation from this pattern, but this was almost entirely due to very special circumstances. At some colleges, BEd students, who early in their college life discovered that teaching was no longer their preferred career choice, were able to transfer to a BA programme by offering education as one of their two degree subjects. Consequently, this subject recruited more than the normal number of students who definitely did not intend to teach. Other slight exceptions to the general pattern included tendencies for an increased proportion of science/maths graduates to opt for scientific analysis and for an increased share of language/area studies graduates to work in the secretarial/clerical field, thus reducing their proportions in teaching.

A supplementary analysis of the levels of occupational status attained by graduates from each of the main subjects provided support for the view that the majority of college graduates' careers were not significantly influenced by the precise nature of the subjects studied. Consequently, apart from a few slight variations, significantly in subjects with fewer students, the employment range and currency of college degrees appear to be generalized and not specific to particular subject offerings.

This interpretation accords with the finding that the bulk of the graduates themselves conceived of their degrees, either positively or negatively, as denoting general rather than subject-specific relevance to occupational selection and performance. In response to an invitation to comment on the extent to which their degree courses may have assisted in the processes of obtaining employment or preparing for work (Q.20i), only a small minority expressed a subject-specific perception of the relevance of their degree to employment. Irrespective of whether they were satisfied with the employment currency associated with their degrees, the vast majority expressed or implied a generalist interpretation of their qualifications. This interpretation was presented in a variety of forms.

The most frequent was the passport or admission ticket view, whereby the degree was allegedly intended to secure entry to occupations regardless of the precise nature and content of the subjects studied. Typical examples included:

(Home economics; showroom manageress) When applying for jobs, the fact that I was a graduate helped by ensuring that I was better qualified than most other applicants, although the actual content of the degree course did not help particularly.

(Business economics/sociology; sales manager) My degree course in economics and sociology left a lot to be desired. The courses in economics, for instance, bordered on O level standard, in fact, I used an O level text book to revise for examinations. My degree has offered no practical usefulness to me and has only helped in a 'status' sense.

Elaborating a little further on the perceived reasons and rationalizations for employers using degrees as a selection device, a second and frequent form of a generalist response pointed to employers' construction of degrees as a measure of IQ. Suggesting that the attraction of a degree for many employers lies in its indication of general and higher intellectual prowess, several graduates offered contributions such as:

(English/history; secretary) As far as employers are concerned, a degree seems to be a measure of intelligence. To employers who don't have degrees themselves, it seems to be an intellectual status symbol surrounded with a certain mystique.

(English/maths; technician) My degree helped me to enter an area [electronics] which I had very little experience in, because it suggested that I was intelligent and quick to learn.

(Religious studies/english; administrative assistant) I do not think the content of an arts degree can help in any career other than teaching. It is merely a measure of intelligence like an A level.

Another group of respondents expounded a parallel interpretation, but from the point of view of their own personal development instead of from the employers' perspective. In this type of response, indications of the generalist conception of college degrees were evident in graduates' descriptions of the broad-based abilities developed as a result of studying their subjects:

(English/history/french/geography; assistant retail manager) Degree course followed was a General Ordinary course, therefore allowing me to study four different subjects — giving great variety and also knowledge to the areas covered. The variation and broad span of knowledge enabled me to consider a vast range of careers and also helped considerably in coping with work that involves constant

variation and instant decision-making. However the courses followed
being general rules out jobs requiring specialist knowledge.

(English/history; teacher) The variety of elements in my degree has
been a positive advantage, showing that I was flexible and capable of
stretching myself.

Other respondents made similar points, but expressed them in the negative
form; they highlighted the generality of their degree courses by citing its
lack of subject-specific relevance to occupational entry and performance:

(Sociology/education; clerical officer) My degree course I have only
found useful as a general qualification. Having found that I am
unable to get another year's grant to train me for a specific career (I
would like to do librarianship), I wish now that I had taken a
vocational degree.

(English/french; clerical assistant) Two-subject course meant wider
superficial knowledge than depth of research into single subject. Very
few degree courses lead to jobs without further training – often not
made clear to students.

The small number of respondents who returned comments which alluded
to a subject-specific perception were predominantly teachers who felt that
their subjects were applicable to their work:

(Music/social administration; Teacher) My degree course gave me a
sound musical education on which I now rely very heavily.

(History/sociology; teacher) Obviously the subjects taken influenced
the subjects I could offer in the teaching profession. My degree also
helped me to obtain a position in an upper school.

(Language studies/history; teacher) I chose a subject that I knew
would be relevant to my career, ie linguistics – language development
is extremely important when working with both mainstream children
and with the mentally handicapped.

While the replies to this item were heavily loaded in favour of generalist
rather than subject-specific perceptions of their degrees, quantitative
indications of satisfaction with the employment currency of their qualifications were more evenly balanced. Approximately seventy-six respondents
volunteered apparently critical answers and appeared to be less than happy
with their degree currency, sixty-six were generally satisfied, forty-five
submitted accounts which were evenly mixed, and about sixteen acknowledged the limited employability associated with their degrees but asserted
that they never intended nor expected that their studies should lead to
enhanced career prospects.

Among those respondents who were disillusioned by the limited
employability engendered by their degrees, seven broad types of dissatisfaction can be identified: first, some thought their degrees failed in a general
and unspecified sense to assist in the procurement of employment and
preparation for work:

(English/history; secretary) I do not think that my degree course has
contributed in any way to my present situation and certainly played no
part in my obtaining this particular post.

Some perceived their degrees' incapacity to fulfil the career expectations
that were raised as a result of studying at college:

(English/drama/history; secretary) . . . I got a lot out of my degree
courses because I felt starved of education, so did other mature

students, but a BA in English and Drama simply doesn't qualify you for a job in any way related to those subjects except teaching. Studying our literary heritage is a wonderful occupation; it may develop self-discipline and reasoned thought, how to tackle a problem but anything more definite? more relevant to a job? . . . In my experience, it was no good toting my degree round employment agencies. I thought I had sufficient back-up with typing, but at 'Graduate Girls Agency' I was offered copy typing for the house magazine of an engineering firm and nothing else, and was turned down for a number of jobs because 'I'd be bored'. They were right, but I needed a job. At the head hunting agency, I was at least working at a level that suited my age and experience and was tempted to stay. When I was supplanted by somebody who could do shorthand, I enrolled for a Pitman's shorthand evening class course the same day and now have the diploma. At the head hunting agency and in my present job I have to deal with job applications myself, and see things from an employer's point of view. When competition is fierce, we can afford to choose kids with practical experience and back-ups like typing etc. I don't think half my problems would have arisen if I'd been a man, like having to do secretarial work, but again I might not have got into theatre administration at all. I don't think its the actual courses that need adapting. If you study literature, you've got to read, research, debate, write about it – there's no other way. But perhaps college authorities might think about beating into the heads of young students the need for self-disipline, application, punctuality and the matter of compromise when doing things they don't enjoy, otherwise the world comes crashing in when they leave college and they turn into dissatisfied, disillusioned people. There is one hell of a gap between the expectations bred into the young and the reality they face, and I think it has something to do with an education system based on academic attainment rather than preparation for work. I sometimes think that humanities courses should be banned, except for people studying for the love of it, or wanting to climb the academic ladder. My boss's daughter – good degree at Bristol – fails to find job – goes back to do PGCE doesn't really want to teach – what else does she do with an English degree? She doesn't know . . . .

Their degrees had a lack of market currency, leading to the acceptance of jobs for which only O and A levels were required:

(Business economics/french; temporary staff consultant) My degree courses have in no way helped me to find my present job – in fact a great deal of employers were rather 'put off' that I did have a degree. However I do feel in the long run they will be of more value. I felt the courses were rather an extension of school than a preparation for work.

(Home economics; unemployed) Many friends who were employed at eighteen are doing better than I was at [my previous employers]. There is always the thought the degree will count more in years to come.

Their degrees were restricted too narrowly to the teaching profession:

(English/education; clerical assistant) I think my degree course was totally irrelevant to my present situation. I don't think it has helped me to obtain employment and it didn't prepare me for work. As my degree was in english and education, I feel it would only be relevant to the teaching profession or anything vaguely related to it.

(English/movement, music, drama; sports centre supervisor) My degree courses were designed for PE teachers, regardless of what my lecturers said. As, after the first year at college, I had no intention of teaching the courses were fairly irrelevant to my chosen career. This opinion is not held by my employers.

Their degrees failed to provide a more specific relevance to other careers:

(Art/education; graphic designer) When I entered college I thought I *might* want to teach and so took a teaching BEd course with art as my main subject. However this was largely due to parental pressure as I really would have preferred art college. After an unhappy year I decided teaching and I could not get along so instead of wasting the year I transferred to a humanities degree keeping both subjects but dropping teaching practice. In my opinion (and in retrospect) this was a rather useless degree, in that it was too wide and didn't prepare me for very much and furthermore [it] meant nothing to most people and they refused to acknowledge the art course.

Their degrees were insufficiently practical and work-orientated:

(Art/education & community studies; office organizer) Some of my practical art course has helped me with the graphics I do now, although I did not actually study graphics. The rest of my degree course has been of little help to my present job. Courses would have been more useful had more practical work in industry etc. been involved.

Finally, their degrees had an inadequate number of vocational courses and components:

(Music; PGCE student) Certainly my degree will be a future factor in looking for a teaching job though was not so for my last two posts. With regard to teaching, a more practically based course would have been better.

Adopting the same approach to the responses which indicated a positive and favourable view of the employment currency of diversified degrees, four broad types of contributions can be identified: first, the degrees provided some general but unspecified assistance in the tasks of obtaining employment and preparing for work:

(Rural science/biology; teacher) My degree course has helped greatly.

(Dance; teacher) Degree courses have helped me obtain my permanent position.

The degrees extended accessibility to employment areas by signifying to employers that the degree holders possessed useful, but unspecified, qualities (most numerous):

(Art/english; social worker) When I obtained my present post I was told that being a graduate got me the job, as they felt that 'I had something to offer'.

(English/sociology; VSO teacher) I wouldn't have got this job if I hadn't had a degree. The 'paper qualifications' does actually count for quite a lot.

The degrees were instrumental in nurturing a range of general skills and attributes which were relevant to occupational performance:

> (English/history; research assistant) I don't think the actual *content* of the courses helped, but the disciplines and skills involved in the study of those subjects were helpful — ie increased literacy, ability to formulate ideas and follow through arguments.

> (English/biology; clerical officer) My degree courses have given me a good educational background for my career. Studying has also taught me self-discipline and use of my own initiative which are both useful qualities in my present job.

The degrees offered subject-specific knowledge and skills which were relevant to occupational performance (predominantly teachers):

> (English/french; teacher) As I studied a foreign language, this is self-evident.

> (Music; teacher) Without my degree, I . . . would not have been accepted in my present post and would not feel qualified enough to teach the A level standard I do teach.

Of those who were assigned to the evenly balanced category, the great majority typically indicated that their degrees delivered some limited employability benefits, but had generally failed in the process of preparation for work:

> (Biology/chemistry; social worker) Apart from having a degree, it did not help me obtain employment.

> (Movement/education; library assistant) The particular course I did has not helped me obtain my present employment but having *a* degree has helped. Though for anyone wishing to do temporary work in catering, for example, it is preferable when applying not to mention one has a degree. My degree course gave me higher expectations about life — they were lowered when I realized the boredom and dissatisfaction of work.

Finally, a further group of respondents recognized the limited employment currency of their degrees, but then went on to explain that, from their point of view, this did not amount to a criticism, since the courses were neither selected nor approached as enhancements of career prospects or preparation for work. The following two extracts typify this kind of comment:

> (English/religious studies; unemployed) My degree course did not help me in any way to make a decision about future careers. I did not regard it as the main function of my degree to do this.

> (English/religious studies; shopowner) A BA in English and religious studies has no relevance to my work. However I *am* glad I did it for personal benefit.

In so far as these comments suggest an attitude of mind which views courses as intrinsic personal enrichment rather than extrinsic career advancement, they closely resemble one of the quantifiable attitudinal statements included in the questionnaire. By way of assessing the generality of this type of comment, respondents were asked to indicate their strength of agreement or disagreement with the statement, 'It is more important that higher education should develop students as people rather than prepare them for a career'.

Graduates' replies were fairly evenly distributed (Table 7.2): approximately a third gave priority to personal development over career preparation; another third marked the neutral category, presumably suggesting equal weighting to both aspects; and the remaining third implied that the emphasis should be placed on career outcomes. Even allowing for the fact that these responses were retrospective, the *collective* message seems clear: college students desire courses which provide both personal enrichment and career enhancement.

There is also the hint in Table 7.2 that teachers were less prepared than workers in other occupations to demote the importance of career benefits, although employees in general administration, with a similar proportion agreeing to the statement as teachers, were an exception in this respect.

'It is more important that higher education should develop students as people rather that prepare them for a career.'

	All	Teaching	Secretarial, Clerical	Gen. Man. and Admin.	Buying, Marketing, Selling	Health, Social Welfare
	%	%	%	%	%	%
Agree	36	28	43	28	44	73
Neutral	31	37	21	44	19	18
Disagree	33	35	36	28	37	9
TOTAL RESPONDENTS (100%)	180	65	33	18	16	11

Table 7.2
Main types of work by attitudes to higher education as personal development rather than vocational preparation.

One of the conclusions emerging from the responses to the open-ended item presented above is that, with the exception of teachers, graduates rarely testify to any direct correspondence of specific skills between their courses and their work, and this receives substantial support from an associated quantifiable question. Of the 41 per cent who indicated their agreement with the statement, 'The particular skills I acquired in my college courses are of close relevance to my present work', two-thirds were working as teachers.

As Table 7.3 shows, whereas 73 per cent of teachers believed that their work utilized specific skills acquired in their degree courses, only 18 per cent of secretarial/clerical workers, and 22 per cent of general administrators indicated that no such relevance existed for them. These, and similar non-teaching employees, also displayed correspondingly low proportions assenting to the statement. The findings endorse the considerable number of open-ended comments highlighting curricular themes within many of the diversified degrees which, intentionally or unintentionally, steer students towards the teaching profession as being the only directly relevant and feasible career outlet for liberal arts subects.

Looking more broadly at the overall experience of college life, rather than just the subjects taken, a considerable proportion of college graduates felt that useful and work-related personality attributes had been fostered during their time in higher education. Two-thirds of college respondents agreed with the statement, 'College life helped me to develop personal qualities which have been useful in my present (or more recent) work'

'The particular skills I acquired in my college courses are of close relevance to my present work.'

	All	Teaching	Secretarial, Clerical	Gen. Man. and Admin.	Buying, Marketing, Selling	Health, Social Welfare
	%	%	%	%	%	%
Agree	41	72	18	22	25	27
Neutral	24	22	12	28	38	36
Disagree	35	6	70	50	37	37
TOTAL RESPONDENTS (100%)	180	65	33	18	16	11

Table 7.3
Main types of work by employed respondents' attitudes to the relevance of course skills to their jobs.

(Table 7.4). However, it is also revealed that appreciable variations occur according to the college attended. While former students from Colleges 1 and 8 demonstrated particularly high proportions affirming the development of useful personal qualites (85 and 76 per cent respectively), graduates from Colleges 2 and 3 displayed the correspondingly lower proportions of 67 and 54 per cent respectively.

'College life helped me to develop personal qualities which have been useful in my present (or most recent) work.'

	Colleges 1, 2, 3 and 4				All
	1	2	3	4	
	%	%	%	%	%
Agree	85	67	54	76	66
Neutral	3	15	24	19	18
Disagree	12	18	22	5	16
TOTAL RESPONDENTS (100%)	34	90	69	21	247

Table 7.4
College by attitudes to colleges' contribution to the development of work-related personal qualities.

One of the open-ended items included in Q.20 of the questionnaire produced many valuable comments which elaborated upon this latter finding. Responses to the question, 'In what ways has the social life of the college campus helped you to obtain employment or prepare you for work?', reflected the same college-based differences as observed in the previous quantifiable item, and suggested that, in the view of the respondents, the development of useful personal attributes owes more to the students' social life than the teaching they received. By way of justifying these interpretations, it was evident that respondents from Colleges 1 and 4 were more inclined to vouch for the benefits associated with the students' social and cultural experience than those from Colleges 2 and 3. The comments of respondents from these latter institutions included several positive ones, but were generally less frequent and enthusiastic, and occasionally more critical.

College 1 graduates, in particular, clearly approved of the extent to which college life extended personal and social skills beneficial to their subsequent occupational performance. Often in very emphatic terms, they declared that the college's social life had helped them to grow in self-confidence, independence, tolerance and maturity. The following two contributions illustrate the flavour of these remarks:

(English/drama/religious studies; trainee houseparent) This area was of the utmost importance for my needs. The experience of living and sharing with people of my own age in a residential setting gave me the impetus I needed to discover my own personal traits and character, strengths and weaknesses. Every opportunity should be made to increase a student's awareness of the unique opportunities that student life enables them to experience.

(English/history/french/geography; assistant retail manager) Provided one involves oneself and contributes to the social life this can be one of the main aids in preparation for employment. Helps you to meet people and socialize, relax, to tolerate and accept a broad selection of personalities from a wide geographical area.

Graduates from other colleges, especially College 2, also expressed a considerable degree of satisfaction with the way in which their social experience at college had advanced their personal development to the point of being advantageous in their occupational roles:

(English/theology; unemployed) Yes, helpful. Contact with other people, students and lecturers helped give me more confidence, listen to others' opinions and views, sort myself out as a person, etc., etc.

(Biology/chemistry; assistant biologist) Good. Learning to deal with other people is most important skill of all: knowing when to say the right thing, how not to offend, or to offend, trying to be important, or at least convincing others you are somebody and making them realize they are.

(English/sociology; VSO teacher) Experience from running various societies and social events has certainly been very helpful. I'm sure my record of this helped me obtain this VSO post.

(History/religious studies; clerical officer) Helps you to mix with a wide variety of different people from different backgrounds. Important when employer is looking to see how you will fit in with the rest of staff.

However, in contrast to those from College 1, respondents from the two larger participating institutions, especially College 3, had smaller proportions offering positive comments and greater proportions who were critical of the social life at college and more sceptical of its value to careers and work:

(English/history; teacher) Did not prepare me for maturity needed in full-time employment.

(Sociology/social administration; personnel officer) College life was really far too insular. More effort should be made either to get the real world in or the students out. Obviously I accept that much is up to the individual but without wishing to sound paternalistic, the world of work comes as something of a culture shock. Ten weeks in vacation time does not enable a student to face the pressure and hum-drum of work.

(English/religious studies; PGCE student) Practically non-existent, apart from a very good summer ball. It would help if the students did not, on the whole, insist on going home at weekends.

(Art/education; teacher) My particular college had little social life due to its close proximity to London.

(History/American studies; trainee accountant) Although students are able to get together and have topical discussions, they live very sheltered lives, even off-campus. They may be well informed on national and international events but still do not seem a part of the 'real' world as the college in many respects was 'over-protective', ie bed-linen distributed, bills paid even in flats outside of college, etc.

The latter comment opens up an awareness of the problems of searching for a secure and close-knit student community without it producing a restrictive and debilitating constraint on students' scope for development. In order to alleviate the degree of culture shock associated with the transition from college to work, it would seem desirable that the initially small and safe community environment, appropriate for the typically rather timid characteristics of the student intake, must progressively open up to a more challenging and demanding set of social circumstances. A final comment comes close to summarizing the tension between matching the appeal of a closely integrated college-based community with the need to encounter a less narrow and inward-looking field of social situations:

(Sociology/social administration; student) The size of the college made for a friendly atmosphere, which in retrospect represented a considerable advantage over a large anonymous university. However, the range and depth of social and cultural activities were somewhat restricted.

In addition to commenting on their experience of college courses and campus life, graduates were given opportunities in the form of both closed and open-ended questions to evaluate the efficacy of other provisions, including careers services and work experience placements, where appropriate. In a quantifiable form, respondents were offered a range of informational sources and provisions, of which they were asked (i) to choose the single most important source through which contact was first established with their initial employer (Table 7.5) and (ii) to rank the three most helpful provisions in their general approach to job-hunting (Table 7.6).

For ease of presentation in the tables, one source, 'Employment Agencies', has been formed by combining two of the original minor response categories and a composite source, 'Careers Service', has been derived by aggregating the frequencies of responses for its specialist constituent elements. It should also be noted that in a few cases respondents answered the question with regard to the careers service at the institution where they studied for a PGCE qualification, instead of the college where they obtained their first degree.

Even allowing for this possible contamination of the results, which if anything should have increased the use of careers services, the contribution of college-based provisions towards assisting graduates in their initial search, and then securing specific employment, is surprisingly low. Table

	All	Colleges 1, 2, 3 and 4			
	%	1 %	2 %	3 %	4 %
National paper/journal	27	32	22	27	43
Local paper	16	17	21	12	9
Friend/relative	9	15	6	9	5
Personal contacts	4	3	2	4	0
Employment agencies[a]	10	9	7	11	5
Speculative approach	8	6	7	9	14
Vacation work contact	3	0	5	4	5
Academic staff	2	3	2	3	5
Careers service:[b]	(10)	(12)	(13)	(11)	(0)
Careers adviser	2	3	3	1	0
Vacancy notices	3	3	4	4	0
DOG, GO, etc.[c]	2	6	4	1	0
CSU vacancy lists[d]	1	0	1	3	0
Employers' visits	1	0	0	1	0
Careers conventions	1	0	1	1	0
Prestel[e]	0	0	0	0	0
Others	5	3	6	4	9
Not applicable	6	0	9	6	5
TOTAL RESPONDENTS (100%)	247	34	90	69	21

Notes

a Combines two categories: 'Employment Services Agency/Professional Employment Register' and 'Private employment agency'.
b Shows the composite percentage for the following specialist facilities offered by careers services.
c Various directories of graduate opportunities.
d Vacancy mailing lists published by the Central Services Unit.
e A computerized informational source on vacancies.

Table 7.5
Sources of information used to establish contact with initial employers.

7.5, for example, shows that only 12 per cent of all respondents learnt about their initial employer through the career services or academic staff. More influential methods of contact included national and local newspapers, external employment agencies, friends, relatives and speculative approaches to employers. Apart from an indication that those institutions with highest proportions of teachers also displayed the highest proportions with respondents who learnt about their employer through a national paper (TES, Guardian, etc.), this finding was consistent across all the major participating colleges.

Moreover, exactly the same pattern emerges when general usefulness rather than specific job placement is considered. Table 7.6 indicates that as many as 30 per cent of respondents were unable to record that any of the sources and provisions were helpful in the task of looking for employment. Once again, only 15 per cent of all respondents ranked the careers service or academic staff as the most helpful, although in this respect College 2 had a higher percentage (24 per cent) than College 1 (18 per cent), which in turn was higher than College 3 (12 per cent). It is believed that this ordering reflects the comparative extent to which each of these institutions had established a college-based careers service for the students who graduated in 1979.

	All	Colleges 1, 2, 3 and 4			
	%	1 %	2 %	3 %	4 %
None	31	14	30	39	29
National paper/journal	26	23	27	23	43
Local paper	9	15	9	4	5
Friend/relative	4	9	3	3	0
Personal contacts	2	3	0	2	5
Employment agencies[a]	7	12	3	7	5
Speculative approach	3	3	1	6	9
Vacation work contact	2	3	3	3	0
Academic staff	3	3	6	2	0
Careers service:[b]	(12)	(15)	(18)	(10)	(0)
Careers adviser	3	0	7	1	0
Vacancy notices	3	6	6	0	0
DOG, GO, etc.[c]	3	6	3	3	0
CSU vacancy lists[d]	3	3	2	6	0
Employers' visits	0	0	0	0	0
Careers conventions	0	0	0	0	0
Prestel	0	0	0	0	0
Others	1	0	0	1	4
TOTAL RESPONDENTS (100%)	247	34	90	69	21

Notes
See Table 7.5.

Table 7.6
Sources of information ranked first as being generally helpful in job-hunting.

Responses to the open-ended item on careers services (Q.20iv) firmly substantiate the findings of the previous question. An overwhelming majority of respondents were clearly dissatisfied by the inadequacy of the provision in the careers area and several returned highly critical and uncomplimentary replies. As could be expected, criticisms were particularly severe from graduates of the institutions which had been slow to develop their careers services, but even graduates from colleges which had extended their provisions were demonstrably unimpressed.

Numerous respondents complained about the lack of properly staffed and equipped careers services and strongly advocated a more thorough and comprehensive provision:

> ... This was virtually non-existent, but a tremendous amount of organization and research needs to go into this sort of service, if it is to be of any use to a student who is more worried, during his 3/4 years, whether he will finish his essays before the deadline.

> ... Was the absolute minimum – it may just as well not have existed.

> ... The college careers service at my college was not particularly dynamic, the main channel of communication being in reality the noticeboard listing potential job opportunities. Sadly though, when one considers the present economic cutbacks, it is unlikely that this situation will improve greatly, especially when college staff have to devote so much of their time to recruitment and promotion campaigns for their colleges so that they can remain employed.

Among those critical of the services provided a common complaint was the over-emphasis placed on careers in teaching:

... This is an aspect of college facilities that I found particularly useless. My careers adviser was under-informed and unimaginative. She knew nothing of careers outside the field of teaching and the Civil Service.

... Non-existent. It was assumed that everyone would enter teaching.

... Found the emphasis was mainly on those students looking for teaching posts – amount of advice and information offered by the Careers Service for students other than teaching was to an extent narrow and short-sighted – duplication of information obtainable in directories.

... At the time of my graduation, the college provided little real help in terms of job contacts. More could be done with regard to building up a careers service which had links with industry and commerce. (However, it does very well as regards the teaching profession.)

... Terrible except a certain amount of literature but bias to further education/teaching.

There were many general remarks (eg 'dreadful', 'hopeless', 'pathetic', etc.) but in the more detailed comments shortcomings which were regularly alluded to included: the tendency to offer information and advice 'too little, too late' for the student to take effective decisions; over-reliance on published material instead of individual counselling; a lack of contact and familiarity with employing organizations and the world of work in general:

... I think they could perhaps do more by visiting college's first-year students. They should also find more detailed information on careers, eg I was told I would be able to do accountancy. I was not told my Maths O level had to be a higher grade. I feel I could have saved myself a lot of time and trouble applying for accountancy vacancies, perhaps I may have considered other jobs more favourably if I'd known. More detailed information is needed. I feel students ought to be consulted in their first year about careers, then the careers advisory services could give them an opportunity for work experience in a field they are interested in, then there is enough time for a student to change his/her mind without any detrimental effect.

... This didn't help me. We have a self-service careers information room, but little or no personal guidance.

... No help whatsoever. Would be improved by treating students as individuals rather than as names on a list to be processed on completion of a degree programme.

... Out of touch with the real world.

... More direct contact with employers.

Only a small proportion in each college expressed satisfaction with the careers services, but a few more made certain allowances for the poor quality of the provision. For example, some appreciated that they were among the first diversified degree graduates and hoped that the services would improve in the future. Similarly, a small number accepted that the onus for careers rested with the student and not the careers service:

... My college careers service was, to be honest, laughable. We had one short session in which we were asked – 'who wants or needs to work anyway?' I understand the situation has improved since.

... In 1979 the college careers service was comparatively new and had little experience in directing BA students, the majority of information was gained by personal contacts and interviews.

... I feel the service was not very adequate, but at the time I was perhaps too anxious to be 'spoon-fed'.

In addition to a careers advisory service, one institution offered a short work experience component for all its non-teaching degree students. Although, as noted earlier, there was no evidence to suggest that the work experience provision improved the colleges' employability rates, the majority of their respondents were favourably disposed towards the scheme and supported its development. Each of the following comments illustrates one of the benefits the graduates believed they had gained from their off-campus work experience placement:

... Work experience was amazing in my case and very rewarding (worked with disabled children).

... Only in that it gave me experience of working environment.

... The work experience placements were particularly valuable in that they gave one time and the opportunity to reflect on whether or not that was what one wanted to do in the future. It could have saved a lot of people from wasting valuable time on leaving college.

... I worked with handicapped children for a month at college. I have found that this experience has helped me to be more understanding towards any underprivileged person (even if, in the present political climate, they be black, etc., etc.)

... Placements in sports centres etc. would be very helpful to those seeking management posts in recreation.

... Should be increased. Encouragement of relationship between students and prospective employers. Not dissimilar to polys (sandwich course) and universities (milk-round).

Criticisms usually focused on the lack of suitable preparation and unstimulating work situations:

... Working on off-campus experience served no purpose in obtaining a post. I felt that we were merely cheap labour.

... An utter waste of time − 2 weeks in a theatre (sweeping the stage) − comprised my off-campus work. Other people fared better, but they were mainly those who could not see beyond a classroom.

... Not much use as so disorganized and short-term.

Although only one of the main participating colleges offered a work experience scheme, many graduates from other institutions also recommended more practical and work-related components in their courses. Overall, these responses reaffirm many of the earlier comments which urged a greater practical relevance in the degree courses offered by colleges.

8

The Evidence Assembled

By way of drawing together the threads of this study, the final two chapters are divided into four main sections:
- A compilation of what appear to be the key reservations for which due allowance must be made when assessing the significance of the results of the study and their implications for future policy development.
- A summary of the main research findings in the form of suggested answers to the empirical questions raised in Chapter 1.
- An analysis of the implications of the results for two of the central problems currently facing higher education and labour market policy formation.
- An initial consideration of the study's implications for the policy-orientated questions raised in Chapter 1 concerning the institutional and curricula development of colleges of higher education.

The first two sections are dealt with in the present chapter, the latter two in the final chapter. Specific implications for the colleges of higher education emerge from the wider perspective of the repercussions of the evidence on policy development in higher education and the labour market in general.

The Results in Context

A number of preliminary points are necessary to put the results of the study in a balanced perspective and give context for an appropriate appraisal of the significance of the findings. Some points show up the boundaries of the present inquiry, often delineating types of questions that the research was quite clearly not designed to answer. There has been earlier recognition in this book of the limits of the study: for example, in the description of research methods and sampling in Chapter 2; it is hoped that the following will help dispel any further impression that the results and interpretations advanced here are grounded in total certainty and confidence.

First, it is certainly prudent to question the typicality of research based exclusively on students graduating in one particular year. It has been argued, for instance, that in comparison to later year groups the 1979 graduates, the first substantial group from the diversified degree programmes to leave the colleges, were especially committed to the teaching profession on entering college and, consequently, were more likely to proceed to PGCE courses on graduation. Although this particular argument is suspect — analyses of the first destination statistics for 1980 and 1981 graduates from former colleges of education show correspondingly higher, not lower, proportions of graduates taking up teacher training – the question of how similar the 1979 group may have been to subsequent year groups in terms of post-graduation experience remains open. The only sure way of answering this question would be to replicate the study for another group, for, say, the 1982 graduates.

Moreover, first destination details of more recent graduates from colleges of higher education do not suggest that graduates' initial placements have changed so substantially as to undermine the validity and relevance of the research findings summarized here. For instance, although the first destination returns for recent years show a decline in the proportion of graduates from *all* types of colleges entering teacher training (eg from 30 per cent in 1980 to 12 per cent in 1983), the statistics do not reveal whether the percentage entering teacher training from *former colleges of education*, the institutions under study in this research, has fallen or risen. This is because the information provided by ACACHE is not disaggregated by college types, namely proto-polytechnics, combination colleges and former colleges of education, the latter of which, according to the results of the research undertaken here, demonstrated a much higher rate of PGCE course entry than the remaining college types. Thus, the overall decline in the percentage entering teacher training may be due to a disproportionate increase in the numbers of graduates from combination colleges and proto-polytechnics included in ACACHE returns rather than a uniform fall in the PGCE entry rate in all three types of colleges. It should also be recalled that of 1979 graduates of former colleges of education, the proportion who had actually entered teacher training two years after graduation (44 per cent, Table 4.4) was substantially higher than the percentage of 1979 graduates of *all* colleges entering teacher training as recorded in first destination returns (22 per cent, Table 3.1). As far as we are aware, the information necessary to calculate the extent of the corresponding increase beyond the 12 per cent recorded in the 1983 first destinations statistics is non-existent.

However, albeit on the basis of guesswork, it would seem reasonable to assume that the percentage of graduates entering teacher training from former colleges of education has decreased in recent years. This may well be a consequence of the restrictions placed on PGCE admission numbers, which has resulted in a fall in available teacher training opportunities, particularly for those with degree subjects in the liberal arts. Such a decline could be a serious concern for the colleges because, as earlier chapters have highlighted, the research indicates that very often a lower proportion of college graduates entering teacher training is associated with a higher proportion encountering problems in finding satisfying alternative careers. Tentative impressions gained from first destination statistics suggest that 1982 and 1983 college graduates demonstrate a similar tendency, although, once again, this presupposes that the career patterns of graduates from former colleges of education can be inferred from the destinations of graduates from *all* college types. However, indications of the reduced opportunities for teacher training leading to other early career problems are to be found in the rise in unemployment, which has increased from 8 per cent in 1979 to 17 per cent in 1983. In addition, although in recent statistics the category 'Secretarial and Clerical Work' has been removed from the available classifications, thus preventing direct comparisons with previous years, the type of work areas most commonly entered by 1983 college graduates closely resemble the ones predominantly entered by 1979 college graduates. Hence, far from indicating that the problems and frustrations recounted by the 1979 respondents are no longer applicable, the first destination statistics for more recent year groups could be taken to suggest that the kind of difficulties encountered by our sample may well have intensified.

Secondly, largely because the 1979 graduates were the first appreciable diversified degree output, the colleges' careers advisory services were very much in their early stages of development. It is generally accepted that many colleges have since extended and improved these services (eg more colleges now receive the benefits to be derived from AGCAS membership), and it is possible that such developments have influenced the early career patterns of subsequent college graduates. Similarly, it seems likely that in 1979 many employers and personnel managers would have been unaware of a small output of graduates from a comparatively obscure sector of higher education. Latterly, it could be assumed that employers are becoming better informed about this group of graduates, and some impact on their careers and employment trends might be expected. Once again, without further extension the research cannot provide any evidence to put these assumptions to the test. Some results from the Brunel project suggest, however, that the majority of employers remain ignorant of the fact that colleges of higher education produce non-teaching degree graduates (Roizen and Jepson 1985).

Thirdly, it must be stressed that the present study has observed graduates' early careers in a period of economic recession and rising graduate unemployment, especially affecting the kind of liberal arts graduates produced by the former colleges of education. As argued in Chapter 1, when evaluating the relevance of the results, some allowance must be made for the extenuating circumstances of a particularly competitive graduate labour market. On the other hand, it would be wrong to overreact: recent indicators suggest that since 1979 general vacancies for graduates have declined still further. This trend has led some observers (Dore 1978; Paci 1977; Teichler et al. 1980) to believe that the widespread experience in Western economies of an oversupply of graduates with non-vocational degrees signals a growing structural problem rather than a temporary aberration from a normally buoyant market for the highly qualified.

Related to the latter point, the extent to which the early careers of 1979 liberal arts graduates from other sectors of higher education progressed along similar lines to those reported here constitutes a further issue about which one can only speculate. Although, on the basis of first destination statistics, some important differences in employment trends were drawn in Chapter 3, no comparable data to that provided by the 'Beyond Graduation' questionnaire for college graduates are available for university or polytechnic graduates in the same year. Such a deficiency underlines the need for a full cross-sector investigation into the initial careers of graduates. It remains to be seen whether the universities and polytechnics, at a time of limited opportunities for many graduates, will actively foster independent research into a sensitive but crucial topic, which would have serious repercussions for thousands of prospective entrants to higher education.

In spite of the limitations imposed by a simple input-output model of educational performance, analyses of the quality of the output of an institution must take some stock of the quality of the relevant input. The survey evidence bears out the generally accepted view that, relative at least to university undergraduates, college entrants had lower A level grades. Putting it bluntly, in the main, colleges are operating at the bottom of the A level market. Additionally, although there is little firm evidence to substantiate the view, some acknowledgement must be made of the opinion often expressed by staff that, relative to university and polytechnic entrants, college undergraduates are more likely to be timid and introverted. To a certain extent then, it is necessary to assess the careers performance of college graduates in relation to their academically inferior entry qualifications, and their allegedly less confident personality attributes. As pointed out in Chapter 1, this point constitutes an additional reason why it would be injudicious to expect the highest of standards in terms of careers performance and employability from the 1979 graduates from former colleges of education. However, too much weight should not be attached to this argument, because it runs counter to the frequently expressed insistence, first, that A levels are poor predictors of degree and careers success and, second, that the particular styles of teaching allegedly provided by the colleges are instrumental in enhancing the fairly modest academic achievements attained in secondary schooling.

In providing a context in which to evaluate the implications of the results for policy formation, a key theme must be recapitulated which first emerged in the review of the historical development of diversification (Chapter 1). Ultimately, the onus of responsibility for the size of the supply of college graduates in the market for the highly qualified rests with the Government, especially the Department of Education and Science, rather than the colleges and institutes of higher education themselves. In overseeing the early stages of diversification, two particular features of the DES involvement were noticeable: first, absence of a coherent and comprehensive strategy for the educational and economic role of colleges of higher education; and second, restriction of diversified curricula development to within the existing resources and staffing associated with the teaching of the traditional BEd degree. Latterly, it has come to be widely considered that DES policies for the colleges have continued to allow the aim of curbing public expenditure to overshadow all others. Bearing this in mind, as well as the depressed state of the labour market, it would be totally unreasonable to perceive the colleges as being solely accountable for the careers experience of their graduates.

Additionally, it is readily acknowledged that there are many other agents and participants in the careers field whose views were not canvassed and represented in this research (eg schools careers staff, employers, parents, etc.). It is accepted that the present findings and interpretations necessarily reflect a partial rather than a global view.

A detailed exposition of all the possible ramifications of the present study's findings is beyond the limits of this book, and a selection has been made of what appear to be the salient issues and problems. Such a selection will be influenced, however, by the authors' own biases and concerns, so it is hoped that other parties (college careers advisers or undergraduates, for example) will be active in drawing their own conclusions from the results.

The following are some among several possible interpretations of the policy implications to be extracted from the findings.

Finally, it is recognized that discussion of the evidence supplied by the present research touches upon sensitive areas and arises at a time when colleges of higher education seem to be locked into a state of perpetual pressure and vulnerability. Although some consider the climate to be so adverse as to preclude the raising of any public debate, it is maintained here that such an approach merely allows decisions to be made without open discussion and rational appraisal of empirical evidence. In this particular case, such a stance leads to a reduction of problems to financial expediency without proper consideration of genuine educational, social and economic objectives. The following discussion is offered in the belief that the benefits of posing the questions arising from the research findings in a frank and open forum outweigh the risks of the results being exploited to justify wholly negative and unconstructive polices.

Summary of the Findings

The empirical questions raised in Chapter 1 will be used in organizing a summary of the main findings to be derived from the research.

1 As indications of economic contribution, what were the main early career and employment patterns displayed by the 1979 non-teaching degree graduates from colleges of higher education which diversified from a teacher training base?

The evidence consistently shows that entry to the teaching profession was, by a substantial margin, the most prevalent type of career route followed by graduates with non-teaching degrees from colleges of higher education that had diversified from a teacher training base. Of those respondents who reported having a career goal on entering the colleges, 70 per cent cited teaching. Thirty months after graduation, 44 per cent had undertaken PGCE courses and a further 15 per cent expressed a desire to do likewise. In the period subsequent to the first year of graduation, teacher training continued to attract more respondents than any other occupational training. At the time of completing the questionnaire, 36 per cent of those permanently employed were working as teachers.

At the end of 1981 the other occupational areas commonly entered by these graduates from those colleges were: secretarial and clerical work (18 per cent of employed respondents); general administration (10 per cent); buying, marketing and selling (9 per cent); and health and social welfare (6 per cent). Apart from teaching, the only other numerically significant form of occupational training entered after leaving college was secretarial work.

The majority of employed respondents were engaged in the public service and education sectors (62 per cent), with comparatively small proportions in industry (14 per cent) and commerce (13 per cent).

At the close of 1979 only a third of the graduates were in permanent employment. At the end of 1980, as a result of the large number of PGCE graduates finding employment, this share had doubled to two-thirds. A year later, in December 1981, the proportion in permanent employment had reached 73 per cent.

Throughout the period of the survey, the rate of unemployment among the graduates remained stable at the 11 per cent level. In addition, by the end of 1981 a further 8 per cent were either not available for employment or were engaged in temporary work.

No more than a minute proportion of the graduates progressed to research or further academic study. Only 1 per cent in any of the three years since graduating advanced their studies to higher degree level.

At the time of responding to the questionnaire, only 13 per cent of the sample had remained in their posts for the major part of the period covered by the survey. The two peak periods for entering latest known jobs were in the late summer months of 1980 and 1981, when the substantial numbers who followed PGCE courses were launched into the labour market.

2 As a further indication of economic contribution, at what levels of occupational status were graduates with non-teaching degrees finding employment?

The survey findings provide support for the indication from the first destination statistics that, relative to university and polytechnic graduates, greater proportions of college graduates were 'filtering down' the market and entering types of work hitherto largely unaccustomed to taking on highly qualified personnel. These areas included 'Buying, Marketing, Selling', 'Secretarial, Clerical', 'General Administration', and 'Health, Social Welfare'. At the time of completing the questionnaire, there were more graduates employed in these areas than at any time since graduation.

Mainly on the basis of their own accounts of the currency standing of their work, each respondent was assigned to one of four categories: not employed, low status employment, medium status employment or graduate status employment. Although 39 per cent achieved graduate status positions, the majority of these were in teaching − only 13 per cent were successful in obtaining work of a similar status in other fields. Broadly conceived, three groups were identifiable: (i) just over a quarter who were not permanently employed; (ii) a third who were in low or medium status jobs generally not associated with graduate entry (mainly secretarial and clerical work); (iii) almost two-fifths who were in graduate status occupations, two-thirds of whom were in teaching.

Furthermore, there were only a small proportion of cases where internal promotion to work of a more suitable and intellectually demanding level had been procured and even fewer incidences of graduates appearing to be in a position to upgrade the quality and skills requirements of the jobs they had entered. Difficulties prohibiting these strategies included being over-qualified and over-educated, 'dead-end' departments, a lack of opportunities for displaying initiative and higher order abilities, the feeling of inertia brought on by prolonged experience of tedious and demeaning tasks, and the problems of constructing and presenting a new identity once stereo-typed, in the eyes of employers and colleagues, as a relatively menial and routine employee.

3 Are there any sub-groups among these graduates whose early careers were markedly different from the rest of the group?

At several points in this study, comparisons have been drawn between the group of graduates who undertook PGCE courses and those who did not. In contrast to those who did not, respondents who belonged to the PGCE group were more likely to find graduate status employment, predominantly in teaching, to experience less unemployment, to command higher salaries, to be more satisfied with their jobs, degree currency and course relevance, and to possess a stronger career commitment to their occupation or employer.

Almost three in every four respondents were women and many of the problems which permeate the research findings (eg the significant effect of the underemployment encountered in secretarial and clerical work) reflect the special difficulties women graduates faced in finding suitable alternatives to teaching. While similar proportions of male graduates found non-teaching graduate status jobs as they did teaching ones, practically three times as many female graduates entered teaching as entered alternative jobs with a parallel standing. Similarly, whereas women were heavily concentrated in the two main types of work categories, 'Teaching' and 'Secretarial, Clerical', a greater proportion of men were more widely dispersed across a range of categories. Women were also less likely to invest their latest jobs with a long-term career commitment. In addition, just under half of women respondents felt that their employment opportunities had been hampered because of their gender. Married women were particularly concerned about incidences of sex discrimination, their most frequent complaint referring to employers' suspicions and questions about the conflicting interests between family and work responsibilities. Subsequent evidence revealed that, at an aggregate level at least, respondents appeared to apply for jobs similar to those obtained. This finding offers some support for the view that the paucity of women in certain sectors and levels of employment (eg industry) is partly attributable to their reticence to apply for vacancies there. This would suggest that, given the continued bias against the recruitment of women, the colleges should make more resources available to provide courses and services to raise the careers consciousness and competitiveness of female undergraduates.

In the period following graduation, single male respondents displayed an increasing vulnerability to unemployment, while married men constituted a small but distinctively successful group with very low unemployment and high employment rates.

Reflecting the colleges' emphasis on recruiting students straight from schools, the number of mature students (over 21 on entry) included in the survey was low. However, the results begin to suggest that unemployment among this group was higher than that among the younger group, and once again this appeared to be associated with single, especially male, rather than married respondents.

Students with above average A levels were more likely to obtain Honours degrees than their peers who were less well qualified on entering college. However, for college graduates at least, the advantages of higher A level grades or of an Honours as opposed to an Ordinary degree produced few detectable effects on their initial career and employment experiences.

The survey provided further evidence of the middle class trend in the colleges' student constituency: only one in four graduates were from working class families. But compared with graduates from a middle class background, a higher proportion from working class families were permanently employed, though they were heavily reliant on entry to the teaching profession, with smaller proportions finding employment in alternative and compatible occupations.

By and large, the dominant patterns in early career routes were the same in all the participating colleges, notable exceptions being the variations in entry to PGCE courses and the proximity of the institutions to favourable employment opportunities. With the exception of the London college, for which the reverse was the case, a higher share of the more successful graduates were to be found among those who were willing to travel further afield to find suitable work.

The limited number of colleges producing diversified degree graduates in 1979, the uniformity of the subjects offered, and the bias towards liberal arts as opposed to science courses, were all factors conspiring to make it virtually impossible to tease out a clear view of graduates' early careers disaggregated according to subjects studied. With the minor exceptions of rather idiosyncratic indicators for certain subject offerings (eg music graduates showed a high propensity to enter teaching rather than any alternative jobs of similar status, while science and maths graduates displayed a reduced orientation towards teaching, with a correspondingly slightly higher than normal entry to non-teaching posts), the trends portrayed throughout the study were apparent for the vast majority of subject and discipline areas offered by the colleges. Since only one of the participating colleges had introduced an early form of careers education programme, it is impossible to isolate the effects of this from other institutionally specific factors. It would appear, however, that although that careers programme might have contributed to a broadening of graduates' career horizons, its impact on employability was not immediatly encouraging since the graduates from the college were among the least successful in terms of salaries, level of employment, and satisfaction with job performance and degree currency.

4 How did the early careers of college graduates compare with graduates from other sectors of higher education?

First destination statistics and previous research indicated that throughout the late 1970s unemployment among liberal arts graduates from all sectors of higher education reached new high levels; moreover, Catto et al. (1981) pinpointed these graduates as being particularly susceptible to the processes of filtering down. On the grounds of Bacon et al.'s (1979) conclusions that degree qualifications from universities and polytechnics were not held in a parity of esteem by employers, it is reasonable to conclude that college credentials would also be perceived as possessing unequal status and currency.

In comparison to 1979 graduates from universities and polytechnics, graduates from former colleges of education displayed low proportions in further academic study and permanent home employment, especially in the industrial sector, and particularly high participation rates in PGCE courses. Furthermore, increased proportions of graduates from former colleges of education were evident in type of work categories lacking a tradition of substantial graduate entry.

By restricting the comparison to graduates in the arts, which represented the main discipline area available in the college, there emerged a more balanced view of the first destinations achieved by graduates from the different sectors. However, for the colleges, this was only attainable at the 'all types' level; once the graduates from the combination colleges and the proto-polytechnics were extracted (the latter of which most closely resembled the trends in the polytechnics' output), arts graduates from the former colleges of education revealed an unusually high involvement in teacher training.

The small number of proto-polytechnic graduates who received the 'Beyond Graduation' questionnaire limits the comparative part of the survey analysis to illustrative purposes only. In comparison to respondents from former colleges of education, those from the proto-polytechnics indicated lower levels of unemployment, substantially fewer of them on teacher training courses, more on training courses for other occupations, slightly more in permanent employment, especially in industry, greater proportions working as sales executives or accountants and less in teaching and hardly any in secretarial and clerical work. Compared to 39 per cent of respondents from former colleges of education, a weighty 67 per cent of proto-polytechnic graduates found graduate status employment, 49 per cent being in non-teaching graduate status positions (13 per cent was the equivalent for former college of education graduates). Reflecting this gulf in careers performance, proto-polytechnic respondents were receiving significantly higher salaries and, in general, were manifestly more satisfied with their career development, job satisfaction and degree currency.

The small group of graduates from combination colleges did not fare so well. Relative to graduates from former colleges of education, they demonstrated very high levels of unemployment (over a quarter) with correspondingly low proportions in permanent home employment and smaller rates of entry to PGCE courses. Of those who were employed, higher proportions were to be found in creative and entertainment work, fewer in teaching and roughly the same proportions in secretarial and clerical work. Compared to the 39 per cent of graduates from former colleges of education, only 22 per cent of combination college graduates obtained graduate status employment, which in turn reflected the lower salaries and levels of satisfaction experienced by respondents from this type of college.

5 What extent were college graduates satisfied with their degree
    currency and occupational circumstances?

For the items concerning respondents' levels of satisfaction and evaluation, a familiar theme reverberated throughout the interpretation of the findings. The most satisfied were more likely to be found among the graduates who were employed in teaching, or, in the case of a minority, in alternative graduate status occupations; the least satisfied were more likely to be employed in lower status jobs, especially secretarial and clerical work, or else not in employment at all. As one of several confirmations of this general trend, a strong correlation existed between occupational status and intellectual satisfaction with latest jobs.

A substantial amount of qualitative and quantitative data testified to the frequency and intensity of mental frustration and underemployment encountered by respondents in the three areas of work most commonly entered outside teaching. For instance, in comparison to 25 per cent of teachers, 73 per cent of secretarial and clerical workers, 61 per cent of those in general administration, and 50 per cent of retail workers expressed dissatisfaction with the lack of intellectual stimulation in their work. Graduates in these areas often described their work as tedious, mundane, repetitive, soul-destroying, requiring a minimum of intelligence and initiative, and capable of being performed by people with low, or even no, qualifications.

Outside teaching, substantial proportions of graduates incurred real difficulties in finding occupations or employing organizations in which they felt they could invest a commitment to long-term career development. By way of illustration, 80 per cent of teachers, but only 30 per cent of secretarial and clerical workers, saw their future career development in line with their latest occupation or employer. As a result, several non-teaching employees felt that their jobs were not fulfilling the career expectations raised through studying for a degree.

Similarly, responses to attitudinal statements revealed that employees in the main non-teaching areas were significantly less satisfied with the currency value of their degrees than those in teaching. Furthermore, the open-ended material tended to reinforce this interpretation and showed that their reasons for feeling disillusioned included working in jobs which did not require a degree qualification, competing with graduates who possessed superior types of degrees, encountering a labour market in which the prestige value of a degree was fading, holding a degree which had little specific relevance to occupations other than teaching, and coping with employers who perceived graduates to be over-qualified and probably over-ambitious for the vacancy under consideration.

The vast majority of graduates perceived their degrees to denote general rather than applied subject-specific relevance to occupational selection. Most respondents believed that employers used degrees as a passport to indicate a general level of intelligence rather than specific occupationally-relevant knowledge.

While almost three in every four teachers indicated that the particular skills acquired in their courses were of close relevance to their occupational performance, less than one in four in other occupational areas expressed the same view. This finding tends to support the considerable number of open-ended comments which drew attention to the continuing predisposition of diversified degrees towards teaching and to the view that teaching is the only directly relevant career outcome for liberal arts graduates.

From a retrospective view, the graduates as a whole indicated support for the view that higher education should provide both intrinsic personal enrichment and extrinsic career advancement. Moreover, two thirds of the respondents considered that college life had helped them develop personal qualities that had proved useful in their latest work. Open-ended comments suggested that the social life of the college campus was the main contributory factor in fostering such personal growth, although in this respect some variations between the colleges were noted.

Respondents severely criticized the absence of, or, at best, the early development of, college-based careers advisory services. Few respondents found the services to be of much benefit in their initial search for employment. Instead, national and local newspapers, external employment agencies, friends, relatives, and speculative approaches to employers, were considered to be of more direct use in establishing contact with their first employer. In comparison to those who entered the teaching profession, non-teaching respondents were more likely not to have thought about a particular career until their final year at college and consequently found the problem of deciding what to do after college almost as difficult as finding a suitable vacancy.

6 Does the diversified degree appear to enhance the career prospects, employability and salaries of its holders?

Without specific comparative information on either the indices of employability open to respondents on completion of their secondary schooling, or on the employment trends for 1975 and 1976 school-leavers of similar ability who did not enter higher education, an 'objective' measurement of the extent to which degree courses may or may not have extended graduates' career prospects is unobtainable. The most that can be offered here is an indication of graduates' own perceptions and evaluations of career enhancement and an impression of the relative range and level of opportunities available to them at the stages of commencing and completing their higher education. It is appreciated that other participants not included in the research (eg schools careers staff, employers, parents, etc.) may also have been able to offer valuable, perhaps diverging, accounts of the opportunities available on leaving school, but this is simply to restate a point which has already been conceded: the research, like most of its kind, is bounded by its own limitation and the view that it presents of the world is inevitably incomplete. However, it is concluded that the accounts of filtering down and underemployment portrayed above are sufficiently persuasive to contest the commonly held assumption that career advancement as a result of obtaining a degree can be taken for granted.

With regard to graduates' latest known employment circumstances, for the two-fifths of the respondents who obtained teaching posts or jobs of a similar status, it is self-evident that they have enhanced their career prospects beyond those open to them as an alternative to entering higher education. For the remaining three-fifths in lower status work or not in employment at all, the case for careers enhancement lacks substance. Virtually all of their jobs were reported to be open to candidates without degree qualifications and a considerable number of these respondents illustrated the disadvantages of possessing a degree when searching for many jobs, occasionally pointing to the superior circumstances of those who entered work immediately after leaving school.

With regard to graduates' perceptions of their potential career prospects, one in every three non-PGCE respondents felt that their future job prospects would have been as good without a degree.

Finally, the salaries acquired by non-teaching employees leave little scope for any significant advantages over those who left school without entering higher education. While 91 per cent of teachers earned gross monthly salaries of over £400, 67 per cent of secretarial and clerical workers earned less than £400 a month. Similarly, as many as 46 per cent of all non-PGCE respondents had salaries of less than £400 a month.

9

The Policy Implications

Consideration of the policy implications of research findings inevitably involves selecting particular contextual parameters in which to locate the analysis. These parameters include choices relating to time scale, the range of institutions incorporated into the conceptual frame, and the 'taken-for-grantedness' of social and political structures. Dichotomizing the options, the analysis could be directed towards long-term, wide-ranging and radical changes or short-term policies focused on specific institutions and immediately applicable to given realities. Neither of the approaches is risk-free. Requiring sweeping social changes, the former runs the risk of remaining in the realm of utopian idealism; the latter often amounts to little more than tinkering with symptoms without dealing with underlying causes. The policy analysis attempted here uses both of these approaches, but, in so doing, the risks associated with both are fully accepted. The first section adopts a wide-angle, radical perspective, while the second considers the more immediate implication for the colleges.

Implications for Graduate Employment and Higher Education

Supplementing much of the policy-orientated literature (Greenaway and Williams 1973; Neave 1976; Teichler et al. 1980; Kelly and Dorsman 1984), the empirical evidence presented in earlier chapters testifies to the urgent need for policy makers to address two particular problems in the graduate labour market:
1 The continuing over-supply of graduates in non-applied subjects, with its attendant problems of unemployment, filtering down, 'vertical substitution' (Teichler et al. 1980), over-qualification and under-employment;
2 The mounting evidence of employers' discrimination in the recruitment of graduates from different sectors of higher education and the associated problems presented by hierarchies of prestige and inequalities of opportunity *within* the provision of higher education.

Writing in 1973, Williams succinctly described the dramatic transformation in the difficulties confronting policy makers in higher education and the labour market:

> For a quarter of a century after the end of the second world war, in developed and developing countries alike, educational planners have been concerned with shortages of qualified manpower. By the beginning of the 1970s the preoccupations of planners had changed.

It was no longer difficult to find the qualified manpower needed by the economy. The problem was rather how labour markets could absorb the output of rapidly expanding higher education systems. (Williams 1973b, p.41)

Since this was written, the difficulties of 'graduate saturation' (Neave 1976) have intensified and, as argued in Chapter 1, the issues have largely been neglected. Moreover, it is arguable that many of the relevant educational policy implementations have tended to aggravate rather than alleviate the problems.

Reports of graduates in routine clerical jobs obviously blunt the argument for investing scarce resources in higher eduction on the grounds that graduates improve productivity and economic well-being. They also undermine the credibility of the claims that higher education can extend equality of opportunities or assist in reducing social inequalities in general (Neave 1976; Teichler et al. 1980). For an illustration of this, the experiences of the 1960 graduates from working class origins described by Kelsall et al. (1972), for whom the entry to an occupational élite was an almost automatic sequel to gaining access to university, may be contrasted with the increased probability faced by their 1980 counterparts of joining non-graduates on the dole queues or in less skilled work.

Furthermore, in concentrating on the social and structural dimensions of the problem of graduate over-supply, namely, declining contributions to economic efficiency and equality of opportunity, there is a tendency to ignore the private pressures and emotional injuries experienced by the victims of filtering down and underemployment. Many of the accounts reported in previous chapters document graduates' experiences of the lack of meaning and social esteem associated with their work, as well as the stressful adjustments involved in coming to terms with un-realized expectations and potential. In view of the dominant definitions of what counts as suitable work for each of the sexes, and what counts as the most suitable subjects for each to study, women graduates were seen to be particularly exposed to underemployment and the psychological strains which it can induce.

Effortless and comparatively minor adjustments to the system seem ill-designed to deal with the ubiquitous and deep-rooted nature of the problems involved. One response, for instance, is to argue the case for a functional dissociation between higher education and occupational selection. Greenaway (1973) has quoted the National Union of Students as having argued along these lines:

The myth about a university degree being a first-class ticket to an executive post must be dispelled and a student must be prepared to value his education for its own sake rather than as a qualification for employment. (p.20)

A similar viewpoint regularly emerged during our discussions with lecturers in the colleges. Reluctantly conceding the rather uncompelling quality of the grounds for establishing a sound employment relevance for the diversified degree programmes, several members of staff rejected the need for courses to be justifiable in employment terms at all, and challenged the ideological frame in which such economic criteria were allegedly placed. For them, the function of the programmes could be overlaid with the single objective of intrinsic benefits, mainly personal enrichment and intellectual growth. Issues of employment and economic relevance were posited as mere epiphenomena of the central business of higher education; as such, they were not a necessary condition to be incorporated in any rationale of colleges' diversified degree provision or of higher education in general.

The weakness of the functional dissociation solution is that the chances of reducing participant's expectations and motivations to purely intrinsic ones appear very slight. From a hindsight perspective, the majority of respondents wanted both the intrinsic and the extrinsic rewards of higher education. Furthermore, given the high probability that employers will continue to use degree qualifications in the process of occupational selection, it seems highly likely that potential undergraduates will also continue to expect, albeit tacitly in many cases, both personal enrichment and career advancement. In addition, the purely intrinsic conception of degree courses completely ignores the often distressing incongruity between the attainment of higher intellectual and critical sensibilities engendered by higher education and the everyday monotony of routine work. As the qualitative material in the present study frequently illustrated, it can be severely frustrating and debilitating for many graduates to experience the 'intellectual explosion' of academic life only to end up in undemanding occupations which offer few or no opportunities for psychological, mental and altruistic satisfaction. Consequently, leaving aside the public subsidy arguments for ensuring economic relevance, it is considered here that the survey evidence underlines the point that degree programmes must be justifiable in extrinsic and economic terms as well as intrinsic and academic ones.

For similar reasons, certain other tenuous reactions and corrective measures seem inadequate to the scale of the problems involved. Manpower planning has a disappointing record and has been roundly criticized on ethical, technical, economic and educational grounds (Greenaway and Williams 1973; Lindley 1981). Improved counselling of sixth formers (Watts 1973), the strengthening of 'market messages' (Lindley 1981), and 'broad steer' measures (Catto et al. 1981) may affect the subject mix within higher education, but, for reasons offered above, seem highly unlikely to reduce the overall public demand for degree qualifications. Likewise, by itself, widening access to higher education (Fulton 1983) to expand its role in facilitating equality of educational opportunity will increase still further the number of graduates needing to be absorbed by a saturated labour market.

Superficially, various 'brakes on' strategies, aimed at curbing the flow into higher education either by directly restricting places or by negative subsidies, appear to offer an effective solution to the problems. On examination, however, it soon becomes apparent that these strategies involve and precipitate other undesirable, counter-productive outcomes. By way of illustration, limiting entry to higher education could only accomplish a reduction in the size of the pool of thwarted and unemployed graduates at the expense of increasing the size of the pool of thwarted and unemployed school-leavers. Over and above the repercussions this may have for social cohesion and the growing alienation of unemployed school-leavers, public expenditure savings accruing from the reduction in higher education places would be largely offset by new welfare benefits and the funding of alternative educational and training services. Moreover, such policies ignore other important educational outcomes, such as higher education as a civilizing force, and impose a socially divisive constraint on educational opportunities, whereby entry to degree courses would be further restricted to the affluent or academically élite sections of the community.

Within a more long-term and radical perspective, there is an alternative solution to the current predicament in the graduate labour market. Assuming a substantive and functional correspondence between the general intellectual capacities stimulated by degree courses and the occupational performance of higher order tasks, it is suggested that in a civilized and advanced industrial society it is not the over-supply of general degree graduates which is problematic and undesirable per se, but the failure of the dominant occupational structures to provide sufficient opportunities for meaningful and challenging work. Thus, according to this alternative proposal, rather than restrictions on the availability of higher level jobs with their wholly negative influence on access to higher education, there should be a much wider distribution of the roles requiring discretionary skills and full use made of the expanding supply of applicants with extended education. In encouraging a more constructive and efficient use of human resources, it is believed that the most convincing justification for sustaining and widening access to higher education is located in a comprehensive government policy to distribute, more evenly than at present, work which offers increased opportunities for social and psychological rewards. Such a policy would involve restructuring the ways in which labour is currently organized and allocated, including implementing job-sharing schemes among professional workers in both public and private sectors. In addition to absorbing more graduates by rationing out the available jobs to a larger number of incumbents by transforming the dominant patterns of designing and distributing work tasks, scope exists for increasing the actual number of jobs requiring discretionary capabilities. Such reforms would involve dismantling the hierarchical and bureaucratic form of work design commonly found in organizations which are based on 'role cultures' and applying the more loosely linked forms of work design associated with 'task cultures' that are characteristic of many of the emergent information technology industries (Handy 1978). As part of the reorganization of work designs and methods of allocating labour, particular attention should be paid to removing the obstacles inherent in existing practices and conditions (eg hours of work and career cycles) which militate against an equal representation of women graduates in professional and discretionary employment. In widening the opportunities for challenging and discretionary employment, such reforms would open up the prospects for fulfilling more of the expectations generated by degree courses.

Although the organizational patterns of work and labour should not be conceived as immutable, it should be recognized that political resistance to such changes is likely to be extensive and that the proposed reforms will only materialize with a matching rise in political consciousness and determination. The frustrations and disillusionment of graduates who are filtering down and underemployed are a potentially powerful source of motivation. Some of this force may be dissipated as expectations are lowered as a result of greater public awareness of the processes of filtering down, but the dissonance between the substantive capabilities extended through higher education and those demanded by the relatively less challenging jobs being entered by many graduates is likely to intensify, thus inflaming the pressure for major changes to occupational structures. In this respect, degree courses, and especially careers–related components, could usefully embrace the task of raising students' critical awareness of the need and scope for reforms in the social organization of work, providing this could be achieved without 'cooling out' and demotivation effects.

Turning to consider briefly the second set of selected problems, it may be noted that a substantial body of empirical evidence is now available to confirm the view that employers do not attribute parity of esteem to institutions of higher education (Bacon et al. 1979; Kelly and Dorsman 1984; Roizen and Jepson 1985). The perceived reality of a rank order in institutional status, what Kelly and Dorsman (1984) term the 'entrenched hierarchy of prestige', is a feature which permeates most aspects of the findings collected during the present research. It is evident, for example, in considerable differences between university and college students' A level scores, in variations in the career performances of graduates from different sectors of higher education, and in respondents' perceptions of the superior status of university degrees. Apart from the official rhetoric to the contrary, which only reflects the hierarchization within higher education, it is difficult to participate in the daily activities of college life without sensing an ethos of institutional inferiority, vulnerability, and at times, paranoia.

The growth of differential status in higher education and its attendant problems for such institutions as the colleges of higher education should not be construed as a peculiarly British experience. Teichler et al. (1980) identify the phenomena as a virtually invariable and universal consequence of the transition from élite to mass higher education. As an example of the cross-cultural quality of the trend towards hierarchization, these authors describe the low status reputations of the American 'community colleges', which one article has described as the 'coming slums of higher education' (Corcoran 1973). Their remarks on this type of institution are particularly apposite to our present concerns, since the colleges of higher education have sometimes been categorized as the British versions of 'community colleges' (Scott 1982). Although the latter author warns against the dangers of the wholesale adoption of the American model, such factors as the low A level scores of their recruits and an uncertain image in the eyes of employers make it exceptionally difficult for British colleges of higher education to resist being forced down the low status road of the American community colleges.

Unequal status and prestige among the different sectors of higher education exacerbate many of the problems which beset the college area of educational provision. For instance, a hierarchical structure in higher education as a whole encourages attempts to upgrade the prestige of low status institutions by emulation of characteristics that are believed to constitute the high status institutions' appeal. Accordingly, the process of 'academic drift' observed in the polytechnics (Pratt and Burgess 1974) can also be witnessed in the colleges, a process with deleterious consequences for the economic relevance of degree courses. It sustains the denigration of several applied subjects within higher education curricula, such as engineering, which in turn produces a 'back-wash effect' of a similar low status for such subjects in the secondary schools.

Differential institutional status also undermines the extent to which higher education can be said to widen the scope for equality of opportunity. The traditional competition for access to higher education in general is in danger of developing into a struggle for advantage over the particular sector to which a student can gain admission. Consequently, as is the experience in other developed countries, a comparatively disadvantaged group *within* higher education is beginning to emerge. By default rather than by design, a tripartite system of higher education is developing, which bears many of the hallmarks of the corresponding state of affairs that troubled secondary education in the 1950s and 60s, including injustices and inequalities for those in the lower status institutions. Moreover, the low status identity of the college sector is passed on to its women graduates, and represents a further limitation on women graduates' already low level of employability. Many colleges would aspire to specialize in promoting the mobility opportunity of women students, but from a female perspective the low status of the college sector renders it a very mixed blessing – at best, it binds them to teaching, very often it results in underemployment.

The only effective solution to the increasing hierarchization between different sectors of higher education ultimately appears to rest in pursuing policies equivalent to those which were used to eradicate the streaming of pupils in the tripartite system of secondary education. Accordingly, higher education would seem to require corresponding comprehensivization strategies, in which the different types of institutions currently offering advanced further education would be integrated into a single system of provision. Such a solution would be in accordance with the experience of countries that have moved closer towards mass higher education, where a number of low status institutions of higher education have actively sought integration into a comprehensive university provision (Teichler et al. 1980).

The integrationist proposal for developing higher education offers several improvements to existing circumstances. Providing all new comprehensive higher education institutions were instructed to admit specific proportions of applicants with low or no A level scores, the conspicuous institutional separation of a comparatively disadvantaged group in higher education would be terminated, as would the psychological effects and low morale among staff and students in low status institutions. In addition to expanding the scope for advancing equality of educational opportunity, a comprehensive system of what we cannot help but dub 'universities' would be less conducive to the processes of 'academic drift' and hence more congenial to increasing the status of applied and vocational subjects such as engineering. Such reforms could create the conditions for extending the contribution that higher education can make to eonomic advancement. Finally, although it would seem unlikely that many of the colleges and institutes of higher education would be sufficiently large to justify being nominated independent universities, amalgamation with existing universities or polytechnics could be so arranged as to preserve their distinctive courses and specialist expertise as integral units within the larger institutions.

To recapitulate, discussion has focused in this section on the wider implications of the research findings for two particular issues which currently confront higher education policy development in general, namely the various problems associated with the over-supply of certain types of graduates and the increasing hierarchization between different sectors of higher education. In response to these problems, it has been argued that future policy formation should concentrate on broadening the number and distribution of occupational tasks involving discretionary work and integrating the different sectors of higher education into a comprehensive provision with all its institutions perhaps called universities.

Implications for Colleges

As a result of their dependency on wide-ranging social change, it is not envisaged that the above analysis and suggestions for reforms should have any immediate and direct bearing on the specific policy issues presently facing the colleges and institutes of higher education. Moreover, they represent long-term strategies which will grow in importance as credentialism continues, and as such they need to be borne in mind when taking current policy decisions. Consequently, it is not being argued that colleges should immediately seek fuller integration with neighbouring universities and polytechnics, but that they should pursue policies and curricula which would strengthen the distinctive contribution they could make within the context of a comprehensive higher education system and reforms to the occupational structure. Such an approach underpins the following responses to the three policy-related questions raised in the opening chapter.

A In view of the early career experiences of diversified degree graduates, would (i) the extending of the occupational relevance of teaching degree programmes or (ii) the continued provision of non-teaching courses represent the most efficient and resourceful method of giving the colleges the required stability to respond flexibly to a fluctuating demand for teachers?

The question is founded on the proposition that the former colleges of education cannot function efficiently and effectively as long as they are continually exposed to the alternating periods of expansion and contraction in the teacher labour market. To avert personal employability problems for their graduates and regular rounds of institutional trauma for their staff, college degree programmes require an element of flexibility if they are to survive and manage the ever-changing demands for recruits to the teaching profession. The research findings provide little support for key assumptions underpinning the so-called 'diversified degree' programme in part (i) of the question above. They do suggest that closer investigation of the potential for alternative, wider based and more flexible 'teaching degree' programmes might be afforded greater priority.

A central, but usually implicit and certainly untested, assumption underlying the introduction of diversified degrees in the mid-1970s was the supposition that, whereas a BEd graduate who did not enter the teaching profession could be considered a wasted resource, a BA/BSc graduate who did likewise would be less of a wasted investment, because of the latter's greater capacity for successfully transferring to other professions. Accordingly, the BA/BSc diversified degree programmes were conceived, not as alternative 'back-door' routes into teaching, but as avenues into a genuine diversity of occupations and careers.

The research findings establish beyond all doubt that teaching constituted the principal employment outlet of 1979 BA/BSc diversified degree graduates. With only 13 per cent of graduates in non-teaching jobs of broadly equivalent standing, the assumption that BA/BSc degrees in colleges would be less teacher-orientated and more easily transferable to other occupations is seriously challenged by the evidence collected. Similarly, in view of the underemployment experienced by respondents and the manifest scale and level of difficulties faced in finding suitable alternatives to teaching, the research failed to provide sufficient evidence to refute the assertion that BA/BSc graduates not entering teaching also amounted to 'wasted resources'.

It must be conceded, therefore, that the findings provide some justification for earlier suspicions that the diversified degrees were serving as alternative avenues to teaching qualifications. Indeed, some college principals and staff actively encourage the view that the diversified degree courses constitute new ways of implementing the colleges' natural commitment and traditional expertise in teacher training. Instead of a three or four-year BEd degree, it is said, the colleges now accentuate the BA-plus-PGCE route. As a logical consequence of this emphasis, it follows that in the main the efficacy of the diversified degree programmes' relevance and responsiveness to economic needs must be judged in terms of their contribution to general preparation for the occupational demands of teaching.

The question that arises from this line of argument is not simply whether the colleges are implementing the most effective method of initial teacher education, but whether or not they are providing the most effective scheme of initial teacher education they can within the overall provision for teacher education. Thus, rather than advocate the case for colleges' teaching degrees (BEd) as the single most effective scheme, it is sufficient, for present purposes, to acknowledge that primary as well as secondary teaching benefits from a diversity in teacher education, and that, as part of the total diversity, the colleges' education degrees foster qualities, skills and insights which are difficult to achieve through other avenues, notably the BA degree followed by a one-year PGCE course. Some indications of the comparative and distinctive strengths and weaknesses of three or four-year teaching degrees are demonstrated in the well-documented study, *The New Teacher in School* (Department of Education and Science 1982a). In shifting the balance of their provision from specialist teaching degrees to general degrees followed by a PGCE, the colleges appear to be in danger of relinquishing, or at least diminishing, their largely unique contribution to initial teacher education in order to adopt a model of teacher education which is uniformly available in other sectors of higher education and which incorporates courses which many consider to be already well-catered for and over-subscribed (eg academic drift, etc.). Furthermore, in the light of the findings presented here, it remains to be demonstrated that the rationale for implementing this shift – namely that BA/BSc degrees purportedly command greater transferable currency value – is based on any empirical evidence or justification.

As a supplementary inquiry, the 'Beyond Graduation' questionnaire was also administered to a small sample of 1979 BEd graduates who were thought not to have entered the teaching profession. It went to 278 BEd graduates from the six CCRG institutions and 130 completed returns were received (a response rate of 47 per cent). Because a higher proportion of the BEd group were oriented towards teaching and fewer had attempted to use their degrees to enter alternative occupations, it would be misleading to contrast the overall frequencies for the BEd and non-BEd samples. However, upon restricting the comparison to those who were not working within the teaching profession, it was found that exactly the same proportion of each sample was employed in graduate status occupations: 16 per cent of the 61 non-teaching BEd graduates from the CCRG sample compared to the same percentage of the 143 non-teaching BA/BSc graduates from the corresponding institutions occupied graduate status positions. Although the small percentages involved underline the need for caution, the data suggest that providing the motivation exists, a similar proportion of BEd graduates can obtain non-teaching graduate status jobs as can BA/BSc diversified degree graduates. If this were the case, even the existing BEd might offer as much potential for occupational transferability as the BA/BSc degrees.

This is not to say that there should be a retreat from diversified degrees and a straight-forward reversion to traditional BEd degrees, but the results do raise the question whether a revitalized form of the latter could not better provide the necessary flexibility and transferability to other occupations, as well as strengthen its contribution to the richness and diversity of initial teacher education. If, for example, a restructured BA degree in education incorporated greater experiential learning based in a variety of work settings, including but not exclusive to the classroom, then its employment relevance for teaching and other professions could be extended simultaneously. (The need for teachers to bring a wiider understanding and experience of work in industry and commerce was a major recommendation of the DES report, *Teacher Training and the Preparation for Working Life* (1982b)). In such a manner, the revived degree would be in a strong position to incorporate many of the more innovatory elements that have been developed within the diversified degree programmes (careers education, experiential learning and so forth.)

The colleges and institutes would also stand to gain a number of benefits from a degree with a greater emphasis on experiential learning. Having a more distinctive degree programme than is currently available through most liberal arts courses, former colleges of education would reduce the risk of directly competing with other sectors and institutions of higher education, and make full use of their specialist resources and expertise. Likewise, because the degree would be distinctive to the college sector, applications could be expected from a larger number of prospective students with higher A level grades and qualifications. Following Bacon et al. (1979), this should have the positive effect of raising employers' perceptions of the academic status of the graduates holding the degree.

    B Assuming the desirability of some provision of diversified courses, do the early career experiences of non-teaching graduates from the former colleges of education lend support to the strengthening of (i) liberal arts degree programmes or (ii) more vocationally-specific courses?

In the opening chapter the hope was expressed that the findings would provide some broad indications of the relative economic and employment merits of fostering the two types of diversification first mentioned in the Robbins Report: (a) general courses in the arts and sciences and (b) more vocationally-specific courses with special reference to various professions in the social services.

The study has pointed to the increased unemployment encountered by liberal arts graduates from all sectors of higher education. Against a background of an over-supply of this type of graduate, the survey findings have highlighted the particular employment problems confronting graduates from former colleges of education, most of whom studied liberal arts subjects. Although this particular project has not covered the employment trends of the output from the more vocational courses offered by the colleges, first destination statistics reveal that it is generally associated with comparatively higher levels of appropriate employment and occupational entry. Thus, in terms of securing suitable career opportunities for their graduates, the results would indicate that the colleges should, wherever possible, increase their commitment to the latter not the former type of courses.

While not implying a wholesale condemnation of the mid-1970s policy of diversification through liberal arts degrees, the results do suggest that the benefits gained by this strategy (eg institutional survival, flexibility for the colleges, satisfying the early 1980s peak in demand for higher education places by providing degrees in the least expensive subject areas) may have been bought at the cost of adding to the pool of graduates who were already experiencing greatest disappointment and frustration in their early years after graduation. Hence, if employment criteria are given their due consideration, colleges should be wary of thinking that diversification through liberal arts degrees constitutes a permanent solution to their problems of institutional flexibility and development. An alternative view would be to consider this form of diversification as a transitional stage, providing a breathing space in which to progress to a more secure type of diversification based on greater emphasis on vocational courses leading to specific occupations other than teaching.

In the context of this latter proposal, the findings have underlined the particular need to extend, wherever the demand allows, the provision of vocational courses which would strengthen women graduates' chances of finding suitable and meaningful work outside of the teaching profession. Because of the colleges' traditional bias towards the enrolment of women, many of whom unwittingly add to their relative economic disadvantages by taking liberal arts subjects, it could be justifiably argued that the colleges inherit a moral duty to encourage more women to study subjects with greater vocational relevance and application.

   C Assuming the continued provision of diversified liberal arts degree programmes, do the results offer encouragement for any distinctive curricula innovations, such as careers education courses, which might enhance the economic relevance and marketability of college graduates?

Barring some association between the provision of careers education and a reduced dependence on teaching, few features of diversified courses were clearly instrumental in extending graduates' employability in non-teaching occupations. The results were consistent with the view that the influence of attributes common to all participating colleges (eg dominant liberal arts subject bias, the perceived status of degrees and institutions, etc.) as well as more penetrating institutional differences (eg the contrasting local employment opportunities for graduates) far outweighed the effects of any supplementary curricula innovations and other provisions.

Although it should be reiterated that insufficient institutions were included in the research to take account of all the possible variables required for a confident verification of this guarded interpretation, the case for augmenting the main degree courses with additional curricula components (such as careers education or work experience) on the grounds that they extend employability is neither immediately nor readily established by the research findings. Thus, at this stage in the development of the additional courses, any interpretation of their value must remain an open one. At best, such schemes may be viewed as mollifying the severest difficulties produced by more powerful determining forces; at worst, they may act as cosmetic presentations, which convey misleading impressions of the currency value of the degrees concerned, and which, in turn, lead to a more intense sense of disillusionment and dissatisfaction after graduation. In view of the evidence suggesting the restricted influence of supplementary provisions, the veracity of either of these two perspectives depends more on the appraisal of the currency value of the degrees themselves than on that of the extra courses and services appended to them.

In the current economic structure and circumstances, and especially if support were forthcoming for the earlier policy recommendations, the justifications for sustaining the present form of diversified degree provision appear rather weak and limited when looked at purely from the angle of individual extrinsic expectations and economic returns. In the labour market for the highly qualified, the programmes duplicate a type of graduate of which an abundant supply already exists; college non-teaching degree graduates seem particularly prone to the problems of underemployment and filtering down; and, taking for granted certain widely held notions of what constitutes suitable graduate employment, their main economic contribution remains the same as that of the programmes they were intended to replace and broaden, namely teaching.

Of course the colleges are committed to providing non-teaching degree programmes and the research results clearly show that graduates of these courses would have appreciated much more assistance on career decision-making than is generally provided. In this more limited respect, careers education appears to have an important contribution to make. Without claiming that such courses will improve the standing of their degrees in the eyes of employers, careers education schemes could help students to acquire the skills of 'vigilant information processing' (Janis and Mann 1977) and to appreciate the links that might be made between academic courses and more experiential forms of learning. Moreover, as suggested in the previous section, providing the demotivation of students could be avoided, a central task of such courses could be the development of undergraduates' critical awareness of the need and potential for change in various facets of the social organization of work.

Nevertheless, given that careers education seems to have produced little impact on graduates' employment performances, the economic and careers-related arguments for maintaining diversified degree programmes, with or without careers education, are not substantiated by the research data. In addition, it would seem likely that, in view of their similarity to courses provided by other institutions of higher education, diversified degree programmes could easily be subsumed under the course structure of merging universities and polytechnics. With such dubious employment relevance and manifest lack of distinctiveness, it may be imprudent of the colleges to commit all their energies to developing their diversified degree programmes in their present form. Instead it may be wiser to concentrate on refining the special qualities of college teaching degrees or expanding provision of other vocational courses. The development of diversified degrees will be productive only if more radical strategies are adopted to give them greater employment currency.

Appendix A

The 'Beyond Graduation' Questionnaire

Summary of Main Items

Q.1 Sex
Q.2 Age: under 21/21−25/over 25
Q.3 Status: single/married/other
Q.4 Children?
Q.5 (a) Full-time employment after school
     (b) Professional qualifications prior to college
Q.6 Present employment circumstances:
        full-time employment
        full-time education
        housewife not seeking full-time employment
        unemployed seeking full-time employment
        unemployed but employment/training arranged
        not available for employment
Q.7 Studying for further qualifications in connection with work?
Q.8 Distances from college and home of job applications
Q.9 Distances from college and home of present work
Q.10 Sources of information about initial employer; rank most helpful*
Q.11 Details of main occupational and training position entered since graduation
Q.12 Jobs applied for other than those listed in Q.11
Q.13 Present job and long-term career expectations?*
Q.14 Career goals – now? when leaving college? when entering college?
Q.15 Ranking of job search problems*
Q.16 Five-point scale responses to various attitude statements on satisfaction with degree and employment*
Q.17 Father's occupation (social class)
Q.18 FOR THOSE NOT IN TEACHING: Attitudes to teaching as career
Q.19 FOR ALL WOMEN: Opportunities hampered because you are a woman?
Q.20 In what ways, if any, have the following items helped you obtain employment and prepare you for work? Have you any criticisms or suggestions on how they could be made more useful to future students?
    (i) Your degree courses
    (ii) Any short 'optional' courses (if applicable)
    (iii) Practical work within your degree programme (including any work experience placements)
    (iv) College Careers Service (if applicable)
    (v) Other Careers Advisory Services (if applicable)
    (vi) The social life of the college campus
    (vii) Vacation work (if applicable)
    (viii) Work experience prior to attending college (if applicable)
Q.21 IF YOU ARE WORKING: What earnings or advice would you offer to present students hoping to enter your current area of employment?

---

* See relevant tables in the text for separate items and statements.

Appendix B

Subject Classification of Diversified Degrees

The following are classifications of diversified degree subjects according to course content rather than the title of the degree. To achieve some consistency with subject classifications in other sectors of higher education, they are based on groupings used in the *First Destinations of University Graduates 1978–79* (UGC). These groupings, with any additional college courses, are listed beneath the main degree subject areas.

1   ARTS

University Group 8 – Language, Literature and area studies

English
Welsh and other Celtic languages and studies
French language and studies
French/German language and studies
German language and studies
Hispanic languages and studies
Other and combined Western European languages and studies
Russian language and studies
Other Slavonic and Eastern European languages and studies
Chinese language and studies
Oriental, Asian and African languages and/or studies
Classical studies
Other, general and combined language, literature and area studies

University Group 9 – Arts other than languages

History
Archaeology
Philosophy
Theology
Art and Design
Drama
Music
Arts general, and combined other arts subjects
plus
Combinations of subjects within university groups 8 and 9

2   SOCIAL STUDIES

University Group 6 – Social, administrative and business studies

Business management studies
Economics
Geography
Accountancy
Government and public administration
Law
Psychology

Sociology
Social Anthropology
Combinations within social studies

University Group 1 — Education

Education
plus
Combinations of subjects within university groups 6 and 1

3   ARTS AND SOCIAL STUDIES

Combinations of degree subject areas 1 and 2

4   SCIENCE

University Group 5 — Science

Biology
Botany
Zoology
Physiology and/or anatomy
Biochemistry
Other, general and combined biological sciences
Mathematics
Mathematics with physics
Physics
Chemistry
Geology
Environmental sciences (other than geology)
Other, general and combined physical sciences
Combinations of biological and physical sciences
plus
Home Economics
Liberal Studies in Science
Combinations of subjects within university group 5

5   OTHERS

Arts (1) and/or social studies (2) combined with science (4)
Physical education
Sports studies
PE or sports studies combined with arts (1), social studies (2), science (4)

References

ACACHE (see Association of Careers Advisers in Colleges of Higher Education)

Adelman, C.L. and Alexander, R.J. (1982) *The Self-Evaluating Institution: Practice and Principles in the Management of Educational Change* London: Methuen

Adelman, C.L. and Gibbs, I. (1979) *Student Choice in the Context of Institutional Change* Final Report to the Department of Education and Science, Bulmershe College of Higher Education

Adelman, C.L. and Gibbs, I. (1980a) The emergence of the colleges of higher education *Educational Research* 22(2) 97–106

Adelman, C.L. and Gibbs, I. (1980b) Curriculum development and the changing constituency of students: the case of the colleges of higher education *Journal of Curriculum Studies* 12(2) 167–71

Association of Careers Advisers in Colleges of Higher Education (1979) *First Destination Statistics 1979 – A Pilot Survey* Chester College of Higher Education

Bacon, C., Benton, D. and Gruneberg, M.M. (1979) Employers' opinions of university and polytechnic graduates *The Vocational Aspect of Education* 41(80) 95–102

Berg, I. 1970) *Education and Jobs: The Great Training Robbery* Harmondsworth: Penguin

Binks, E.V. (1979) The alternative way: career prospects *The Guardian* October 30th

Bone, A. (1980) *The Effect on Womens' Opportunities of Teacher Training Cuts* Manchester: Equal Opportunities Commission

Brunel (1984) *The Expectations of Higher Education Project* Department of Government, Brunel University

Burns, T. (1980) Science and arts: the job gap widens *Employment Gazette* November, 1182–1184

Campbell-Stewart, W.A. (1980) Tapping the barometer: higher education since 1950 *Studies in Higher Education* 5(2) 149–160

Catto, G., Goodchild, A. and Hughes, P. (1981) *Higher Education and the Employment of Graduates* Research paper No. 19, Department of Employment, London: HMSO

Central Register and Clearing House (1982) *The handbook of degree and advanced courses in Institutes/Colleges of Higher Education: Colleges of Education, Polytechnics and University Departments of Education* National Association of Teachers in Further and Higher Education, Bradford: Lund Humphries

Committee on Higher Education (1963) *Higher Education* (Robbins Report) London: HMSO

Cook, T. and Reichardt, C.S. (1979) *Qualitative and Quantitative Methods* London: Sage

Corcoran, T.B. (1973) Community colleges: the coming slums of higher education? In Change Magazine (Eds) *On Learning and Change* New Rochelle: Change Magazine, 104–119

Dent, H.C. (1977) *The Training of Teachers in England and Wales 1800 – 1975* London: Hodder and Stoughton

Department of Education and Science (1972a) *Teacher Education and Training* (James Report) London: HMSO

Department of Education and Science (1972b) *Education: A Framework for Expansion* London: HMSO

Department of Education and Science (1973) *Development of Higher Education in the Non-university Sector* (Circular 7/73) London: HMSO

Department of Education and Science (1974) *Development of Higher Education in the Non-university Sector: Interim Arrangements for the Control of Advanced Courses* (Circular 6/74) London: HMSO

Department of Education and Science (1980) *First Destinations of Graduates and Higher National Diplomates 1975–76 to 1977–78* (Statistical Bulletin 2/80) London: HMSO

Department of Education and Science (1982a) *Teacher Training and Preparation for Working Life* London: HMSO

Department of Education and Science (1982b) *The New Teacher in School* London: HMSO
DES (see Department of Education and Science)
Dore, R. (1978) *The Diploma Disease: Education, Qualification and Development* London: George Allen and Unwin
Dowie, J. (1980) Bounds and biases. In Dowie, J. (Ed.) *Risk and Rationality* Block 1, U201, Milton Keynes: The Open University Press, 99–156
Fay, B. (1975) *Social Theory and Political Practice* London: George Allen and Unwin
Fulton, O. (Ed.) (1981) *Access to Higher Education* Guildford: Society for Research into Higher Education
Gedge, P.S. (1981) The Church of England colleges of education since 1944 *Journal of Educational Administration and History* 13(1) 33–44
Gibbs, I. and Cree, S. (1982) *Opening a Closing Door* Unpublished paper, SRHE Annual Conference 1981. Available from CCRG
Greenaway, H. (1973) The impact of educational policies. In Greenaway, H. and Williams, G. (Eds) (1973) *Op. cit.*, 1–23
Greenaway, H. and Williams, G. (Eds) (1973) *Patterns of Change in Graduate Employment* London: Society for Research into Higher Education
Halsey, A.H., Heath, A.F. and Ridge, J.M. (1980) *Origins and Destinations: Family, Class, and Education in Modern Britain* Oxford: Clarendon Press
Hammersley, M. and Atkinson, P. (1983) *Ethnography: Principles in Practice* London: Tavistock
Hampson, K. (1977) Murder, he says *The Guardian* July 19th
Handy, C.B. (1978) *Gods of Management* London: The Souvenir Press
Hebron, C.C. (1971) Are BA general graduates employable? *Bulletin of Educational Research* 1, 17–20
Hencke, D. (1978) *Colleges in Crisis: The Reorganization of Teacher Training 1971–7* Harmondsworth: Penguin
Hunter, L.C. (1981) Employers' perceptions of demand. In Lindley, R. (Ed.) (1981) *Op. cit.*, 4–48
Hutt, R. and Parsons, D. (1981) *The Mobility of Young Graduates* Brighton: Institute for Manpower Studies
Janis, I.L. and Mann, L. (1977) *Decision Making: A Psychological Analysis of Conflict, Choice and Commitment* New York: The Free Press
Karabel, J. and Halsey, A.H. (Eds) (1977) *Power and Ideology in Education* New York: Oxford University Press
Kelly, M. and Dorsman, M. (1984) *An Investigation of the Employment Market for 1982 Graduates from Universities and Polytechnics in the United Kingdom: Policies and Practices of Employers* Staff Development Unit, Manchester Polytechnic
Kelsall, R.K., Poole, A. and Kuhn, A. (1970) *Six Years on* Department of Sociological Studies, Sheffield University
Kelsall, R.K., Poole, A. and Kuhn, A. (1972) *Graduates: The Sociology of an Elite* London: Methuen
Lindley, R. (Ed.) (1981) *Higher Education and the Labour Market* Guildford: Society for Research into Higher Education
Locke, M. (1979) *Colleges of Higher Education: Constraints and Opportunities* Commentary No. 19, Centre for Institutional Studies, Anglian Regional Management Centre, North East London Polytechnic
Locke, M. and Russell, M. (1979) *Colleges of Higher Education: The Emergence* Commentary No. 17, Centre for Institutional Studies, Anglian Regional Management Centre, North East London Polytechnic
Lynch, J. (1979) *The Reform of Teacher Education in the United Kingdom* Guildford: The Society for Research into Higher Education
McNamara, D.R. and Ross, A.M. (1982) *The BEd Degree and its Future* Final Report to Department of Education and Science, Department of Educational Research, University of Lancaster
Morris, V. (1973) Investment in higher education in England and Wales: the human capital approach to educational planning. In Fowler, G., Morris, V. and Ozga, J. (Eds) *Decision-making in Britain* London: Heinemann Educational, 284–308
Morris, V. and Ziderman, A. (1971) The economic return on investment in higher education in England and Wales *Economic Trends* London: HMSO, xx–xxvii
Murray, R.G. (1978) Planning for diversification *Journal of Further and Higher Education* 2(1) 57–65
Neave, G. (1976) *Patterns of Equality: The Influence of New Structures in European Higher Education*

upon the Equality of Educational Opportunity Windsor: NFER Publishing

Office of Population Censuses and Surveys (1980) *Classification of Occupations* London: HMSO

Paci, M. (1977) Education and the capitalist labor market. In Karabel, J. and Halsey, A.H. (Eds) (1977) *Op. cit.*, 340–355

PCA (see Polytechnic Careers Advisers)

Polytechnic Careers Advisers: Statistics Working Party (Annually) *First Destinations of Polytechnic Students* Annual Reports, London: Committee of Directors of Polytechnics

Pratt, J. and Burgess, T. (1974) *Polytechnics: A Report* London: Pitman

Pratt, J., Russell, M. and Locke, M. (1979) *Colleges of Higher Education: The Students* Commentary No. 18, Centre for Institutional Studies, Anglian Regional Management Centre, North East London Polytechnic

Raggett, M. and Clarkson, M. (1976) *Changing Patterns of Teacher Education* London: The Falmer Press

Roizen, Judith and Jepson, Mark (1985)*Degrees for Jobs: Employer Expectations of Higher Education* Guildford: SRHE & NFER-NELSON

Russell, M. and Pratt, J. (1979) Numerical changes in the colleges of higher education *Higher Education Review* 12(1) 13–39

Scott, N. (1980) Graduate supply and demand. In *Employment Gazette* February, 133–135

Scott, P. (1982) Colleges for the common man *Times Higher Education Supplement* February 19th

Spradley, J.P. (1979) *Participant Observation* New York: Holt, Rinehart and Winston

Standing Conference of Principals and Directors of Colleges and Institutes in Higher Education (1982) *Guide to the Colleges and Institutes of Higher Education* The Secretary of the Standing Conference, Worcester College of Higher Education

Stodd, G.J. (1980) An alternative approach for the colleges of higher education *Higher Education Review* 12(2) 55–66

Stodd, G.J. (1981) The colleges of higher education and the academic time-bomb *Journal of Further and Higher Education* 5(1) 3–9

Syrett, M. (1983) Jobs: New hopes for graduates *The Sunday Times* July 10th

Tarsh, J. (1982) The labour market for new graduates *Employment Gazette* May, 205–215

Teichler, U., Hartung, D. and Nuthmann, R. (1980) *Higher Education and the Needs of Society* Windsor: NFER Publishing

Thorburn, D. and Parker, F. (1978) Beyond integration: new directions in the public sector *British Journal of Teacher Education* 4(2) 93–101

Thorburn, D. and Parker, F. (1980) New vocationalism in the colleges of education *British Journal of Teacher Education* 6(1) 62–70

Times Educational Supplement (1983) Polys losing out in graduates job race. November 11th

UGC (see University Grants Committee)

Universities Central Council on Admissions *Statistical Supplement to the Fifteenth Report 1976–7* Cheltenham: UCCA

University Grants Committee (Annually) *First Destinations of University Graduates* (Annual Reports) Cheltenham: Universities Statistical Record

Watts, A.G. (1973) Career influences on students' educational choices. In Greenaway, H. and Williams, G. (Eds) (1973) *Op. cit.*, 59–66

Whitehead, L. and Williamson, P. (1980) On the way up: an analysis of first jobs from the early careers survey of graduates *Employment Gazette* May, 472–477

Willey, F.T. and Maddison, R.E. (1971) *An Enquiry into Teacher Training* London: University of London Press

Williams, G. (1973a) First employment of university graduates. In Greenaway, H. and Williams, G. (Eds) (1973) *Op. cit.*, 25–34

Williams, G. (1973b) The economics of the graduate labour market. In Greenaway, H. and Williams, G. (Eds) (1973) *Op. cit.*, 41–58

Williamson, P. (1979a) Going into industry: trends in graduate employment *Employment Gazette* January, 18–25

Williamson, P. (1979b) Moving around in the room at the top *Employment Gazette* December, 1220–1228

Williamson, P. (1981) *Early Careers of 1970 Graduates* Unit for Manpower Studies, Research Paper No. 26, Department of Employment

Woodhall, M. (1973) The economic returns to investment in women's education *Higher Education* 2, 275–99

Ziderman, A. (1973) Does it pay to take a degree? The profitability of private investment in university education in Britain *Oxford Economic Papers* July, 262–74

Abbreviations

ACACHE	Association of Careers Advisers in Colleges of Higher Education
AFE	Advanced further education
AGCAS	Association of Graduate Careers Advisers
BA/BSc	(See page 24)
BCombined Studies	Bachelor of Combined Studies
BEd	Bachelor of Education
BHum	Bachelor of Humanities
CCRG	Combined Colleges Research Group
CertEd	Certificate of Education
CNAA	Council for National Academic Awards
CSU	Central Services Unit
DES	Department of Education and Science
DHSS	Department of Health and Social Security
DipHE	Diploma of Higher Education
HND	Higher National Diploma
LEA	Local Education Authority
PCA	Polytechnic Careers Advisers
PGCE	Postgraduate Certificate of Education
SCOEG	Standing Conference of Employers of Graduates
SRHE	Society for Research into Higher Education
UMS	Unit for Manpower Studies

The Society for Research into Higher Education

The Society exists both to encourage and co-ordinate research and development into all aspects of the field of higher education, including policy studies concerned with the future; and also to provide a forum for debate on issues in this field. Through its activities, it draws attention to the significance of research and development and to the needs of those engaged in the area. (It is not concerned with research generally, except, for instance, as a subject of study or in its relation to teaching.)

The Society's income is derived from its subscriptions, book sales, conferences and specific grants. It is wholly independent. Its corporate members are universities, polytechnics, institutes of higher education, research institutions and professional and governmental bodies. Its individual members include teachers and researchers, administrators and students. Members are found in all parts of the world and the Society regards its international work as amongst its most important activities.

The Society discusses and comments on policy, organizes conferences and sponsors research. Under the imprint SRHE & NFER-NELSON it is a specialist publisher of research, having over 30 titles in print. It also publishes Studies in Higher Education *(three times a year),* Higher Education Abstracts *(three times a year),* International Newsletter *(twice a year), a* Bulletin *(six times a year), and jointly with the Committee for Research into Teacher Education (CRITE)* Evaluation Newsletter *(twice a year).*

The Society's committees, study groups and local branches are run by members, with help from a small secretariat, and aim to provide a forum for discussion. Some of the groups, at present the Teacher Education Study Group, the Women in Higher Education Group, and the Staff Development Group, have their own subscriptions and organization, as do some Regional Branches. The Governing Council, elected by members, comments on current issues and discusses policies with leading figures in politics and education. The Society organizes seminars on current research for officials of the DES and the other ministries, and is in touch with bodies in Britain such as the CNAA, NAB, CVCP, UGC and the British Council; and with sister-bodies overseas. Its current research projects include one on the relationship between entry qualifications and degree results, directed by Prof. W.D. Furneaux (Brunel) and one on 'Questions of Quality' directed by Prof. G.C. Moodie (York).

The Society's annual conferences take up central themes, 'Standards and criteria in HE' (1986), 'Re-structuring' (1987). Joint conferences are held, viz. on 'Information Technology' (1986, with the Council for Educational Technology, the Computer Board and the Universities of Glasgow and Strathclyde) and on 'The Freshman Year' (1986, with the University of South Carolina and Newcastle Polytechnic). For some of the Society's conferences, special studies are commissioned in advance, as 'Precedings'.

Members receive free of charge the Society's Abstracts, *annual conference proceedings (or 'Precedings'), and* Bulletin *and* International Newsletter, *and may buy SRHE & NFER-NELSON books at booksellers' discount. Corporate members receive the Society's journal* Studies in Higher Education *free, individuals at a heavy discount. They may also obtain* Evaluation Newsletter *and certain other journals at discount, including the NFER* Register of Educational Research.

Further information may be obtained from the Society for Research into Higher Education, At the University, Guildford GU2 5XH, UK.